Linguistic Studies Presented to John L. Finlay

Linguistic Studies Presented to John L. Finlay

Edited by H.C. Wolfart

Memoir 8

ALGONQUIAN AND IROQUOIAN LINGUISTICS

1991

ALGONQUIAN AND IROQUOIAN LINGUISTICS

John D. Nichols, Editor
H.C. Wolfart, Associate Editor (Supplements)
A.C. Ogg, Typographer

Algonquian and Iroquoian Linguistics
Fletcher Argue Building
28 Trueman Walk
Winnipeg, Manitoba R3T 2N2

Canadian Cataloguing in Publication Data

Main entry under title:

Linguistic studies presented to John L. Finlay

(Algonquian and Iroquoian linguistics. Memoir ; 8)
  Includes bibliographical references.
  ISBN 0-921064-08-X

1. Algonquian languages – Manitoba. 2. Indians of North
America – Manitoba – Languages. 3. Language and languages.
I. Wolfart, H. Christoph, 1943-. II. Finlay, John L., 1939-.
III. Series.

PM601.L564 1991   497/.3   C91-097104-8

CONTENTS

STUDIA LINGUISTICA IOANNI LAURENTIO FINLAY OBLATA

In presenting these studies to John Finlay,
the dean extraordinary whose decree established
the Linguistics Department at Manitoba, we pay
homage to a true scholar and good friend.

John Beaverbone's Story
as
Retold by Joseph Tootoosis

Edited and Translated by
Freda Ahenakew & H.C. Wolfart

The historical text here presented (as transcribed by us from the audio-recording, analysed, edited and translated) was given to Freda Ahenakew on 19 June 1989 by Joseph Tootoosis, a respected Plains Cree story-teller in his seventies, originally from Poundmaker's Reserve (near Battleford, Saskatchewan) but long resident at Hobbema, Alberta.[1] The story had been told to him by another old man, John Beaverbone, about whom we have no biographical information beyond that contained in the text.[2]

According to his own story, as retold, John Beaverbone came from Jackfish Lake (also near Battleford) and was about 12 years old at the time of the great influenza epidemic which swept the Prairies after World War I and still figures prominently in many Plains Cree historical narratives. Having travelled across the Prairies with his family, he then lived, at least for some time, in the foothills of the Rocky Mountains.[3]

Aside from a preface and an equally brief conclusion, the story is told entirely from the perspective of the original narrator – in his own words, as is emphasised by the frequent repetitions of *itwêw* 'so he said'.[4] While this mode of narration may look strange on the printed page, it is common enough in oral tradition.

[1]   ---~ niya mân ômatowihk [*gesture*] mihcêtwâw kâ-~
kâ-pîkiskwêyân, mihcêt ayisiyiniw ninitohtâk mâna.

[2]   niya, 'côsap côhcôsis' k-êtikawiyân, *Poundmaker Reserve* ohci;
mâk ôta ôma *Hobbema* ê-ay-atoskêyân. êkota mâna mihcêtwâw, awa
ayisiyiniw ôt[a] ôhci, nanâtohk ohc âyisiyiniw, kâ-pê-nitohtawit mâna,
kâ-pê-nâh-~-nâh-~-nâh-nitomicik, ka-pîkiskwêyân pikw îta.
nîst ê-kî-sîhkimikawiyân, êkosi ka-tôtamân; kik-âsônamawak
nîc-âyisiyiniw, êkây ka-wanisimôhâwasot, êkây ka-wanisimikot
wâpiskiwiyâsa.

[3]   êwak ôm ôta, ôma kâ-wî-âcimoyân, kisêyiniw pêyak
ê-kî-âcimostawit, iyikohk ê-kî-koskwêyihtahk; "tâpwê ês ôma, no-~
[*sc:* nôsisim], ê-kitimahikoyahkok wâpiskiwiyâsak," ê-kî-isit. ê-âcim-~
êkwayâk ê-mâmiskôtamâhk, tânisi iyikohk ê-kî-kakwâtakêyihtamihâcik
mihcêt ayisiyiniwa pêci-nâway, êwakw ânim ê-mâmiskôtamân.
êwakw âwa kisêyiniw kâ-kî-âcimostawit, '*John Beaverbone*'
kî-isiyîhkâsow.

---

[4]   nistam ê-pê-sipwêhtêyâhk, **itwêw**, kinosêwi-sâkahikanihk
ohci, ôtê *Saskatchewan*, **itwêw**, nîsosâp ê-itahtopiponêyân, **itwêw**,
kâ-pê-sipwê-piciyâhk êkotê ohc, **îtwêw**. kîhtwâm ê-pê-nakîyâhk
manitowi-sâkahikanihk, êkota nôhtâwiy pê-mîskotônikêw [*sic*]
misatimwa, êkwa otâpâna, **itwêw**. kîhtwâm êkwa
ê-pê-sipwê-piciyâhk, ôta ôma maskwacîsihk kâ-kî-pimi-nakîyâhk âsay
mîna, ê-ayipi-~ ê-ayiwêpihastimwêyâhk, **itwêw**; awa maskawi-nâpêw
kâ-kî-ayât, êkota kâ-nakîyâhk, **itwêw**; êkwa ê-nôcihtât nôhtâwiy
kîkway kika-nîmâyâhk, **itwêw**; tâpwê wiya kâhtitinamwak, **itwêw**.
êkota ohci kâ-sipwê-piciyâhk, **itwêw**, ôma *Lacombe*, êkota
nitati-pimi-picinân, **itwêw**. êkotê ohc ê-sipwê-piciyâhk, **itwêw**,
â, êwak ôm êkwa 'kâ-cawacinâsik' k-êtamihk, **itwêw**, êwak ôm êkota
nitati-pimohtânân, **itwêw**. â, kapê-nîpin ôm ê-pê-pimi-piciyâhk,
itwêw, ê-pê-ay-âsônakîyâhk, **itwêw**; êkot[a] ê-takohtêyâhk, **itwêw**.
êkospîhk k-êskwânêhk, **itwêw**, âstamispîhk anima kâ-pê-sipwêhtêyâhk,
itwêw.

[5]   kayâs ôm âyisiyiniw, mistah ê-kî-sâkihitot, **itwêw**;
kâ-nanânistipitikoyahk aw êkwa wâpiskiwiyâs, **itwêw**. anima mîn
ôtitwêwin, k-âti-wanihtâ-~, kâ-wanihtâyahk kititwêwininaw,
kinêhiyawêwininaw, **itwêw**; ôm êkwa k-âti-cî-~ [*sc:* -cîhkêyihtamahk],
k-ât[i]-âyiwâkêyihtamahk âkayâsîmowin, **itwêw**. namôya ês ânim
êwako, kiyânaw, ka-kî-pimohtahikoyahk êwakw ânima pîkiskwêwin,
itwêw; kiwî-wanisininânaw, kitawâsimisinawak wî-wanisinwak,
ê-kî-itwêt.

[1]   --~ as for me, having spoken on this kind [tape-recorder] many times, many a person has listened to me.

[2]   I am from Poundmaker Reserve and my name is *côsap côhcôsis* [Joseph Tootoosis]; but I have been working here at Hobbema. There have been many occasions when the people from here and people from various places have come to listen to me and have also come to invite me to speak elsewhere. I, too, had been encouraged [as a young man] to do this; to pass it [the traditional teachings] on to my fellow-people so that they will not lead their children astray, so that they [themselves] will not be misled by the Whites.

[3]   A certain old man had told me the story I am going to record here, he had been greatly surprised by it; "It is true, Gran-~, the Whites have brought misery upon us," he had said to me. We were discussing how they had brought so much suffering upon many people from the earliest times onwards, I was discussing that. It had been this old man who told me the story, John Beaverbone had been his name.

---

[4]   When first we left to come here, **he said**, from *kinosêwi-sâkahikanihk* over there in Saskatchewan, **he said**, I was twelve years old, **he said**, when we left from there to move here, **he said**. We next stopped on our way at *manitowi-sâkahikanihk*, there my father traded the horses and the wagon, **he said**. The next time we left in our move, we stopped again in our travel here at *maskwacîsihk* and gave the horses a rest, **he said**; we stopped where *maskawi-nâpêw* used to live, **he said**; and then my father hunted so that we would have something to take along, **he said**; and they did indeed get some, **he said**. When we moved camp from there, **he said**, we moved towards Lacombe, **he said**. We moved camp from there, **he said**, well, and then we travelled towards the place they call *kâ-cawacinâsik*, **he said**. Well, our move over there took us all summer, **he said**, we had been stopping here and there along the way across the prairies, **he said**; then we arrived, **he said**. It was at the time of all the deaths, **he said**, it was after that when we left to move here, **he said**.

[5]   Long ago, people had greatly loved one another, **he said**; now the White-Man has torn us apart, **he said**. And it is also his language, as we have been losing -~, as we are losing our language, our Cree language, **he said**; more and more we are embracing the English language, **he said**. But as for us, evidently that language is not for us, it will not sustain us, **he said**; we are going to be lost, our children are going to be lost, **he had said**.

[6]   êkota anim, îtwêw, ê-ati-sa-sâkêwêtâpâsoyâhk ê-otâkosik
anima kâ-cawacinâsik, itwêw, misatimwak kâ-wâpamâyâhkok, êkwa
otâpânâskwak, itwêw. ôki misatimwak ê-nânapwahpisocik, itwêw,
"ââ, kitôtihtânawak ayisiyiniwak," k-êtwêcik, itwêw. otâpânihk
nâway nipim-ây-apin niy, îtwêw, tâpwê niwâpamâwak ôki
misatimwak, itwêw; ayisiyiniwak ôki, iskwêwak nâpêwak, itwêw,
kâ-pê-mâh-matâwisicik, itwêw – ês ôk ê-pê-nitâmisohk, itwêw.
â, konita mînisa kâ-pê-nâh-nayôhtahkik âtiht, itwêw, askihkohk.

[7]   êkos ânitê as-~, ita ôm ê-cahcakwahcâsik, êkota ôk
ê-wawêyapicik ôk âyisiyiniwak, itwêw; nika-kitâpamâwak, itwêw;
kêtahtawê kâ-pasikôcik, itwêw, ê-âh-âkwaskitinitocik, itwêw, êkos
ê-isi-mâtocik, itwêw; "yââw! kîkwây êtok ôki ê-mawîhkâtahkik?"
k-êtêyihtamân, itwêw. êcikw âni [sic], ê-kôtawêyimâcik âtiht
owâhkômâkaniwâwa, namôy êkota ê-wîcihiwêyit, môy ê-wâpamâcik,
itwêw, êkospîhk k-êskwânêhk [sic] ayisiyiniw, itwêw. êkot[a]
ê-kî-wâpahtamân iyikohk ayisiyiniw, ê-sâkihitot, itwêw, êkospîhk,
itwêw, mâk ânohc êkwa, môy kisâkihitonânaw, itwêw.

[8]   êkota êkwa, itwêw, â, êkonik êkwa
ê-ati-sipwê-wîcêwâyâhkok, itwêw, itê anima kâ-~
kâ-pê-ohci-nitâmisocik, êkotê êkwa ê-takohtêyâhk, itwêw. êkota
nitay-ayânân, itwêw, niwîci-piponisîmânânak, itwêw. â, kêtahtaw âwa
pêyak kisêyiniw k-êtasiwêt, itwêw, kik-âsowahamihk ôma sîpiy,
akâmihk ka-nitaw-âyâhk, itwêw; kahkiyaw, kahkiyaw têpêyimowak,
itwêw. êkw êkwa k-âsowakâmê-picihk ôm, îtwêw, Saskatchewan River,
itwêw, anim êkwa Sunchild ita k-âyâcik, itwêw, êkota, itwêw,
ê-nitawâpahtamihk anim âskiy, itwêw, êkota miywêyihtamwak,
itwêw, sakâhk; kinwês ka-miyo-pimâcihohk, ê-mihcêtit pisiskiw,
itwêw.
[9]   kâ-kî-oyôhtâwîyân aw, îtwêw, "hâw, mahti!
kiwâhkômâkaninawak nitawi-nitonawâtânik! ôm ôtê, 'Hinton'
k-êsiyîhkâtêk, êkotê," itwêw; "sisonê asinîwacîhk, aspin ôm êkotê
kâ-kî-isi-sipwêhtêcik," k-êtwêt, itwêw. êkot[a] ôhc âsay mîna
kâ-sipwê-piciyâhk, itwêw, êkw êkwa, ê-at-ây-ayâyâhk, itwêw.

[10]   âsay mîna nimiskawânânak êkotê ayisiyiniwak, itwêw. âsay
mîn êkonik ê-môsko-miywêyihtahkik ê-wâpamikoyâhkok, itwêw; konit
âtiht ôki kêhtê-ayak ê-pê-oy-ocêmicik [sic], iyikohk ê-mâtocik, itwêw,
ê-miywêyihtahkik ê-otihtâyâhkok, itwêw. êkota êkwa, itwêw,
nôhtâwiy êkwa, itwêw, misatimwa ôh, îtwêw, ê-âpacihât ê-mâh-mâcît,
itwêw; â, ê-kiskinohamâht anim îtê ê-mihcêtiyit pisiskiwa, itwêw;

[6]   It was there, at *kâ-cawacinâsik*, **he said**, as we began to drive into view in the evening, **he said**, that we saw horses and wagons, **he said**. The horses were hobbled, **he said**, and they said, "Well! We have come upon people," **he said**. As for me, I was sitting in the back of the wagon, **he said**, I did indeed see the horses, **he said**; and the people, women and men, **he said**, coming out from the bush, **he said** – they had evidently gone there to pick berries, **he said**. Well, some came carrying berries on their backs, **he said**, in pails.

[7]   And then the people settled down and sat over there where the ground was level, **he said**; I kept watching them, **he said**; suddenly they arose, **he said**, and hugged one another, **he said**, and simply wept, **he said**; "By gosh! What might they be crying about?" I thought, **he said**. It must have been that some of them realised the loss of their relatives, the fact that they were not with the group and that they did not see them, **he said**, it was at the time of all the deaths, **he said**. There I saw that people really used to love one another, **he said**, at that time, **he said**, but today we do not love one another, **he said**.

[8]   And then, **he said**, well, we left with them now, **he said**, and returned with them to where they had come from to pick berries, **he said**. There we stayed, **he said**, and spent the winter with them, **he said**. Well, at one time a certain old man announced, **he said**, that the camp should be moved across the river, that the camp should go and live on the other side of the river, **he said**; all of them, all of them agreed, **he said**. And then the camp was moved across the river, **he said**, the Saskatchewan River, **he said**, to the place, **he said**, where the Sunchild band live, **he said**, that land was checked over, **he said**, and they liked it there, **he said**, in the bush; you could live a good life there for a long time, the animals were plentiful, **he said**.

[9]   It was my late father, **he said**, who said, "Well, let us go and look for our relatives! Over there, at the place called Hinton," **he said**; "they have gone over there, the last I know, in the foothills of the Rocky Mountains," he said, **he said**. And once again we left from there and moved, **he said**, and then, **he said**, we kept moving along, **he said**.

[10]   Once again we found people over there, **he said**. And once again these people were moved to tears with joy when they saw us, **he said**; some of the old people came over to kiss me, they wept so much, **he said**, and they were happy that we had come to them, **he said**. And there now, **he said**, my father now, **he said**, made use of the horses, **he said**, in his hunting, **he said**; well, he was shown where the animals were plentiful, **he said**; oh my, we lived a good life, **he said**.

wahwâ, nimiyo-pimâcihonân, **itwêw**. êkos âsay mîn ê-pipohk ôm,
îtwêw, ê-mâci-nôcihcikêt, **itwêw**, wahwâ, ahtayak! mistahi miywâsin,
itwêw, ê-pimâcihoyâhk, **itwêw**.

[11]   kêtahtawê êkotê ê-ay-ayâyâhk, **itwêw**, kâ-takohtêt ayisiyiniw,
itwêw, ê-nayôhtahk, ê-nayôhcikêt, **itwêw**, mihkostikwânêw awa,
âpihtawikosisân, **itwêw**; "ââ, kinitôc [sic] kiciwâmisinaw takohtêw,"
itwêwak, **itwêw**. â, ê-wa-wîcihiwêt êkwa êkota, **itwêw**, wahwâ,
miywâpatisiw aw âpihcaw-âyis, **itwêw**, kêhtê-ayak ôki
miywâpacihêwak, **itwêw**; ê-âkayâsîmot, ê-itwêstamawât ayisiyiniwa,
itwêw, ôh âhtaya k-êtohtahâcik, **itwêw**; â, miywâpatisiw, **itwêw**;
wahwâ, miyw-âyâwak -~ miyw-âyâw, **itwêw**. êkwa iyikohk
ê-oyotôtêmit, **itwêw**; nânitaw isi, ôma mâna, â, nânitaw k-êsistâhk,
itwêw, mawimoscikêwina ôh, **îtwêw**, êkota wîsta ê-wîcihtâsot, **itwêw**;
wahwâ, miywâpacihêwak, **itwêw**. o-~, kinwêsîs ay-ayâw, **itwêw**,
â, wîsta *he's had his own trapline* ayâw, **itwêw**, nôcihcikîwaskiy [sic]
wîst êkotê isi, êkotê ê-miyiht, **itwêw**, â, wîst êkotê, atimwa at-âyâwêw,
itwêw, ê-nôcihcikâkêt, **itwêw**; ê-kiskinohamâht k-êsi-nôcihcikêt, **itwêw**;
wahwâ, miywâpatisiw, **itwêw**.

[12]   kêtahtawê, **itwêw**, ayamihêwiyiniw kâ-takohtêt, **itwêw**,
kinwâpêkasâkêw, **itwêw**. "wah, ayamihêwiyiniw kitôtihtikonaw,"
â, ê-itwêcik mâna kisêyiniwak; mâninakis aw âyamihêwiyiniw, **itwêw**,
ê-papâ-mwêstât-~-mwêstâcîhkawât ôh âyisiyiniwa, **itwêw**;
ê-kakwê-kwêskinât, **itwêw**. êkon ôh âpihcaw-âyisa, **itwêw**, wahwâ,
mwêstâcîhkawêw, **itwêw**; ayis êkoni ê-~ ê-itwêstamâkot, **itwêw**, piyis
ati-sâkôcimêw, **itwêw**. piyis êkwa ê-sâ-sipwêhtahât, **itwêw**, nêhi nêtê
wâhyaw ayisiyiniwa ê-papâ-nitonawât, **itwêw**; mâh-miskawêwak,
itwêw. kêtahtawê âpihcaw-âyis aw, **îtwêw**, kâ-mâtahpinêt, **itwêw**.
môy êkwa awa -~, môy êkwa awa kî-nanâtawihêw awa
ayamihêwiyiniw, **itwêw**, nêhiyawa êkwa ôhi pê-wêpinamawêw,
itwêw. â, kêtahtawê êkosi miton âh-êtatawisiw, **itwêw**; kahkiyaw
ôki kisêyiniwak, **itwêw**, mêh-mîskoc [sic] ê-nipiskâtâcik, **itwêw**, môy
kî-kiskêyihtamwak tânis ê-itâspinêyit, **itwêw**.

[13]   kêtahtawê awa pêyak, **itwêw** – mêtoni mân ê-wî-nipit
aw âpihcaw-âyis, **itwêw**, kâwi mân ê-âpisisihk, **itwêw**; wahwâ,
kakwâtakihik, **itwêw** -~ kakwâtakihtâw, **itwêw**. kêtahtawê awa pêyak
kisêyiniw, **itwêw**, ê-saskahamâht, **itwêw**, mêton âciyaw kâ-nikamot,
itwêw. ê-kîsi-nikamot, **itwêw**, "hâw, niwâhkômâkanitik! namôy âw
ê-âhkosit aw âyisiyiniw; mahti pêhotân, wâpahki, tânisi kiy-ês-âyât!
êkosi ka-kiskêyihtênânaw," k-êtwêt, **itwêw**.

And so it was winter once again, **he said**, and he began trapping, **he said**, oh my, the pelts! It was a very good life, **he said**, we lived, **he said**.

[11]   It was at one time while we were living over there, **he said**, that someone with a backpack arrived, **he said**, he had a backpack on, **he said**, and he had red hair, he was a halfbreed, **he said**; "Well! Our brother has arrived," they said, **he said**. Well, then he stayed on with the people there, **he said**, oh my, this halfbreed was useful, **he said**, the old people made good use of him, **he said**; he spoke English and interpreted for the people, **he said**, when they took the pelts to the post, **he said**; well, he was useful, **he said**; oh my, they had a good life -~ he had a good life, **he said**. And he was so friendly, **he said**; any kind, well, when any kind of ceremony was held, **he said**, the rites of worship, **he said**, he, too, helped with that, **he said**; oh my, they made good use of him, **he said**. He lived there for quite a while, **he said**, well, he, too, had his own trapline, **he said**, he, too, had a trapline assigned to him over there, **he said**, well, eventually he had his own dogs over there, **he said**, and trapped with them, **he said**; and he was taught how to trap, **he said**; oh my, he was useful, **he said**.

[12]   At one time, **he said**, a priest arrived, **he said**, in a long robe, **he said**. "Wow, a priest has come to us," well, the old men would say; and the priest kept on, **he said**, going about bothering the people, **he said**; trying to convert them, **he said**. And that halfbreed, **he said**, oh my, he [the priest] did bother him, **he said**; for that one interpreted for him, **he said**, and at last he came to convince him, **he said**. Then, at last, he kept taking him away with him, **he said**, and went looking about for those people far away over yonder, **he said**; and they did find some here and there, **he said**. After a time the halfbreed, **he said**, began to be ill, **he said**. And then -~, and then the priest could not doctor him, **he said**, and then he brought him back and left him with the Crees, **he said**. Well, after a while, then, he was about to die, **he said**; all the old men, **he said**, took turns treating him, **he said**, but they could not discover the nature of his illness, **he said**.

[13]   After a while one of them, **he said** – the halfbreed would be very close to death, **he said**, and again he would be coming back to life, **he said**; oh my, it [the illness] made him suffer, **he said** -~ he suffered, **he said**. After a while a pipe was lit, **he said**, for one of the old men, **he said**, and he sang for a very short time, **he said**. When he had finished singing, **he said**, "Now, My Relatives! This person is not ill; let us wait and see how he is tomorrow! In that way we will know," he said, **he said**.

[14] â, kêtahtawê, **itwêw**, ê-ati-wâpaniyik, **itwêw**,
kâ-wâwâstaminaw-~ kâ-wâwâstinamawât ôhi pêyak, **itwêw**, ê-nitomât,
itwêw; kîkway ka-minihkwêsit ê-nitawêyihtahk, **itwêw**, sêmâk, **itwêw**,
mîcimâpoy, **itwêw**, ê-mâh-minahiht, **itwêw**; êkwa ê-sêsâwiniht ôhi
wiyawihk, **itwêw**, wâskikanihk, **itwêw**.

[15] kêtahtawê, **itwêw**, ê-wâh-ostostotahk ôm, **îtwêw**, kâ-kaskihtât
êkwa, mitoni kwayask ê-ostostotahk, **itwêw**. "pakâhkam ôm êkwa,
nikâh-kaskihtân ka-pîkiskwêyân," k-êtwêt, **itwêw**. "hêhêhêêhahê,
niwâhkômâkanitik! êkây nânitaw itêyimik, iyikohk
kâ-kakwâtakihitakok! êkây nânitaw itêyihtamok, niwâhkômâkanitik!
aw âwa, aw ôta kâ-kinwâpêkasâkêt, kâ-kî-takohtêt, êwakw âw âwa
kâ-mi-~ kâ-misiwanâcihit, kêkâc kâ-misiwanâcihit," **itwêw**, itwêw,
itwêw. "mâk êkwa, môya wîhkâc kîhtwâm, isko ka-pimâtisiyân, môy
kîhtwâm êkotowahk nika-nitohtawâw, kêkât nimisiwanâcihik,"
k-êtwêt, **itwêw**. "kiyawâw ês ôma, anima kâ-kî-isi-miyikowisiyêk,
anima kitisi-mawimoscikêwiniwâw kâ-wîci-tôtamômitakok, êwakw ês
ôma nîsta ka-pimitisahamân. êkosi, nika-pihkohon."
[16] "kêtahtawê ôma mâna, sôskwâc ôma kâ-êtatawisiyân,
ê-sipwêhtêyân ôma mâna, aw ôtê kihc-ôskâpêwis ê-otihtak. 'yôôôh,
kitakohtân!' ê-isit mân," **îtwêw**, " 'hâw, ôm ôma mêskanaw
kâ-kî-miyikowisiyan, mâka nêma kâ-pimitisahaman, nêma kotak;
niyâ! wâwonî! êwako pimitisaha!' ê-isit mân," **îtwêw**, "êkosi mâna
kâ-pê-wâwonîyân; kâ-pê-wâwonîyân anima mâna k-âpisisiniyân. âsay
mîna kîhtwâm mîna mâna kêkâc kâ-nipiyân; âsay mîn ânima mân
ê-sipwêhtêyân, êwak ôma môniyâwi-mêskanaw, nêtê mân
ê-takohtêyân. 'â, kiwanisinin! â, piko ka-wâwonîyan; nêhiyaw-mihko
ôm ê-kikiskaman,' ê-itikawiyân mân," **îtwêw**, "kâ-pê-wâwonîyân kâwi
mâna – ayis ninêhiyawân! mitoni kinisitohtâtinâwâw, êwak ôma
kâ-pâh-pimohtahikoyân," k-êtwêt, **itwêw**.

[17] "kapê-ayi ôm îyikohk kâ-kakwâtakihtâyân, kapê-ay ôm
êkosi ê-itahkamikisiyân. ôm êkwa iskwêyâc kâ-sipwêhtêyân, ôma
nêhiyawi-mêskanaw kâ-mitimêyân. nêtê an[a] ôskâpêwis k-ôtihtak,
ê-mâtoyân anima. 'yaw, kimâton!' – 'êha, nimâton. nimihtâtên,
kâ-wanisiniyân kêkâc,' ê-itak. 'hâw, niyâ! wâwonî! nêtê takohtêyani,
êkotê ka-wîhtamâkawin,' k-êsit," **itwêw**. "ê-takohtêyân ôta, ayisiyiniw
kî-pimisin," **itwêw**, "ôtê ayisiyiniw kâ-miciminit, ôtê [*gesture*], ômis
[*gesture*] ê-isi-pakamisimit, êkota ôma k-âpisisiniyân," k-êtwêt, **itwêw**;
"êkosi kâwi kâ-pêkopayiyân, kâ-wâpamitakok ôma. namôy ôm

[14]   Well, suddenly, **he said**, when dawn was approaching, **he said**, he [the halfbreed] waved at one of them, **he said**, beckoning him to come, **he said**; he wanted something to drink, **he said**, and right away, **he said**, he was given sips of soup, **he said**, to drink, **he said**; and then he had his limbs exercised, **he said**, on his body, on his chest, **he said**.

[15]   After a while, **he said**, as he kept coughing, **he said**, then he was able to cough properly, **he said**. "Now, I believe, I might be able to speak," he said, **he said**. "Hey hey heey hahey, My Relatives! Forgive me that I have caused you so much suffering! Do not hold it against me, My Relatives! It was he, the one who had arrived here in a long robe, it was that one who has destroyed me, who has almost destroyed me," **he said**, he said, **he said**. "But now I will never again, so long as I live, I will never again listen to that kind, he has almost destroyed me," he said, **he said**. "It is that which you, for your part, have been given by the powers, your way of worship in which I participated with you, it is that which I, too, must follow. With that I will be released."

[16]   "At times, when I was close to death, I would depart and, over there, I would come upon the Great Server. 'Oooh, you have arrived!' he would say to me," **he said**, " 'Now, this is the road which you were given by the powers, but you followed that one yonder, that other one; go! turn around! follow this one!' he would say to me," **he said**, "and so I would turn around hither; it was when I turned around hither that I would come back to life. And again, once again, I would be almost dead; and once again I would depart and arrive over yonder on the White-Man's road. 'Well, you are lost! Well, you must turn around; you have Cree blood in you,' I would be told," **he said**, "and I would turn back hither again – for I speak Cree! I fully understand you, that is what has been sustaining me," he said, **he said**.

[17]   "During the times when I was suffering greatly [at the crisis], this is what I was doing during that time. The last time now, when I departed, I followed the Cree road. And when I reached that Server, I was weeping. 'Lo, you are weeping!' – 'Yes, I am weeping. I regret that I was almost lost,' I said to him. 'Now, go! turn around! When you arrive over yonder, there you will receive your instructions,' he said to me," **he said**. "When I arrived here, a human being lay there," **he said**, "and a human being held me here [*gesture*] and threw me down like this [*gesture*], and it was then that I came back to life," he said, **he said**; "and so it was that, when I awoke again, I saw you.

ê-ohc-âhkosiyân [nb: ê-ohc-âhkosíyân] – ê-kî-pâstâhoyân ôma,"
k-êtwêt, itwêw.

[18] nêw-âskiy nikî-wîcêwânân an[a], îtwêw; kêtahtawê
kâ-mâyamahcihot, itwêw, tâpiskôc ê-nipât, itwêw, êkosi; êkosi
nikî-nakatikonân, itwêw. êkos êtokwê kî-pihkohow; anima
kâ-kî-isi-miyikowisit, wîst îtê kik-êtâcih-~ [sc: kik-êtâcihot]
kik-êsi-sipwêhtêt, êkos êtokwê kî-pihkohow, ê-kî-isit ana kisêyiniw,
êwak ôma âcimowin mâna k-âtotamân.

[19] ka-mâmitonêyihtahk ayisiyiniw, ê-otawâsimisit, ê-oyôsisimit,
nêhiyaw-mihko kê-kikiskahk, tânêhk ânima kâ-kî-kanâtahk
kimihkonaw [nb: kimihkónaw] – môy tâpiskôc wâpiskiwiyâs,
pâstâhowi-mihko k-âyât, ê-kî-itwêt ana, ana kisêyiniw.

---

[20] êwako mân ôm ê-mâmitonêyihtamân mâna, ôki
nitawâsimisak, mistahi mâna k-âhkwâtisiyân, ê-ohti-nâkatôhkêyân; ayis
nîsta nisâkihâwason, nisâkihâwak niwâhkômâkanak.

[21] âyiman, âyimanohk kipimohtânaw. âyiman, âyimanohk
kitakohtahikonaw, nanâtohk ôhi ayamihâwina k-âti-pimitisahamahk,
nanâtohk ita k-âti-wîcihiwêyahk, k-âti-tâpwêhtawâyahk awa
wâpiskiwiyâs – wîst âna pîtos ê-kî-isi-miyikowisit. "êkây êkosi
tôtamôhkan!" ê-kî-isit mâna, ôta mân ê-kî-wa-wîcêwak ana kisêyiniw.

[22] hâw, êkwayikohk.

I was not ill at all – I had committed a breach of the natural order,"
he said, **he said**.

[18]   We had him with us for another four years, **he said**; at one
time he came to feel unwell, **he said**, it seemed as though he were
sleeping, **he said**, that was the end; thus he left us, **he said**. Thus he
must have been released; thus, where he, too, had been given by the
powers to go, to that place he must have been released, **that old man
had said to me, this is the story I usually tell.**

[19]   Let people with children and grandchildren think about it,
those who will have Cree blood in them, why our blood used to be
pure – not like the White-Man's who has sinful blood, **that old man
had said.**

---

[20]   I usually think about this when I am so strict with my
children and watch over them; for I, too, love my children, and I love
my relatives.

[21]   It is difficult, we walk a difficult road. It is difficult, the
Whites have led us into a difficult situation now that we begin to
follow religions of various kinds, participate in various rites, and
believe the Whites – they, too, were given their own religion by the
powers. "Don't ever practise theirs!" that old man used to say to me
when I used to have him living here with me.

[22]   Now, that is enough.

NOTES

1   Freda Ahenakew wishes to acknowledge above all the gift of the text by Joseph Tootoosis.

The Cree Language Project under whose auspices the text was recorded and prepared for publication is supported by the Social Sciences and Humanities Research Council of Canada.

2   Not all the proper names, whether of people or places, have been identified as fully as they might be: additional enquiry *in situ* or in the archives might well yield further details.

3   The itinerary from *kinosêwi-sâkahikanihk* 'at Fish Lake' [Jackfish Lake] (where both Cree and Saulteaux [Ojibwe] are spoken in an area often subsumed under the regional term Cochin) roughly follows the valley of the Battle River, south of which lies *manitowi-sâkahikanihk* 'at God's Lake' [the modern Manito Lake], to *maskwacîsihk* 'at the Bear Hills', an area now collectively referred to as Hobbema.

kâ-cawacinâsik 'The-Opening-between-the-Hills' is almost certainly to be sought in the vicinity of Rocky Mountain House, on the south side of the Saskatchewan and with the Sunchild Reserve across the river; the foothills area which stretches north from here (the town of Hinton lies on the Jasper-Edmonton road) remained a favourite hunting terrain until it was at last destroyed by the petroleum developments of the past fifteen years.

4   The QUOTATIVE use of *itwêw* appears to have been discussed for the first time in our introduction to *wâskahikaniwiyiniw-âcimowina / Stories of the House People, Told By Peter Vandall and Joe Douquette* (F. Ahenakew, ed., Publications of the Algonquian Text Society, Winnipeg: University of Manitoba Press, 1987; pp. xiii-xiv).

It was a rather unusual Dean of Arts who during the summer of 1982 annotated an experimental edition of these texts with helpful comments.

Women in the History of Linguistics

Donna H. Breyfogle

Surprisingly little appears to have been published concerning women in the history of linguistics. Women linguists and the rôle of women in linguistics do not figure prominently in standard surveys of the field, such as R.H. Robins' *Short History of Linguistics* (1984); collective biographies of linguists frequently do not include women (for example, Davis 1980; Sebeok 1967); the *Cambridge Encyclopedia of Language* (Crystal 1987) does not address the topic of women linguists or women in the history of linguistics. Indeed, the state of the field is such that library tools such as *Books in Print* (1990) and *Library of Congress Subject Headings* (1989) do not even give the terms "Women in linguistics" or "Women linguists" as subject headings, although they do include such headings as "Women in medicine," "Women in science," "Women anthropologists," "Women musicians," and "Women mathematicians".

While the history of women in linguistics has been largely neglected, the past two decades have seen a great deal of research on their rôle in other disciplines. The substantial work that has been done, for example, on the history of women in the sciences and in art[1] suggests the direction which research on women in linguistics might take.

SCIENCE

The history of women in science – a term which is here restricted to the "pure" sciences[2] – has captured widespread attention. The review articles of Carolyn Merchant (1982), Dorinda Outram (1987) and Londa Schiebinger (1987) identify a variety of approaches to the study of women in the history of science – biographical, historical, and psychoanalytical.

Biographical works have the longest tradition, one of the earliest examples of the genre being George Ballard's *Memoirs of British Ladies who have been Celebrated for their Writings or Skill in the Learned Languages, Arts, and Sciences*, published in 1752. Much collective biography has been published since, including H.J. Mozans' 1913 work, *Woman in Science: With an Introductory Chapter on Woman's Long Struggle for the Things of the Mind*, and Margaret Alic's *Hypatia's Heritage: A History of Women in Science from Antiquity Through the Late Nineteenth Century* (1988). Mozans and Alic draw attention to the contributions of women scientists which have been ignored. In addition to biographical dictionaries of general scope, such as Marilyn Bailey Ogilvie's *Women in Science, Antiquity Through the Nineteenth Century: A Biographical Dictionary with Annotated Bibliography* (1986), some work has focussed upon women in particular fields, such as mathematics (e.g., Osen 1974) and astronomy (e.g., Rizzo 1954).

Individual biographies have been devoted to such outstanding figures as Margaret Cavendish, Duchess of Newcastle (Sarasohn 1984; Paloma 1980) and Anne Conway (Merchant 1979). The more recent publications of this genre, including the three mentioned here, are significant for placing the individuals' work within the social and intellectual context of the time rather than treating their involvement with science as curiosities.

The more general histories which have appeared concentrate more sharply on the context of women's participation in science. Rather than asking, "Why are there no women scientists?", the question they put might be phrased: "Why are there so few women scientists *that we know about?*" (Schiebinger 1989:2). In *Women Scientists in America: Struggles and Strategies to 1940* (1982), for example, Margaret W. Rossiter examines the social and institutiofial factors affecting the limited participation of women in science. She documents the relegation of female scientists to subordinate status within the scientific enterprise, both as to the type of work they were expected to perform and in terms of the double standard of recognition and advancement. Rossiter's survey includes revealing statistics regarding university degrees awarded, employers of female scientists, relationship of marital status to unemployment for female scientists, and notable couples in science before 1940.

Londa Schiebinger's historical study, *The Mind Has No Sex? Women in the Origins of Modern Science* (1989), examines the increasing restrictions placed upon women's participation in science in the seventeenth and eighteenth centuries. In tracing the effect of the professionalisation and institutionalisation of science upon the limited access of women to the field, she stresses "the tendency in early modern science to make women and their work peripheral, to constrain them within very narrow circuits of thought and reputation" (Geertz 1989:20). As Schiebinger adds, some scientists stopped at very little – even publishing illustrations of women with disproportionately small skulls and large pelvises – in trying to justify their exclusion. In an earlier essay (1988), Schiebinger had explored the iconography of science – the replacement, by the beginning of the nineteenth century, of the image of science as Woman, with that of an efficient, serious, self-sufficient White male wearing a white lab coat.

The significance of metaphor and imagery is pursued, as well, by Carolyn Merchant in *The Death of Nature: Women, Ecology, and the Scientific Revolution* (1979), where she links the decline of women's participation in science and a changed, less sympathetic perception and portrayal of nature with the masculinisation of science as a result of the Scientific Revolution.

Both historical studies (e.g., Merchant 1979; Easlea 1981) and works in the philosophy of science (e.g., Fee 1983; Harding 1986; Keller 1985) portray science as masculine in nature – "reflecting traditional stereotypical male values: it is 'hardnosed', objective, value-free" (I. Mitroff & R. Kilmann, quoted in Bentley & Watts 1986:121). In terms of the dichotomies linked to sex in Western civilisation – masculine/feminine, public/private, active/passive, reason/emotion, objective/subjective – it is apparent that the stereotypical articulation of feminine characteristics and values is seen as antithetical to scientific pursuits. Feminist historians of science, by contrast, would argue for a direct correlation between the limited participation of women in science, past and current, and the masculine nature of science.

Both Merchant (1979) and Schiebinger (1989) point to the Scientific Revolution as a turning point in this defining and delimiting process. Merchant focusses on the sixteenth and seventeenth centuries, while Schiebinger pays greater attention to the seventeenth and eighteenth centuries – the time period when, she claims, modern norms of science and femininity were being established.

Explanations for the alienation of women from science have also been offered from the perspective of psychoanalysis. The theory of object relations is used, for example, in an analysis of Cartesian thought by Susan Bardo (1986) and a study of Bacon's impact on the intellectual origins of the masculine character of science by Evelyn Fox Keller (1985).

Feminist philosophers of science have gone beyond exploring the relationship between the under-representation of women in science and the discipline of science, and have raised the question whether a "feminist science" is possible at all (e.g., Harding 1986; Longino 1989). There is little consensus on this point. In a recent review of the field, Sue Curry Jansen (1990:236) emphasises the change of focus:

> Unlike earlier feminist attempts to correct or reform science, the new feminist epistemologies raise fundamental questions about the nature of truth, objectivity, observation, empiricism, verification, and rationality.

The argument for an approach to science which is feminist in nature is put most persuasively by Evelyn Fox Keller (1981:418):

It is not the case that the history of science lacks instances of the kinds of thinking regarded as feminine (relational, contextual, intuitive), but rather, that both the paradigms that emerge as dominant and the image that is projected of how these theories have emerged appear suspiciously consonant with what is regarded as masculine.

Keller advocates a scientific methodology that would embrace subjectivity and thinking "just like a woman" –

the unique contribution feminism makes to more traditional studies of science is the use of that expertise that has traditionally belonged to women – not simply as a woman's perspective – but as a critical instrument" (quoted in Bentley & Watts 1986:127).

The application of critical thinking interpreted as more relational and more "feminine" in approach is exemplified in "The Force of the Pacemaker Concept in Theories of Aggregation in Cellular Slime Mold" (Keller 1985) and *A Feeling for the Organism: The Life and Work of Barbara McClintock* (Keller 1983).

Much has already been accomplished in the study of women in the history of science. "Lost" women scientists have been identified and studied; historical surveys have been written; for some areas statistical analyses have been completed to help provide a clearer image of the representation of women in the scientific world. Both historians and philosophers have considered the reasons for the under-representation of females in science and its effects. Finally, the question has been raised whether the increasing involvement of women in science will have an impact upon the discipline, perhaps to the extent that a "feminist science" will become recognisable.

ART

The study of women in the history of art is defined by similar issues.[3]
It would be difficult to overrate the influence of Linda Nochlin's 1971 essay, "Why Are There No Great Woman Artists?" (1988). Rather than identifying previously overlooked female artists, Nochlin criticises the assumptions behind the very question she poses. She points to institutional and social limitations upon the participation of women in the arts (to whom, for example, nude models were simply not available) and argues against the primacy of individual genius, "the myth of the Great Artist" (Nochlin 1988:153), in the assessment of artistic achievement.

Since 1971, the participation of women in the history of art has been documented in a variety of forms: in biographical and bibliographical works such as Chris Pettey's *Dictionary of Women Artists: An International Dictionary of Woman Artists Born Before 1900* (1985) and Eleanor Tufts' *American Women Artists, Past and Present: A Selected Bibliographic Guide* (1984); surveys of art history such as Elsa Honing Fine's *Women and Art: A History of Women Painters and Sculptors from the Renaissance to the 20th Century* (1978) or Wendy Slatkin's *Women Artists in History from Antiquity to the 20th Century* (1990); and exhibition catalogues, such as Ann Sutherland Harris' and Linda Nochlins' *Women Artists 1550-1950* (1976).

Criticism of such work has focussed upon its perceived readiness "to place women artists within the traditional historical framework" (Gouma-Peterson & Mathews 1988:327) of the study of art history. More recent scholarship, inspired by a feminist critical perspective, the methodology of social history, Marxist theoretical and methodological approaches, criticism based upon deconstruction, psychoanalysis and Lacanian critical theory, offers more fundamental challenges to the discipline of art history. Rather than attempting to integrate women into the existing framework, many current writers question virtually all the assumptions and presuppositions of the discipline. In short, there has been a clear shift in focus from the study of women in the history of art to feminist art history.

A feminist art historian whose work encompasses many of these critical approaches is Griselda Pollock. A work she co-authored with Roszika Parker, *Old Mistresses: Women, Art, and Ideology* (1981), emphasises the necessity of taking the social environment into account in analysing the position of women artists – analysing their position "structurally and relatively, to ask how the social categories 'women' and 'artist' intersect at given moments to allow or inhibit a woman artist's choices and possibilities" (Zemel 1990:337).

In a more recent work, *Vision and Difference: Femininity, Feminism and the Histories of Art* (1988), Pollock pursues this approach further, arguing that "complementing the task of deconstruction is feminist rewriting of the history of art in terms which firmly locate gender relations as a determining factor in cultural production and in signification" (1988:12). Pollock points to the eighteenth and nineteenth centuries as the critical phase in the evolution of both gender relations and our current conception of the artist (1988:48-49):

By the nineteenth century, with the consolidation of a patriarchal bourgeoisie as the dominant social class, women were increasingly locked into place in the family... Femininity was exclusively domestic and maternal. At the same time the bourgeois notions of the artist evolved, associating the creator with anything that was anti-domestic, whether it was the Romantic ideal of outsiderness and alliance with sublime Nature or Bohemian models of free living, sexually energetic, socially alienated outcasts. As bourgeois femininity was to be lived out in rigidly enforced reproductive and prescribed supportive rôles, a profound contradiction was established between the ideological identities of the artist and of woman.

Feminist art historians, taking note of the under-representation of women in the field of art, have also challenged the "authority or validity of the male-defined notion of greatness and artistic achievement" (Gouma-Peterson & Mathews 1988:327) and "the meaning and pervasiveness of the equation between art by women and femininity, and between femininity and bad art" (Pollock 1983:40). It is a matter of theoretical and practical consequence alike that "a large part of traditional female creative output that conveyed a female experience had been invalidated as art or relegated to the category of 'craft' through the creation of an aesthetic hierarchy qualitatively differentiating 'high' from 'low' art" (Gouma-Peterson & Mathews 1988:332). Should women's art be judged by different standards from men's? Is there, based upon their sensibility and experience, a "women's imagery that can be distinguished from that of men" (Gouma-Peterson & Mathews 1988:336)?

Research on women in the history of art has led to the identification of "lost" and undervalued female artists, and explored the reasons for their restricted access to the field. Above all, however, feminist art historians have challenged basic assumptions in the fields of art and art history, bringing about a sharp transition: from an effort to minimise the differences in the artistic contribution of men and women to the assertion of very basic differences.

LINGUISTICS

The history of women in linguistics is, at most, in its infancy. Its future path might well follow the general pattern outlined by Gerda Lerner (1976:357-365): (1) "compensatory history" – the history of notable women; (2) "contribution history" – documenting "women's contribution to, their status in, and their oppression by male-defined society;" (3) "transitional history" – an approach that would introduce new questions relevant to women's experience of the world, rather than accepting existing methodological approaches.

At this point, the history of linguistics has not even identified its "women worthies." There are no dictionaries of women linguists, no collective biographies of females who have been involved in linguistic pursuits. Ballard's compendium of 1752 might provide a useful point of departure. General surveys such as Antonia Fraser's *The Weaker Vessel: Woman's Lot in Seventeenth-Century England* (1984) also identify a number of women involved in language-related pursuits. Such works, however, do not consider their subjects from the perspective of the history of linguistics.

Individual biographies are available for many women who would figure in an historical dictionary of female linguists; for instance, the eighteenth-century Saxonist, Elizabeth Elstob (Green 1980); the Dutch scholar, Anna Maria van Schurman (Irwin 1980); and Bathsua Makin, a seventeenth-century English scholar (Brink 1978, 1980; Myers 1985).[4] Only rarely, however, do such studies focus on the language-related work of these women, and the question of their significance as women in linguistics is not addressed.

One of the few linguists to have written about a woman linguist is Vivian Salmon (1987). Ironically, however, Salmon does not present her study of Bathsua Makin as a contribution to the history of women in linguistics (1987:304):

> It cannot be claimed that she [Makin] was a linguist of any great originality, though as a woman she was a pioneer; but an account of her life and works may be of value to educationalists who argue that "scholarly biographies of educated women are needed before the history of women's education is complete" ... and to social historians who acknowledge that the "recent feminist revival has its priorities, and a systematic revaluation of lesser known feminists in history has clearly not been one of them."

While she considers Makin to be significant, Salmon appears convinced that her work on Makin is more important to the history of education and social history than to the history of linguistics.

Clearly, more "compensatory" documentation (to follow Lerner's scheme) needs to be gathered about women in linguistics before the next step, to "contribution" and "transitional" history, can be taken. The examples from science and art suggest some of the issues to be addressed: differences in the ways in which men and women function within a discipline; sexist assumptions and stereotypes embedded within supposedly neutral and objective disciplines; and challenges to the very nature of the disciplines themselves.

In the meantime, however, some introspective analysis has begun, for example in Deborah Cameron's *Feminism and Linguistic Theory* (1985). Her aims (1985:2) include a critique of academic linguistics:[5]

> This is not just a matter of pointing out sexist assumptions and practices, important though they may be: more radically it involves questioning the whole scientific/objective basis of linguistics and showing how the practices of linguists are implicated in patriarchal ideology and oppression.

In her critique of linguistic theory, for example, Cameron argues that linguists are wrong to claim that there is no connection between grammatical gender and sex, and proceeds to claim that sexism is found not only in language, but in the analyses which linguists have made of it.

What is noticeably absent from Cameron's work is any analysis of the part which the limited participation of women has played in the development of linguistic theory and analysis. It would be interesting to determine if, as suggested for the history of women in science (Schiebinger 1989), women had been comparatively active in the field at one time and subsequently found their involvement curtailed.

Valuable insights into the discipline might also be gained by investigating the nature of women's participation in linguistics: are (or were) female linguists working predominantly in particular areas, and, if so, what can we learn from this about the discipline, about socially acceptable areas of work for women, or about institutions which train linguists? In the sciences, for example, proportionately greater numbers of women work in cell and molecular biology (Gornick 1990:25) and primatology (Bleir 1988:186-187).

Has the work of female linguists been primarily of a supportive and secondary nature? An example from anthropology suggests the type of gender-specific task distinctions which might be discovered in linguistics. In her study of Camilla Wedgwood, Nancy Lutkehaus observes that "some of the projects she was engaged in, such as her museum work at Cambridge and the editing of [Bernard] Deacon's fieldnotes,... had the connotation of gender-specific preoccupations" (1986:791).

Should it turn out that the history of women in linguistics differs from that in other disciplines, it would be equally interesting to ask why this should be the case, and what effect it might have. The increasing interest in women in the history of various disciplines is clearly linked to concerns about their current status. Even in the field of art, Gouma-Peterson & Mathews (1987:329) draw attention to the practical impact of the early feminist movement of the 1960s, with female artists seeking "economic parity and equal representation in exhibitions."

Among the obstacles which historians of women in linguistics will have to overcome, the first is that of identifying female scholars in earlier time periods. Name changes aside, the negative association between femininity and scholarship may have caused them to publish anonymously or under a pseudonym.

Many successful artists were the daughters of artists or had a close personal connection with a more prominent male artist (Orenstein 1975:510; Nochlin 1988:168-169). In literature, too, there are well-known cases of supportive and collaborative relationships, for example, the friendship between Hester Thrale and the lexicographer Samuel Johnson; a number of these are examined in *Mothering the Mind, Twelve Studies of Writers and Their Silent Partners* (1984) by Ruth Perry and Brownley Martine Watson. In trying to identify "lost" women in the history of linguistics, one might well begin by looking for similarly associated male linguists.

Rossiter has stressed the value of manuscript sources for the study of women in the sciences, particularly for the light they shed on "the motivation, attitudes, and behaviour behind the statistics" (1982:xi). Manuscripts frequently do not survive, however, and those belonging to women may be particularly endangered. It is reported (Reynolds 1929:57) that the seventeenth-century prophetess Eleanor Davies was married twice and had her manuscripts burnt by both husbands.

Perhaps the greatest challenge for the history of women in linguistics is the need for triple expertise on the part of the researcher. In order to study print and manuscript sources that have survived, to assess the contribution of female linguists and to critically examine the discipline of linguistics in the light of women's participation, the researcher must have an understanding of the history of the discipline and of linguistic theory. In addition, she/he needs to be sensitive to the historical experience of women and, if we are to move beyond "compensatory" and "contribution" history, willing and able to adopt a feminist theoretical perspective.[6]

NOTES

1   The brief reviews which follow are not intended to be comprehensive, but merely to suggest and illustrate the range and variety of publications in these fields.
2   For feminist perspectives on such applied sciences as medicine and various technological fields see Donnison 1977, Smith 1976 or Rothchild 1983.
3   An extensive review of research in this field is provided by Thalia Gouma-Peterson and Patricia Mathews in "The Feminist Critique of Art History" (1987). For a critique of this review, with a response, see Broude & Garrard 1989.
4   That a majority of examples deal with seventeenth-century England is only in part due to personal interest; this is also the period upon which extended investigations regarding women in the history of linguistics have focussed.
5   Cameron's work is distinct from the feminist critiques of language and language use (as opposed to the discipline of linguistics and linguistic theory) which have flourished in the past fifteen years; see, for example, Lakoff 1975 or Spender 1980.
6   Synchronic data on many of these issues may be found in a book which arrived while this essay was in proof: Alice Davison & Penelope Eckert, eds., 1990. *Women in the Linguistics Profession: The Cornell Lectures*. Washington, D.C.: Committee on the Status of Women in Linguistics, Linguistic Society of America.

REFERENCES

Alic, Margaret. 1986. *Hypatia's Heritage: A History of Women in Science from Antiquity Through the Late Nineteenth Century*. Boston: Beacon Press.
Ballard, George. 1752. *Memoirs of British Ladies who have been Celebrated for their Writings or Skill in the Learned Languages, Arts, and Sciences*. London: T. Evans. [reprinted Detroit: Wayne State University Press, 1985]
Bentley, D., & D.M. Watts. 1986. Courting the Positive Virtues: A Case for Feminist Science. *European Journal of Science Education* 8:121-134.
Bleir, Ruth. 1988. A Decade of Feminist Critiques in the Natural Sciences. *Signs: Journal of Women in Culture and Society* 14:182-195.
Books in Print, 1990-91 – Subject Guide, vol. 4. New York: R.R. Bowker.
Brink, J.R. 1978. Bathsua Makin: Scholar and Educator of the Seventeenth Century. *International Journal of Women's Studies* 1:417-426.

—. 1980. Bathsua Makin: Educator and Linguist. J.R. Brink, ed., *Female Scholars: A Tradition of Learned Women Before 1800*, 86-100. Montreal: Eden Press.

Broude, Norma, & Mary D. Garrard. 1989. Discussion: An Exchange on the Feminist Critique of Art History. *Art Bulletin* 71:124-127.

Cameron, Deborah. 1985. *Feminism and Linguistic Theory*. New York: St. Martin's Press.

Crystal, David. 1987. *The Cambridge Encyclopedia of Language*. Cambridge: Cambridge University Press.

Davis, Boyd H., & Raymond K. O'Cain, eds. 1980. *First Person Singular: Papers from the Conference on an Oral Archive for the History of American Linguistics*. Amsterdam: John Benjamins.

Donnison, Jean. 1977. *Midwives and Medical Men: A History of Inter-Professional Rivalries and Women's Rights*. London: Heinemann.

Easlea, Brian. 1981. *Science and Sexual Oppression: Patriarchy's Confrontation with Nature*. London: Weidenfeld & Nicolson.

Fee, Elizabeth. 1983. Women's Nature and Scientific Objectivity. M. Lowe & R. Hubbard, eds., *Woman's Nature: Rationalizations of Inequality*, 9-27. New York: Pergamon Press.

Fine, Elsa Honig. 1978. *Women and Art: A History of Women Painters and Sculptors from the Renaissance to the 20th Century*. Montclair, New Jersey: Allanheld & Schram.

Fraser, Antonia. 1984. *The Weaker Vessel: Woman's Lot in Seventeenth-Century England*. London: Weidenfeld & Nicolson.

Geertz, Clifford. 1989. A Lab of One's Own [reviews of *Feminism and Science* by Nancy Tuana; *The Mind Has No Sex? Women in the Origins of Modern Science* by Londa Schiebinger; *Primate Visions: Gender, Race, and Nature in the World of Modern Science* by Donna Haraway]. *New York Review of Books* 37 (8 November 1990):19-23.

Gornick, Vivian. 1990. *Women in Science*, rev. ed. New York: Touchstone.

Gouma-Peterson, Thalia, & Patricia Mathews. 1987. The Feminist Critique of Art History. *Art Bulletin* 69:326-357.

Green, Mary Elizabeth. 1980. Elizabeth Elstob: The Saxon Nymph (English, 1683-1765). J.R. Brink, ed., *Female Scholars: A Tradition of Learned Women Before 1800*, 137-160. Montreal: Eden Press.

Harding, Sandra. 1986. *The Science Question in Feminism*. Ithaca, New York: Cornell University Press.

Harris, Ann Sutherland, & Linda Nochlin. 1976. *Women Artists 1550-1950*. New York: Random House.

Irwin, Joyce. 1980. Anna Maria van Schurman: The Star of Utrecht (1607-1678). J.R. Brink, ed., *Female Scholars: A Tradition of Learned Women Before 1800*, 65-85. Montreal: Eden Press.

Jansen, Sue Curry. 1990. Is Science a Man? New Feminist Epistemologies and Reconstructions of Knowledge. *Theory and Society* 19:235-246.

Keller, Evelyn Fox. 1981. Women and Science: Two Cultures or One? *International Journal of Women's Studies* 4:414-419.

—. 1983. *A Feeling for the Organism: The Life and Work of Barbara McClintock*. New York: Freeman.

—. 1985. *Reflections on Gender and Science*. New Haven, Connecticut: Yale University Press.

Lakoff, Robin. 1975. *Language and Woman's Place*. New York: Harper & Row.

Lerner, Gerda. 1976. Placing Women in History: A 1975 Perspective. B.A. Carroll, ed., *Liberating Women's History: Theoretical and Critical Essays*, 357-367. Urbana: University of Illinois Press.

Library of Congress Subject Headings, 12th ed., vol. 3. 1989. Washington, D.C.: Library of Congress.

Longino, Helen E. 1989. Can There Be a Feminist Science? N. Tuana, ed., *Feminism and Science*, 45-57. Bloomington: Indiana University Press.

Lutkehaus, Nancy. 1986. 'She was *very* Cambridge': Camilla Wedgwood and the History of Women in British Social Anthropology. *American Ethnologist* 13:776-798.

Merchant, Carolyn. 1979. *The Death of Nature: Women, Ecology, and the Scientific Revolution*. San Francisco: Harper & Row.

—. 1979. The Vitalism of Anne Conway: Its Impact on Leibniz's Concept of the Monad. *Journal of the History of Philosophy* 17:255-269.

—. 1982. Isis' Consciousness Raised. *Isis* 73:398-409.

Mozans, H.J. 1913. *Woman in Science: With an Introductory Chapter on Woman's Long Struggle for Things of the Mind*. Cambridge, Massachusetts: MIT Press. [reprinted 1974]

Myers, Mitzi. 1985. Domesticating Minerva: Bathsua Makin's "Curious" Argument for Women's Education. *Studies in Eighteenth Century Culture* 14:173-192.

Nochlin, Linda. 1988. Why Have There Been No Great Women Artists? *Women, Art, and Power and Other Essays*, 145-178. New York: Harper & Row. [reprint, with revised title, of 1971 essay, "Why Are There No Great Women Artists?"]

Ogilvie, Marilyn Bailey. 1986. *Women in Science, Antiquity Through the Nineteenth Century: A Biographical Dictionary with Annotated Bibliography*. Cambridge, Massachusetts: MIT Press.

Orenstein, Gloria Feman. 1975. Art History. *Signs: Journal of Women in Culture and Society* 1:505-525.

Osen, Lynn M. 1974. *Women in Mathematics*. Cambridge, Massachusetts: MIT Press.

Outram, Dorinda. 1987. The Most Difficult Career: Women's History in Science. *International Journal of Science Education* 9:409-416.

Paloma, Dolores. 1980. Margaret Cavendish: Defining the Female Self. *Women's Studies* 7:55-66.

Parker, Rozsika, & Griselda Pollock. 1981. *Old Mistresses: Women, Art and Ideology*. New York: Pantheon Books.

Pettey, Chris. 1985. *Dictionary of Women Artists, an International Dictionary of Women Artists Born Before 1900*. Boston: G.K. Hall.

Pollock, Griselda. 1983. Women, Art and Ideology: Questions for Feminist Art Historians. *Woman's Art Journal* 5:39-47.

—. 1988. *Vision and Difference: Femininity, Feminism and the Histories of Art*. London: Routledge.

Reynolds, Myra. 1920. *The Learned Lady in England, 1650-1760*. Gloucester, Massachusetts: Peter Smith. [reprinted 1964]

Rizzo, P.V. 1954. Early Daughters of Urania. *Sky and Telescope* 14:7-9.

Robins, R.H. 1984. *A Short History of Linguistics*, 2nd ed. London: Longman.

Rossiter, Margaret W. 1982. *Women Scientists in America: Struggles and Strategies to 1940*. Baltimore: Johns Hopkins University Press.

Rothchild, Joan, ed. 1983. *Machine Ex Dea: Feminist Perspectives on Technology*. New York: Pergamon Press.

Salmon, Vivian. 1987. Bathsua Makin: A Pioneer Linguist and Feminist in Seventeenth Century England. B. Asbach-Schnitker & J. Roggenhofer, eds., *Neuere Forschungen zur Wortbildung und Historiographie der Linguistik*, 303-318. Tübingen: Gunter Narr Verlag.

Sarasohn, Lisa. 1984. A Science Turned Upside Down: Feminism and the Natural Philosophy of Margaret Cavendish. *Huntington Library Quarterly* 47:289-307.

Schiebinger, Londa. 1987. The History and Philosophy of Women in Science: A Review Essay. *Signs: Journal of Women in Culture and Society* 12:305-332.

—. 1988. Feminine Icons: The Face of Early Modern Science. *Critical Inquiry* 14:661-691.

—. 1989. *The Mind Has No Sex? Women in the Origins of Modern Science*. Cambridge, Massachusetts: Harvard University Press.

Sebeok, Thomas A., ed. 1967. *Portraits of Linguists: A Biographical Source Book for the History of Western Linguistics, 1746-1963*, 2 vols. Bloomington: Indiana University Press.

Slatkin, Wendy. 1990. *Women Artists in History from Antiquity to the 20th Century*, 2nd ed. Englewood Cliffs, New Jersey: Prentice Hall.

Smith, Hilda. 1976. Gynecology and Ideology in Seventeenth-Century England. B.A. Carroll, ed., *Liberating Women's History: Theoretical and Critical Essays*, 97-114. Urbana: University of Illinois Press.

Spender, Dale. 1980. *Man Made Language*. London: Routledge & Kegan Paul.

Tufts, Eleanor. 1984. *American Women Artists, Past and Present: A Selected Bibliographical Guide*. New York: Garland.

Zemel, Carol. 1990. Review of *Vision and Difference: Femininity, Feminism, and the Histories of Art* by G. Pollock. *Art Bulletin* 72:336-341.

Old Man Coyote and the Wild Potato:
A Mandan Trickster Tale

Richard T. Carter

The first modern research on the Mandan language was conducted by the late Edward Kennard during the summers of 1933 and 1934. Kennard's only publication of this research was his "Mandan Grammar" of 1936, an excellent account of the phonetics, phonology, and morphology of the language. The formal description was augmented with a traditional narrative text, "Speckled Arrow", presented with an interlinear English translation and grammatical notes at the end of the grammar. Although this was the only text published by Kennard, he actually collected twenty-eight narrative texts from several Mandan raconteurs. These texts, in typescript with free English translations, are held in the Library of the American Philosophical Society at Philadelphia.

As part of my ongoing research on Mandan syntax I am currently editing and annotating the Kennard texts; with the exception of three very short texts published by Robert Lowie in 1913, they constitute our oldest and fullest record of Mandan narrative. This effort has been greatly facilitated by examination of the unpublished work of the late Robert C. Hollow, who re-elicited Kennard's texts from Mandan speakers in the middle 1970's. Hollow's versions of the Kennard texts, in typescript with interlinear English translation, are held in the Archives of the North Dakota Heritage Center, Bismarck, North Dakota.[1]

The text which is presented here is one of those collected by Kennard from Mr. Stephen Bird, probably in 1934. I have chosen this text to include in the present volume, in part because its humourous nature will, I hope, prove entertaining to the honoree, but also to exemplify a number of working hypotheses regarding Mandan syntax, as well as the structure of Mandan narrative. Accordingly, the text is followed by notes on both its grammatical structure and content.[2]

The text consists of seventy-four sentences. Each sentence is presented with an identifying reference number, a phonetic representation (labelled TX), an interlinear, abstract morphemic representation (labelled MR), an interlinear English gloss of the morphemic representation (labelled GL), and a free English translation.[3]

It must be emphasized from the outset that the phonetic representation of the text has been heavily edited; it does not precisely correspond either to Kennard's original representation or to Hollow's revision thereof. Kennard was quite inconsistent in his recording of such phonetic details as vowel length, accent placement, and glottal stricture; Hollow did not record vowel length at all. Such details have thus been "restored" here, based on my own research with contemporary Mandan speakers.[4] There are undoubtedly many remaining errors in the phonetic representation, as I have not yet re-elicited all of the morphemes which this text contains. In addition, I have chosen to alter some of Kennard's word boundaries to better fit my own interpretation of Mandan word structure, as largely dictated by the complexities of the pitch-accent system. (The interlinear English gloss representation makes use of a number of abbreviations, as listed below. As usual, *lexical* glosses are entirely in lower case, while *grammatical* morphemes have glosses which begin with an upper case letter.)

ABBREVIATIONS

ABS	Absolutive		NPST	Narrative Past
ADV	Adverbial		PL2	2nd Pers. Plural
AL	Alienable Possession		PL3	3rd Pers. Plural
A1	1st Pers. Active Case		POT	Potential
A2	2nd Pers. Active Case		PPV	Positional Postverb
CAUS	Causal		PRF	Perfective
CNJ	Conjunctive		PRG	Progressive Aspect
DEF	Definite		PST	Past Tense
DEM	General Demonstrative		PV	Preverb
DIR	Directional		P1	1st Pers. Possessive
DSJ	Disjunctive		P2	2nd Pers. Possessive
FUT	Future		R	Reduplication
IMPma	Imperative, Male		SIM	Simultaneous Action
INC	Inceptive Aspect		SMT	Similitive
INST	Instrumentive		SUB	Subordinative
INTma	Interrogative, Male		SV	Stem Vowel
IPfrc	Instrumental, by force		S1	1st Pers. Stative Case
IPhnd	Instrumental, by hand		S2	2nd Pers. Stative Case
IPtmp	Instrumental, by heat		TOP	Topic, New or Reactivated
LOC	Locative		TR	Transitive
MV	Middle Voice		TYP	Typifier
NEG	Negative			

Old Man Coyote and the Wild Potato
(kinúmą?kšinį pą́·xe)

TX	kinúmą?kšis	kasí·mįro·mąko?š.
MR	ki-ruwą?k-ší -s	ka -si· -wį -o·wąk-o?š
GL	? -man -good-DEF	INC-travel-PRG-NPST -Pma

1 Old Man Coyote started travelling.

TX	warú·textanį	sí·mįro·mąko?š.
MR	waru·te-xtE -rį	si· -wį -o·wąk-o?š
GL	hungry -very-CNJ	travel-PRG-NPST -Pma

2 He was very hungry, so he was travelling.

TX	té·hąta	dé·ho·mąko?š.
MR	te·hą-ta	rE·h-o·wąk-o?š
GL	far -LOC	go -NPST -Pma

3 He went a long way.

TX	kaškáʔnįk	wá·ʔonąpe	mįkó·mąko?š.
MR	ka -škaʔ-rįk	wa·-o=rąp-E	wįk-o·wąk-o?š
GL	be?-DSJ -SUB	ABS-find -SV	no -NPST -Pma

4 But there was nothing to be found.

TX	kánį	óʔharanį	mą́·ta íwakata
MR	ka -rį	oʔ -hrE -rį	wą·ta í -waka -ta
GL	be?-CNJ	be?-cause-CNJ	river DIR-edge?-LOC

TX	dé·ho·mąko?š.
MR	rE·h-o·wąk-o?š
GL	go -NPST -Pma

5 From there he went toward the river bank.

TX	dá·ha·mį	híro·mąko?š.
MR	rE·h-ha·-wį	hí -o·wąk-o?š
GL	go -SIM-PRG	get there-NPST -Pma

6 Going along, he arrived there.

TX	hínį	mą́·ta íʔa·kita	dé·ho·mąko?š.
MR	hí -rį	wą·ta í -a·ki-ta	rE·h-o·wąk-o?š
GL	get there-CNJ	river DIR-up -LOC	go -NPST -Pma

7 Arriving there, he went up the river.

TX	dá·ha·mį·mį·	mą́nąrok	pą́·xe
MR	rE·h-ha·-wį -R	·wrą-rok	pą·x -E
GL	go -SIM-PRG-R	tree-in	potato-SV

TX híro·mąko⁷š.
MR hí   -o·wąk-o⁷š
GL get there-NPST -Pma
8   While he was going along, he came to some wild potatoes in the
    woods.

TX í⁷ahe   hánį   nátka šíro·mąko⁷š.
MR í   -ah -E hE -rį rátka ší -o·wąk-o⁷š
GL INST-cover-SV see-CNJ heart good-NPST -Pma
9   He saw their tops, and he was happy.

TX kánį   ó⁷haranį   dasé   kimá·xero·mąko⁷š.
MR ka -rį o⁷ -hrE -rį ras -E   kiwą-xE-o·wąk-o⁷š
GL be?-CNJ be?-cause-CNJ name-SV ask   -NPST -Pma
10 And he asked one his name.

TX "pą·xe,   nįnás   taškáha éhero⁷ša?"
MR   pą·x -E rį-ras taškaha e=he-o⁷ša
GL   potato-SV P2-name how   say -INTma

TX éhero·mąko⁷š.
MR e=he-o·wąk-o⁷š
GL say -NPST -Pma
11 "Potato, what is your name?" he said.

TX káki   pą·xese·ną   "mįnáse   á⁷tenąk
MR ka -ki pą·x -E -s -e· -rą wį-ras -E   ą⁷t -rąk
GL be?-SUB potato-SV-DEF-DEM-TOP P1-name-SV that-PPV

TX nąnátak,"   éhero·mąko⁷š.
MR ra-rąt   -ak e=he-o·wąk-o⁷š
GL A2-mention-SUB say -NPST -Pma
12 And the Potato said, "That's my name, what you just mentioned."

TX "kašká⁷nįk   nųmą⁷kšiki   dasé   nųpó⁷š,"
MR   ka -ška⁷-rįk ruwą⁷k-ší -ki ras -E   rųp-o⁷š
GL   be?-DSJ -SUB man   -good-SUB name-SV two-Pma

TX éhero·mąko⁷š,   kinúmą⁷kšiną.
MR e=he-o·wąk-o⁷š ki-ruwą⁷k-ší -rą
GL say -NPST -Pma ? -man   -good-TOP
13 "But if one is a chief, there are two names," said Coyote.

TX káki   pą·xese·ną   "mįkó⁷š, mįnáse
MR ka -ki pą·x -E -s -e· -rą   wįk-o⁷š wį-ras -E
GL be?-SUB potato-SV-DEF-DEM-TOP   no -Pma P1-name-SV

```
TX  iška   á⁷tenąk  nąnáto⁷š,"       éhero·mąko⁷š.
MR  iška   ą⁷t -rąk  ra-rąt    -o⁷š  e=he-o·wąk-o⁷š
GL  truly  that-PPV  A2-mention-Pma  say -NPST -Pma
14  Then the Potato said, "No, my name is truly the one you
    mentioned."
```

```
TX  kaška⁷nįk      inák    kimá·xero·mąko⁷š,
MR  ka -ška⁷-rįk   irąk    kiwą·xE-o·wąk-o⁷š
GL  be?-DSJ -SUB   again   ask      -NPST -Pma
```

```
TX  kinúmą⁷kšise·ną.
MR  ki-ruwą⁷k-ší  -s   -e·  -rą
GL  ? -man      -good-DEF-DEM-TOP
15  But Coyote asked him again.
```

```
TX  káki    "mįkó⁷š,"  éhero·mąko⁷š,
MR  ka -ki  wįk-o⁷š    e=he-o·wąk-o⁷š
GL  be?-SUB no -Pma    say -NPST -Pma
```

```
TX  pą·xese·ną.
MR  pą·x  -E -s   -e·  -rą
GL  potato-SV-DEF-DEM-TOP
16  "No," said the Potato.
```

```
TX  káki    kinúmą⁷kšis         íkxąhinį
MR  ka -ki  ki-ruwą⁷k-ší   -s   i=kxąh-rį
GL  be?-SUB ? -man      -good-DEF laugh -CNJ
```

```
TX  "nįnúmą⁷kši⁷š.
MR  rį-ruwą⁷k-ší  -o⁷š
GL  S2-man      -good-Pma
17  Then Coyote laughed, and said "You're a chief."
```

```
TX  nįnáse      ónųpo⁷š.
MR  rį-ras  -E   ó  -rųp-o⁷š
GL  P2-name-SV   FUT-two-Pma
18  "You must have two names."
```

```
TX  kaška⁷nįk      wá·rakiną·nįxo⁷š.
MR  ka -ška⁷-rįk   wa·-ra-kirą·-rįx-o⁷š
GL  be?-DSJ -SUB   NEG-A2-tell -NEG-Pma
19  "But you're not telling."
```

```
TX  mąkíną⁷ta."
MR  wą-kirą·-ta
GL  S1-tell -IMPma
20  "Tell me!"
```

```
TX   "ho· ų́·škarote⁷š
MR   ho· ų·ška    -ote-o⁷š
GL   yes like that-PRF-Pma
21   "Yes, that's right."
```

```
TX   mįnáse        írehekinį     é·rerehsonįk
MR   wį-ras -E     ra-i=hek-rį   ra-e·=reh-so  -rįk
GL   P1-name-SV    A2-know -CNJ  A2-want   -CAUS-SUB
```

```
TX   mįníkiną·kto⁷š,"        éhero·mąko⁷š.
MR   wa-rį-kirą·-kt -o⁷š      e=he-o·wąk-o⁷š
GL   A1-S2-tell -POT-Pma     say -NPST -Pma
22   "Since you want to know my name, I'll tell you," he said.
```

```
TX   kánį      ó⁷haranį        "wá·wa·hų·       éte⁷š.
MR   ka -rį    o⁷ -hrE   -rį   wa·-wa·-hų       ra-e=he-o⁷š
GL   be?-CNJ   be?-cause-CNJ   ABS-ABS-much     A2-say -Pma
23   Then, "You said a lot."
```

```
TX   mąnánųtinį      é·rerehki       mąnánųtinį
MR   wą-ra-rut-rį    ra-e·=reh-ki    wą-ra-rut-rį
GL   S1-A2-eat-CNJ   A2-want    -SUB S1-A2-eat-CNJ
```

```
TX   tektó⁷š.
MR   te -kt -o⁷š
GL   be?-POT-Pma
24   "If you want to eat me, then you will eat me."
```

```
TX   káki      mįnáse        máxaną mįníkiną·kto⁷š."
MR   ka -ki    wį-ras -E     wáxrą  wa-rį-kirą·-kt -o⁷š
GL   be?-SUB   P1-name-SV    one    A1-S2-tell -POT-Pma
25   "And I'll tell you one of my names."
```

```
TX   káki      "píhkaxoke,"         éhero⁷š, "mįnáse
MR   ka -ki    píh -ka    -xok -E   e=he-o⁷š  wį-ras -E
GL   be?-SUB   fart-IPfrc-lift-SV   say -Pma  P1-name-SV
```

```
TX   máxaną."
MR   wáxrą
GL   one
26   "Fart-Lift," he said, "that's one of my names."
```

```
TX   káki      ó⁷haranį        kinúmą⁷kšise·ną
MR   ka -ki    o⁷ -hrE   -rį   ki-ruwą⁷k-ší   -s -e· -rą
GL   be?-SUB   be?-cause-CNJ   ? -man    -good-DEF-DEM-TOP
```

```
TX   "ą́·skak,        nįnúmą⁷kši⁷š,        épeso⁷š,"
MR   ą·ska    -ak    rį-ruwą⁷k-ší   -o⁷š  wa-e=he-s  -o⁷š
GL   like this-SUB   S2-man    -good-Pma  A1-say -PST-Pma
```

TX éhero·mąko[?]š.
MR e=he-o·wąk-o[?]š
GL say -NPST -Pma
27 Then Coyote said, "That's right, I said you were a chief!"

TX ó[?]harani   ké[?]ni   dutó·mąko[?]š.
MR o[?] -hrE -ri   ke[?]-ri   rut-o·wąk-o[?]š
GL be?-cause-CNJ dig-CNJ eat-NPST -Pma
28 Then he dug and ate them.

TX ó[?]harani   warú·tesonik   wá·xtani   hų
MR o[?] -hrE -ri   waru·te-so -rik wa··xtE-ri   hų
GL be?-cause-CNJ hungry -CAUS-SUB ABS-big-CNJ much

TX dutó·mąko[?]š.
MR rut-o·wąk-o[?]š
GL eat-NPST -Pma
29 Since he was hungry, he ate a lot of them.

TX káni   é·xohini   kasí·miro·mąko[?]š.
MR ka -ri   e·xi   -ohi -ri   ka -si· -wi -o·wąk-o[?]š
GL be?-CNJ stomach-full-CNJ INC-travel-PRG-NPST -Pma
30 Then he was full, so he started to travel.

TX dá·ha·mi·mi·   e·s   íku[?]eška   dé·hak
MR rE·h-ha·-wi -R e· -s   í -ku[?] -eška rE·h-ak
GL go -SIM-PRG-R DEM-DEF DIR-there-SMT go -SUB

TX pího·mąko[?]š.
MR píh -o·wąk-o[?]š
GL fart-NPST -Pma
31 Going along, having gone a little way, he farted.

TX píhak   širóte duxókinitero·mąko[?]š.
MR píh -ak širote ru   -xok -rite-o·wąk-o[?]š
GL fart-SUB heel   IPhnd-lift-?   -NPST -Pma
32 Having farted, his heels lifted up.

TX káki   kinúmą[?]kšise·ną   tašíro·mąko[?]š.
MR ka -ki   ki-ruwą[?]k-ší -s -e· -rą taši-o·wąk-o[?]š
GL be?-SUB ? -man   -good-DEF-DEM-TOP like-NPST -Pma
33 And Coyote liked it.

TX inák   e·s   íku[?]eška   dé·hak   inák
MR irąk   e· -s   í -ku[?] -eška rE·h-ak irąk
GL again DEM-DEF DIR-there-SMT go -SUB again

TX pího·mąko⁷š.
MR píh -o·wąk-o⁷š
GL fart-NPST -Pma
34 Again, having gone a little farther, he farted again.

TX ó⁷harąnį   xámąha   í⁷a·ki⁷eš   duxók
MR o⁷ -hrE -rį   ·xwąh -ha   í -a·ki-eš ru   -xok
GL be?-cause-CNJ little-ADV DIR-up -?   IPhnd-lift

TX píhak   duxóko·mąko⁷š.
MR píh -ak   ru   -xok -o·wąk-o⁷š
GL fart-SUB   IPhnd-lift-NPST -Pma
35 When he farted this time, he lifted up a little higher.

TX káki   kinúmą⁷kšis   tašíxtero·mąko⁷š.
MR ka -ki   ki-ruwą⁷k-ší -s   taši-xtE -o·wąk-o⁷š
GL be?-SUB   ? -man   -good-DEF   like-very-NPST -Pma
36 And Coyote liked it very much.

TX inąk   íku⁷eška   dé·hak   pího·mąko⁷š.
MR irąk   í -ku⁷ -eška   rE·h-ak   píh -o·wąk-o⁷š
GL again DIR-there-SMT   go -SUB   fart-NPST -Pma
37 Again, having gone a little farther, he farted.

TX káki   í⁷a·kita   dé·ho·mąko⁷š.
MR ka -ki   í -a·ki-ta   rE·h-o·wąk-o⁷š
GL be?-SUB DIR-up -LOC   go -NPST -Pma
38 And he went upward.

TX ó⁷harąnį   dó·pxanį   hú·nį   kamį́⁷šo·mąko⁷š.
MR o⁷ -hrE -rį   ro-pxE-rį   hu· -rį kawį⁷š-o·wąk-o⁷š
GL be?-cause-CNJ go in -CNJ come-CNJ hurt   -NPST -Pma
39 Then he came back down, and was hurt.

TX dá·ha·mį   píhe   xú·tak   mánątere·ną
MR rE·h-ha·-wį   píh -E xų·t -ak   ↓wrą-trE-e· -rą
GL go -SIM-PRG fart-SV break-SUB   tree-big-DEM-TOP

TX dupó·mąko⁷š.
MR rup -o·wąk-o⁷š
GL hold-NPST -Pma
40 Going along, when he thought he was going to fart, he held on to
    a big tree.

TX ó⁷harąnį   pího·mąko⁷š.
MR o⁷ -hrE -rį   píh -o·wąk-o⁷š
GL be?-cause-CNJ fart-NPST -Pma
41 Then he farted.

```
TX  mánateres       orúskani                í?a·kita
MR  ·wrą-trE-s      o -ru  -skE    -rį  í -a·ki-ta
GL  tree-big-DEF PV-IPhnd-pull up-CNJ DIR-up  -LOC

TX  dé·ho·mąko?š.
MR  rE·h-o·wąk-o?š
GL  go  -NPST -Pma
```
42 He pulled up the big tree, and went upward.

```
TX  ímąpeta         kuhíni              waxtáni
MR  í -wąpe-ta  kuh     -rį  wa -xtE-rį
GL  DIR-down-LOC come back-CNJ ABS-big-CNJ

TX  kamį?šo·mąko?š.
MR  kawį?š-o·wąk-o?š
GL  hurt  -NPST -Pma
```
43 He came back downward, and was really hurt.

```
TX  ó?harani        tí·hį·ke            kirúšani
MR  o? -hrE  -rį  ta-í  -hį·  -kE  ki-rušE-rį
GL  be?-cause-CNJ AL-INST-drink-NOM MV-take-CNJ

TX  oksúkero·mąko?š.
MR  oksuke-o·wąk-o?š
GL  fill   -NPST -Pma
```
44 Then he took his pipe and filled it.

```
TX  oksúkini  ó?harani       waxópinįta
MR  oksuk-rį  o? -hrE  -rį  wa -xoprį-ta
GL  fill -CNJ be?-cause-CNJ ABS-holy -LOC

TX  tí·hį·ks             á·pteho·mąko?š.
MR  ta-í  -hį·  -kE -s   a·-ptEh-o·wąk-o?š
GL  AL-INST-drink-NOM-DEF TR-run -NPST -Pma
```
45 Filling it, he then ran with his pipe to the Spirits.

```
TX  ó?harani        "mámąhanįsta,"           éhero·mąko?š,
MR  o? -hrE  -rį  wa·-wą-hE -rįt-ta    e=he-o·wąk-o?š
GL  be?-cause-CNJ ?  -S1-see-PL2-IMPma say -NPST -Pma

TX  kinúmą?kši?e·ną.
MR  ki-ruwą?k-ší  -e·  -rą
GL  ? -man   -good-DEM-TOP
```
46 Then Coyote said, "Look at me!"

```
TX  káki   "má·ną   omįkitire    mįkó?š"
MR  ka -ki  wa·rą  o -wįk-itire wįk-o?š
GL  be?-SUB someone PV-no -?    no -Pma
```

TX éhekerero·mąko⁷š.
MR e=he-krE-o·wąk-o⁷š
GL say -PL3-NPST -Pma
47 "No one can stop that," they said.

TX ó⁷haranį   wá·xťanį   tí·hį·ks
MR o⁷ -hrE -rį   wa·-xtE-rį   ta-í   -hį·   -kE -s
GL be?-cause-CNJ ABS-big-CNJ AL-INST-drink-NOM-DEF

TX ké·kanį   mákaha   ptého·mąko⁷š.
MR ke·ka -rį   wákah-E   ptEh-o·wąk-o⁷š
GL carry?-CNJ exist-SV   run -NPST -Pma
48 Then he carried his pipe to many that were there, and ran on. (?)

TX mákah íkašešeka "hú·ta   e·ną
MR wákah íkašešeka hu· -ta   e· -rą
GL exist buckbrush come-IMPma DEM-TOP

TX íruteta   á·hu·ta,"   éhero·mąko⁷š.
MR í -rute   -ta a·-hu· -ta   e=he-o·wąk-o⁷š
GL DIR-this way-LOC TR-come-IMPma say -NPST -Pma
49 A Buckbrush that was there said "Come, bring it this way!"

TX káki   tí·hį·ks   dušánį
MR ka -ki ta-í   -hį·   -kE -s rušE-rį
GL be?-SUB AL-INST-drink-NOM-DEF take-CNJ

TX karáptehara   kú⁷ro·mąko⁷š,
MR ka -rá   -pte -hrE ku⁷ -o·wąk-o⁷š
GL INC-IPtmp-burn-cause give-NPST -Pma

TX kinúmą⁷kšis.
MR ki-ruwą⁷k-ší   -s
GL ? -man   -good-DEF
50 Then Coyote took his pipe and lit it for him.

TX kánį   "híre íkašešekahu·se·ną
MR ka -rį híre íkašešeka-hu· -s -e· -rą
GL be?-CNJ now buckbrush-stalk-DEF-DEM-TOP

TX nįšíta   íkaskata,   kxúhinį,"
MR rį-ši   -ta í   -ka -skE-ta   kxųh   -rį
GL P2-foot-LOC DIR-IPfrc-tie-IMPma lie down-CNJ

TX éhero·mąko⁷š.
MR e=he-o·wąk-o⁷š
GL say -NPST -Pma
51 "Now, lie down and tie these buckbrush trunks to your feet," he
    said.

TX káki   ó'haranį   íseko·mąko'š.
MR ka -ki   o' -hrE -rį   i=sek-o·wąk-o'š
GL be?-SUB be?-cause-CNJ   do   -NPST -Pma
52 Then he did it.

TX "nú'ke   íruminįta   núpšaška mą·
MR rį-ųk   -E   ru -i=wrį-ta   rųp-šaška wą·
GL P2-hand-SV   IPhnd-twist-IMPma   two-?   ?

TX mihápmą'k wá·rarusara·to'š.
MR wįhapwą'k wa·-ra-ru   -sra·t -o'š
GL today   ABS-A2-IPhnd-let go-Pma
53 "Wrap both your hands around it, today you might lose hold."

TX ká·re   dusará·ta.
MR ka·re   ru   -sra·t -ta
GL NegImp IPhnd-let go-IMPma
54 "Don't let go!"

TX dú'kasa írušata."
MR ru'kasa í -rušE-ta
GL tight? DIR-take-IMPma
55 "Hang on tight!"

TX kánį   íseko·mąko'š.
MR ka -rį i=sek-o·wąk-o'š
GL be?-CNJ do   -NPST -Pma
56 And he did it.

TX kxųhinį   ą·me íseko·mąko'š.
MR kxųh   -rį   ą·we i=sek-o·wąk-o'š
GL lie down-CNJ   all do   -NPST -Pma
57 Lying down, he did it all.

TX ó'haranį   pího·mąko'š.
MR o' -hrE -rį   píh -o·wąk-o'š
GL be?-cause-CNJ   fart-NPST -Pma
58 Then he farted.

TX á·kita   wára·hinįxo'š.
MR a·ki-ta   wa·-rE·h-rįx-o'š
GL up -LOC NEG-go -NEG-Pma
59 He didn't go up.

TX kaška'nįk   wá·xtanį   pé·ši má·'ąk
MR ka -ška'-rįk wa·-xtE-rį   pe·ši wa·'ąk
GL be?-DSJ -SUB ABS-big-CNJ belly ground

TX í·tkimą·kero·mąkoʔš.
MR i·-tki-wą·kE-o·wąk-oʔš
GL ? -hit-stay -NPST -Pma
60 But his belly kept hitting the ground a lot.

TX ų·škamą·ka   té·hąxtero·mąkoʔš.
MR ų·ška   -wą·kE te·hą-xtE -o·wąk-oʔš
GL like that-stay far   -very-NPST -Pma
61 It went on like that for a long time.

TX káni̜   kipxék   kínątani̜
MR ka -ri̜ ki-pxe -ak ki-rątE -ri̜
GL be?-CNJ MV-land-SUB MV-get up-CNJ

TX kasí·mi̜ro·mąkoʔš,   kinúmąʔkšis.
MR ka -si·   -wi̜ -o·wąk-oʔš ki-ruwąʔk-ší -s
GL INC-travel-PRG-NPST -Pma ? -man   -good-DEF
62 Coyote landed, got up, and started travelling.

TX káki   pą́·xese·ną   kinúmąʔkši
MR ka -ki   pą·x -E -s -e· -rą ki-ruwąʔk-ší
GL be?-SUB potato-SV-DEF-DEM-TOP ? -man   -good

TX "taškᠨ·k mą́·mąnąrutini̜xoʔša?"   éhero·mąkoʔš.
MR taška·k wa·-wą-ra-rut-ri̜x-oʔša e=he-o·wąk-oʔš
GL why   NEG-S1-A2-eat-NEG-INTma say -NPST -Pma
63 And the Potato said to Coyote, "Why don't you eat me?"

TX káki   kinúmąʔkšise·ną   "wakíkarahoʔš,"
MR ka -ki   ki-ruwąʔk-ší -s -e· -rą wa-ki-krah-oʔš
GL be?-SUB ? -man   -good-DEF-DEM-TOP A1-MV-fear-Pma

TX éhero·mąkoʔš.
MR e=he-o·wąk-oʔš
GL say -NPST -Pma
64 And Coyote said, "I'm afraid."

TX "ą́·skak   nųšínąša   mi̜níki̜nąsoʔš,
MR ą·ska   -ak rų-ší -rąš-ha wa-ri̜-kirą·-s -oʔš
GL like this-SUB ? -good-TYP-ADV A1-S2-tell -PST-Pma

TX mi̜nąse   mą́xaną ʔš, épek.
MR wi̜-ras -E wáxrą-oʔš wa-e=he-ak
GL P1-name-SV one -Pma A1-say -SUB
65 "That's why I told you nicely, my name is just one, I said."

TX nųmąʔkšiki   dasé   núpoʔš, émąnątesoʔš.
MR ruwąʔk-ší -ki ras -E rųp-oʔš wą-ra-e=he-s -oʔš
GL man   -good-SUB name-SV two-Pma S1-A2-say -PST-Pma
66 "If one is a chief, there are two names, you said to me."

TX mįnáse   mįnį́kiną·so⁷š.
MR wį-ras -E   wa-rį-kirą.-s -o⁷š
GL P1-name-SV   A1-S2-tell -PST-Pma
67 "I told you my name."

TX é·ną   mąną́kikaraho⁷š."
MR e· -rą   wą-ra-ki-krah-o⁷š
GL DEM-TOP   S1-A2-MV-fear-Pma
68 "And now you're afraid of me."

TX "hų́·, mįnį́kikaraho⁷š,   píhkaxoka.
MR hų· wa-rį-ki-krah-o⁷š pih -ka   -xok -E
GL yes A1-S2-MV-fear-Pma fart-IPfrc-lift-SV
69 "Yes, I'm afraid of you, Fart-Lift."

TX wá·xte·ną   mą·hį·ku   íwaseko⁷š.
MR wa·-xtE-e· -rą   wą-hi·kų   wa-i=sek-o⁷š
GL ABS-big-DEM-TOP S1-difficult A1-do -Pma
70 "I really had a hard time."

TX wapíhtiki   mą́ną̨tere warúpanį   í⁷a·kita
MR wa-ṕíh -tiki   ·wrą-trE wa-rup -rį   í -a-ki-ta
GL A1-fart-SUB   tree-big A1-hold-CNJ DIR-up -LOC

TX owáruskanį   á·ware·hto⁷š
MR o -wa-ru   -skE   -rį   a·-wa-rE·h-kt -o⁷š
GL PV-A1-IPhnd-pull up-CNJ TR-A1-go -POT-Pma
71 "When I farted, I held on to a big tree, and I pulled it out and
    took it upward."

TX kánį   ówaptiktiki   mą́·kamį⁷ška⁷š,"
MR ka -rį   wa-o=ptik-tiki   wą-kawį⁷š-ka   -o⁷š
GL be?-CNJ A1-fall -SUB   S1-hurt -IMPRF-Pma

TX éhero·mąko⁷š,   kinúmą⁷kšiną.
MR e=he-o·wąk-o⁷š   ki-ruwą⁷k-ší -rą
GL say -NPST -Pma   ? -man   -good-TOP
72 "And when I fell back down, it hurt me," Coyote said.

TX kánį   ó⁷haranį   híre⁷oška
MR ka -rį   o⁷ -hrE -rį   híre-oška
GL be?-CNJ be?-cause-CNJ now -even?

TX kasí·mįkto⁷š.
MR ka -si· -wį -kt -o⁷š
GL INC-travel-PRG-POT-Pma
73 And even now he's probably started travelling.

```
TX   í⁷ohąko⁷š.
MR   í  -o -hąk  -o⁷š
GL   DIR-PV-stand-Pma
74   That's all.
```

OBSERVATIONS ON FORM AND CONTENT

Sentence 1: It has become customary to translate the Trickster's name as "Old Man Coyote", at least in the humourous Trickster myths. In other, more serious contexts, such as the Creation myth, the Mandan prefer "First Creator" as the most appropriate translation. Neither are literal interpretations of the Mandan name, which is built upon the word for 'chief', itself a compound of 'man' and 'good'. The prefix in this word is of unknown function. This sentence is formulaic: the Trickster is *always* starting to travel in a myth of this type.

Sentence 2: Also formulaic, as the Trickster is always hungry, and is always looking for something to eat. The first clause ends with the Conjunctive suffix, which seems to mark peripheral cosubordination. A clause so marked is dependent upon the following clause for specification of such peripheral operators as illocutionary force. This type of construction is quite frequent in Mandan. It is interesting to note that the complement of the verb 'want' always takes this suffix, as in sentences 22 and 24. One would assume that the strength of the semantic link here would be too strong for a peripheral juncture.

Sentence 3: Mandan makes extensive use of the Time = Space metaphor, hence the root 'far' refers either to space or time. The reference here is to space, as shown by the Locative suffix; in sentence 61 the same root refers to time.

Sentence 4: What constitutes a sentence boundary in Mandan? In the absence of such things as intonational cues, for example, what criteria are available for deciding where one sentence stops and another begins? This question seems of interest here, as an English speaker might well want to argue that sentences 3 and 4 are peripherally coordinated clauses, rather than independent sentences. Mandan discourse behaves rather differently from English, however, in that peripheral coordination seems relatively rare. In brief, a Mandan sentence *in narrative discourse* typically begins with either a one-word *resumptive clause*, as in sentences 6 and 7, or with a conjunction-like *discourse connector*, as in sentences 4 and 5. That these are not "simple conjunctions" is shown by their *verbal* morphology; i.e., they always terminate in one of a set of suffixes that mark *dependent clauses.* The argument here, in essence, is that sentence-initial discourse connectors are historically derived from resumptive clauses. The initial *ka-* in these forms appears to be an old verbal root, which I have tentatively glossed as 'be'. In addition, with the rare exception of true peripheral coordination, and the trivial exception of direct quotation, a sentence boundary is assumed to be marked by an illocutionary force suffix. This is problematic only when material is "postposed", making the main verb nonfinal. See sentence 13 for an example.

Sentence 7: Mandan uses the same directional metaphor we find in English: 'toward the head of a stream' and 'away from the surface of the earth' are both *upward.*

Sentence 8: The 'potato' referred to here is the edible root of the Jerusalem Artichoke, a plant of the composite family which looks much like the common sunflower.

Sentence 9: The word I have translated as 'tops' means literally 'covering', and can be used for 'skin', 'nails', 'hooves', or 'tree bark'. I assume here that it refers to the stalks and foliage which 'cover' the underlying edible roots.

Sentence 13: Problematic here is the position of the initial discourse connector: is it inside or outside the direct quotation? In the context of the "discussion" between Coyote and Potato, I have assumed that the word should be attributed to Coyote, and not to the narrator. Note also the postposed subject, producing apparent OVS order. This order is quite frequent when the object is "heavy", as in the case of direct quotation. For example, sentence 14 shows basic SOV order with a heavy object, while sentence 16 shows the OVS form. Also of interest here is the Subordinative suffix *-ki*, which seems to mark peripheral subordination, temporal and conditional clauses in particular. Since temporals and conditionals are adjacent on the Interclausal Relations Hierarchy (cf. Foley & Van Valin 1984:270), it is to be expected that they might be signalled with the same subordinative construction.

Sentence 18: It is possible that this sentence and the one following might be in peripheral coordination, as the semantic linkage seems fairly tight. How high is the semantic "threshold" for clause linkage to take place?

Sentence 22: The suffix sequence which ends the first line of text seems to mark causal subordination, as first noted by Kennard (1936:21).

Sentence 23: The intent of this sentence is not clear to me; my suspicion is that Potato is being sarcastic, in the vein of "You've got such a big mouth, let's see you eat me!"

Sentence 26: This name is the centerpiece of the story, of course. Its humour comes from the use of the instrumental prefix *ka-* 'by sudden application of force'. The stem means 'to lift suddenly, unexpectedly, by forceful action'.

Sentence 27: Coyote pays no attention to the significance of the name, of course; he is only interested in being proven right about the matter of the two names!

Sentence 32: The unidentified suffix in the main verb is in the right position to be an aspectual marker, but as yet I have no other examples of it.

Sentence 35: The instrumental prefix *ru-* is the unmarked member of its paradigm. While it literally means 'by hand', it is frequently used to mark unspecified instrumentality, as here.

Sentence 39: The root *ro·pxE* means 'to enter, as a house'; its use here is presumably idiomatic.

Sentence 40: The root *pih* is inherently verbal, 'to fart'. Here it appears in a derived noun, the object of 'to break', providing yet another shared metaphor with English.

Sentence 44: When Coyote reaches for his pipe, we know he is about to run to the Spirits for assistance. The filled pipe is the offering he will make to any Spirit that he can prevail upon to help him.

Sentence 49: Buckbrush is noted for its tough, tenacious roots.

Sentence 50: As in many languages, serialization of a verb with the predicate 'give' serves to introduce a Dative or Benefactive argument.

Sentence 51: Here we see an extraposed clause terminating the direct quotation.

Sentence 54: The Negative Imperative has no cognates in other Siouan languages, but is identical to a form in Caddoan languages. Hence, it would appear that this useful morpheme is a borrowing from Arikara.

Sentence 62: Coyote 'landed', meaning he stayed *permanently* on the ground, without bouncing up and down.

Sentence 67: Again, this sentence and the one which follows might well be in peripheral coordination; the leading word in sentence 68 looks suspicious as the first word of a sentence.

Sentence 73: This sentence, and the one which follows, are again formulaic. Trickster tales always end with Old Man Coyote starting off travelling again, while sentence 74 is the traditional last word of any myth performance.

NOTES

[1] Hollow also collected new texts from contemporary consultants, including new versions of some of the traditional stories that were recorded by Kennard. Nine of these new versions were published, with free English translations only, as part of the Mandan pedagogical materials issued by Mary College (Parks et al., 1978). I would like to express my thanks to the North Dakota Heritage Center, and to its Director, James Sperry, for permitting me to copy Hollow's unpublished Mandan materials.

[2] It is also interesting to compare this older version of the story with the newer version published by Hollow in 1978. Hollow's version was told by the late Annie Eagle, probably in 1967, and is considerably richer and more detailed than the one presented here.

[3] This is actually the third time that a morpheme-by-morpheme analysis of a Mandan text has been attempted. In addition to Kennard's own "Speckled Arrow" text, Mary Schramm Coberly (1979) presented an analysis of Kennard's text "Trickster Challenges the Buffalo" in a format of this type, based upon the morphological analyses provided in the Kennard grammar (1936), and in Hollow's unpublished *A Mandan Dictionary* (1970). The analysis presented here was prepared with the aid of IT, an interactive interlinear text glossing program designed and distributed by the Summer Institute of Linguistics.

[4] I would like to take this opportunity to thank my Mandan consultants, Mrs. Otter Sage and Mr. Edwin Benson, for their unstinting assistance and their continual patience.

REFERENCES

Coberly, M. 1979. A Text Analysis and Brief Grammatical Sketch Based on "Trickster Challenges the Buffalo": A Mandan Text Collected by Edward Kennard. *Colorado Research in Linguistics* 8:19-94.

Foley, W.A., & R.D. Van Valin, Jr. 1984. *Functional Syntax and Universal Grammar*. Cambridge: Cambridge University Press.

Hollow, R.C. 1970. *A Mandan Dictionary*. Ph.D. Dissertation, University of California, Berkeley.

Kennard, E. 1936. A Mandan Grammar. *International Journal of American Linguistics* 9:1-43.

Lowie, R. 1913. Societies of the Hidatsa and Mandan Indians. *Anthropological Papers of the American Museum of Natural History* 11:219-358.

Parks, D.R., A.W. Jones, & R.C. Hollow. 1978. *Earth Lodge Tales From the Upper Missouri*. Bismarck: Mary College.

Motivation, Repetition and Emancipation: The Bureaucratisation of Language

John Haiman

Like all things, human languages change over time. Like human institutions in particular, languages and grammars change through use. In what follows, I want to look at varieties of change which are brought about through routine repetition: I will use the term *ritualisation* as a cover term for all of these related changes. Unlike many linguists who insist on the uniqueness and autonomy of language, I have found it profitable (at least for my approach to this discussion) to compare language not only with other human institutions, but with the development of language-like behaviour (including ritual and play) in other animals. In fact, I shall argue that much of the apparent "autonomy" of language (as of many other human institutions) arises precisely through ritualisation.

The first part of this essay accordingly deals with emancipation, habituation, and automatisation in both human and non-human *non-linguistic* behaviour. The second part deals with the linguistic analogues of these: habituation as grammaticalisation, automatisation as double articulation, and emancipation as the genesis of coded forms (language in general) and ritual or formulaic language (language that is, in one sense, meaningless). In my conclusion, I hope to suggest that both the infinite creativity of human language and its frequent apparent lack of motivation provide evidence for nothing more hardwired than this same process of ritualisation.

NON-LINGUISTIC RITUALISATION

EMANCIPATION

Wishing to copulate with the female dancing fly, the male signals his availability by giving her as a "wedding present", a balloon of silk. While her attention is distracted in unbundling the package, he mounts her and then, if he is lucky, makes his getaway. The package is empty.

Closely related species evince fragments of this all-too-human routine. On the basis of comparative observations of attested behaviour from these species, Kessel (1955) surmised that the extraordinary courtship of the dancing fly may have become established in the following way: Originally, the male dancing fly distracted the predaceous female with the gift of a dead insect: at this (attested) point, the gift was purely instrumental. Later, the gift was interpreted as a signal to the female, a signal whose message was something like "this fly is available for mating." Originally, also, the male partially wrapped his tiny prey up in silk exuded from his anal glands, probably in order to subdue it: the silk, like the dead insect, had an instrumental function, and its similarity to "wrapping" was incidental. (This behaviour also is attested.) Finally, however, the male achieved his original "purpose" by giving the female the elaborated wrapping alone, and it is the wrapping which serves as the mating signal.

This is a paradigmatic example of what ethologists since Tinbergen have been calling *ritualisation* (cf. Tinbergen 1952; Morris 1956; Blest 1963; J. Smith 1966:168; Gleitman 1986):

> in the course of evolution, both locomotory movements and acts (concerned with comfort, with heat regulation, and with the capture of prey) have been selected and modified to produce signals.

In other words, ritualisation in the sense employed here by Blest (1963:102) and others is nothing other than the evolution of (a) language.

Ethologists and anthropologists have noted, incidentally, that ritual in many cases is akin to play. In both cases, an activity is found to occur when the animal is free of environmental and physiological pressures or in effect can take a holiday from the otherwise exceptionless rules of biological necessity and/or social hierarchy (Loizos 1966; Miller 1973).

Ritualisation describes the process whereby phylogenetically instrumental actions are *emancipated* from their primary motivation and free to serve a communicative function instead (Tinbergen 1952; Morris 1956; Blest 1963; Manning 1967). A ritual is identified as one when it ceases to be a purely instrumental act and becomes a sign.

Codification, the creation of signs, is structurally a dual transformation: on the one hand, the ritualised activity is standardised so that its form is relatively autonomous from (emancipated from) its original stimulus (Morris 1956:1):

> It is a basic property of simple signals, when these are contrasted with other types of response, that they remain constant in form regardless of any change in the circumstances which cause them.

A corollary to this *autonomous fixity of form* is that the ritualised act does not necessarily even occur in the same context as the act which is presumed to be ancestral to it (Blest 1963:116).

On the other hand, the form (of the ritual or the play) may become elaborated and (when viewed in purely instrumental terms) hyper-trophied to the point where it is not only useless, but actually dysfunctional (Morris 1956; Loizos 1966:7; Miller 1973:89, 92). This *hypertrophied stylisation* is characteristic not only of ritual, but of art in general (Mumford 1960:69):

> [There is] a tendency on the part of human fantasy, once it is emancipated from the restraint of practical needs, to run riot... In medieval cathedrals, this sometimes went so far that Ruskin even discovered carvings in places where no human eye but his own – if we except the original worker – had probably ever beheld it.

Examples abound of art which originates as propaganda (whether for the Catholic Church, or for Diet Coke). Only too often (or perhaps, not nearly often enough), the propagandist gets carried away and makes works of art which are aesthetically pleasing, all right, but fail to sell the product. Ars gratia artis.

It has been suggested that stylisation (insofar as it involves standardisation) is nevertheless functionally motivated in two ways: first, a stylised signal is easier to recognise (Morris 1956:1, Manning 1967:138); and, second, it is easier to reproduce (Fónagy et al. 1983:173-174; Bolinger 1986:231) than a spontaneous gesture. I will yield once again to the irresistible urge to quote the wisdom of Lewis Mumford (1960:69) on the related transition from handwriting to movable type:

> For the sake of legibility and universality, it was important that the human being who copied a book should achieve a certain kind of neutrality and impersonality,... making each letter conform to a common type, rigorously standardizing the product... After a copyist repeated the same letter a thousand times, his letters would achieve that impersonal quality... at which [they] could be transferred into movable types.

The emancipation of art from its instrumental functions, succinctly summed up in the familiar slogan "art for art's sake", is a characteristic of almost every human institution which "takes on a life of its own."

Any bureaucracy affords a good illustration of an organisation which has become "emancipated" both from the original purpose for which it was created (cf. Merton 1968:253), and from the laws of the marketplace (cf. Beetham 1987:44-45).

So, too, the familiar institution of the six o'clock news, or even of the daily newspaper, illustrates emancipation from empirical motivation. True news is a report of real events. Inevitably, there are days when nothing much has happened: on such days, we can therefore expect no true news. But we still expect the daily "news," which must appear as a matter of routine. In order to satisfy the demands of routinisation, events are replaced by ritualised "pseudo-events," press conferences and photo opportunities (cf. Boorstin 1962).

In Marxist sociology, a term which closely corresponds to the ethologists' *emancipation* is *reification*. Manufactured objects in general have a *use value* which corresponds exactly to the instrumental function which ethologists observe in animal behaviour: the use value of shoes is to be worn, of tobacco to be smoked, etc. In a subsistence economy, all objects have use value or instrumental function only. In an economy where surpluses can be created, objects may also have an *exchange value*, or symbolic function: the exchange value of surplus shoes, tobacco and so forth is the other objects for which they can be traded, and for which, in a sense, they can stand. Reified objects, or *commodities*, may be defined as those which have been entirely emancipated from their original use value, and which have exchange value alone (Israel 1971:58):

> When an object is transformed into a commodity, it is no longer used for its original purpose... It can be independent of the goals for which it was created and, moreover, can even thwart these goals.

The prototypical exemplar of such a reified object is of course money, whose only function is to represent other things.

The parallels between ritualised signs and reified objects are very deep. It is notable, first, that reified objects are typically objects which are invested with symbolic value in addition to their use value. A Cadillac still has a use value as a means of transportation, but its far more important value is as a status symbol. Reification in Marxist sociology then, like ritualisation in ethology, is a process which creates *signs* by investing objects with the capacity for representing other objects, while emancipating them from their instrumental functions.

Another way of thinking about reification is that it occurs whenever original means to achieve some purposes replace those purposes and become ends in themselves.

Mass production (or repetition) is only one of the ways in which this can happen, but it is the one which seems to me the most relevant to language.

HABITUATION

An often repeated ritual can pall. With staleness comes very often a reduction of its formal manifestation and, although not always, a diminution of its meaning. (We express this familiar insight with idioms like "issuing a ritual apology" or "going through the motions" of doing something.) Almost any abbreviated or sublimated gesture or verbal symbol of greeting or farewell, from a handshake to *goodbye* (cf. Firth 1972) is a ritual in this sense, as is any cliché, or the signing of one's own name. Ethologists sometimes use the term *ritualisation* for this process of formal reduction also. Thus, Plooij (1978:123) in his discussion of beckoning behaviour among wild chimpanzees uses *ritualisation* to describe the change whereby the abbreviated gesture of leaning slightly backwards comes to replace the original gesture of lying down.

Clichés and formulas are good examples of the outcome of a process that psychologists call *habituation* or adaptation: a decline in the tendency to respond to stimuli that have become familiar due to repeated or persistent exposure (Bassett & Warne 1919, Karsten 1928, Lambert & Jakobovitz 1960, Smith & Raygor 1956, Gleitman 1986:88, 160, 200). These investigators have provided quantitative proof for the homely proverbs that "you can get used to anything," that "familiarity breeds contempt," that "what we look at habitually, we overlook" (Mumford 1960:103). Repetition may lead to formal reduction (think of your signature), but, independently of this, it may drain meaning away also. As Mumford observes, "there are paintings by van Gogh and Matisse and Picasso that are descending the swift slippery slope to oblivion by reason of the fact that they are on view at all times and everywhere" (Mumford 1960:102).

It is this trivialisation of "the work of art in the age of mechanical reproduction" Walter Benjamin lamented in his famous essay of that title.

AUTOMATISATION

But other, more "desirable" things come with repetition as well. For example, the sequence of numbers

149162536496481100121144169196225...

may seem impossible to learn as long as the student relies on memory alone. But as the sequence

1, 4, 9, 16, 25, 36, 49, 64, 81, 100, 121, 144, 169, 196, 225,...

it is learned in a moment. In the same way, while it is relatively difficult to learn a seven-digit telephone number, it *seems* easy to learn a seven-letter mnemonic like L-A-W-Y-E-R-S, or F-O-R C-A-R-S where each letter corresponds to a number. Or again: an expert telegraph operator receiving a coded message can keep six to twelve words behind the instrument when receiving: this means storing, on an average, about 200 clicks – a truly amazing achievement. On the other hand, if the clicks represent disconnected numbers, the most skilled operators can hold only three or four numbers at a time – a maximum of about twenty clicks (Bryan & Harter 1899:353-4). These are paradigm examples of *chunking* or *automatisation*: the acquisition of what Bryan & Harter called "a hierarchy of habits" (cf. Gleitman 1986:233, 270). Although, objectively, *learning seven digits involves less information processing than learning a sequence of seven letters*, and the digits in the ascending sequence of squares are identical with the digits in the seemingly random list above it, nevertheless, the work seems to be less when the "principle" which generates the sequence has been learned. Strangely, this is true whether the principle is a real generalisation, one which can be expressed as a mathematical formula (as in the case of the sequence of squares), or where the "principle" is simply a painfully acquired skill (as in the case of reading or reconstructing spelling from Morse). In either case, some computation is done automatically and in a sense "doesn't count" as a burden on the person who performs it. Mere repetition leads to automatisation as effectively as possession of a formula: "sheer plod makes plow down sillion shine," as Gerard Manley Hopkins once put it.

I have sketchily reviewed three processes in evolution that are driven (at least in the world of human institutions) by mere repetition: the creation of signs, illustrated most vividly by the mating language of the balloon fly and the institution of money; the replacement of instrumental substance by "empty ritual," illustrated by the pseudo-events in the daily news and the trivialisation of "the work of art in the age of mechanical reproduction;" and automatisation, illustrated by the virtuosity of the experienced telegraph operator. The second and third processes find familiar analogues in traditional linguistics, where they are known as grammaticalisation and double articulation. I will start my discussion of ritualisation in human language with these.

RITUALISATION IN LANGUAGE

GRAMMATICALISATION

So common indeed was [the word *fuck*] in its adjectival form that after a short time the ear refused to acknowledge it and took in only the noun to which it was attached... Far from being an intensive to express strong emotion, it became merely a conventional excrescence. By adding -ing and -ingwell, an adjective and an adverb were formed and thrown into every sentence. It became so common that an effective way for the soldier to express emotion was to omit this word. Thus, if a sergeant said 'Get your —ing rifles!' it was understood as a matter of routine. But if he said 'Get your rifles!' there was an immediate implication of emergency and danger.   (Brophy & Partridge 1931:16f.)

This is a paradigmatic example both of markedness reversal (Andersen 1972) and of ritualisation in the sense used by Plooij. Other paradigmatic cases of grammaticalisation, quite parallel to the degeneration of the F--- word, are: (a) the erosion of referential pronouns with argument status to verbal agreement markers, the mechanics of which have been described in many languages (cf. Meinhof 1936, Givón 1970, 1976, 1979, Haiman 1989a), (b) the erosion of the numeral 'one' to the indefinite article (which, in some languages, now functions in a similar way as an agreement marker, cf. Haiman & Benincà 1991), and (c) the erosion of the demonstrative pronouns to the bound prefix, our familiar definite article 'the' in English.

DOUBLE ARTICULATION

    – My kid said his first word today!
    – Well, my kid can say half a word.
    – Oh yeah, what's that?
    – Mother.   (Urban ghetto joke)

    – Well, here's two words comin' your way: shut the fuck up.
                                    (from the film *Midnight Run*)

In the end result of automatisation, of course, we can also recognise *double articulation*: the smallest meaningful signs are made up of still smaller units which are themselves perceived as meaningless (or, better still, are not perceived at all, as in the examples above).

    Double articulation is a language universal the origins of which are almost as disreputable a subject of study as are the origins of human language itself.

    The standard model of erosion whereby morphemes are reduced, first to bound affixes, then to phonemes and finally to silence, may provide the observable mechanism whereby languages evolved double articulation (cf. Wescott 1967, and now Hopper 1990). Sounds now meaningless may have evolved originally from meaningful morphemes.

    The physiologically mysterious process whereby for example the phone number L-A-W-Y-E-R-S is easier to remember than the corresponding sequence of digits, bears witness to automatisation (cf. the well-known Stroop effect, Gleitman 1986:17 et passim), chunking, and double articulation. The recognised word *lawyers* involves a sequence of letters, but we count remembering this as a simpler act than remembering a sequence of random letters, or a sequence of digits, because the effort of having learned the spelling of the word is taken as a given. Before chunking, or automatisation, learning the spelling of *lawyers* (or of any other word) involves no less work than learning any sequence of random letters. Automatisation, it need hardly be emphasised, is the result of repetition. (The linguistically naive, who believe that what we do in reading is "spell out" the sounds of the letters, can be easily persuaded that this is not the case by attempting to read a passage of English in the accurate but unfamiliar IPA.) Erosion through repetition may be a major source (although not the only one) of meaningless phonemes (and of "half-words" like *mother* in the epigraph) in all human languages.

I think it is highly likely that the converse of double articulation – a kind of codification or sign creation – also often arises through repetition. What I have in mind is the creation of phonaesthemes like English ⟨gl-⟩, or ⟨cr-⟩, which are now associated with "a vague impression of light" or an equally vague "impression of crushing" as a result not of onomatopoeia, but of a number of coincidences. That is, ⟨gl-⟩ has the associations that it does because of the prior existence of words like *gleam, glare, glow, glisten, glimmer*. (As Barthes puts it [1972:119, cited in Goffman 1974:34fn]: "chance is supposed to vary events; if it repeats them, it does so in order to signify something through them: to repeat is to signify.") More homely is the repeated aphorism from the James Bond novels: "the first time it's coincidence; the second time it's happenstance; the third time it's enemy action." Similar "promotion from the ranks" of the originally meaningless is observed in innovative forms like *mono-kini* and *tele-thon*, which have created meaningful morphemes *kini* and *thon* where etymologically there were none before.

Rather than accepting double articulation as an irreducible given, we might get a handle on its origins by thinking of degrees of significance, with signs arranged in a hierarchy:

biggest (most "wordlike"):	(1)	words, lexical morphemes
	(2)	affixes, grammatical inter-mediate signs: morphemes
	(3)	sub-morphemic sounds with associations
smallest (most "soundlike"):	(4)	phonemes

Through etymologically coincidental associations which are often repeated, phoneme sequences (4) may become phonaesthemes (3), thus *acquiring* significance. Through frequent repetition, lexical morphemes (1) may become grammatical affixes (2), thus *losing* significance. The first process corresponds to codification (of which more below), the second to habituation and automatisation.

Excursus on Suprasegmental Double Articulation
On the segmental level, morphemes may through erosion be reduced to the status of phonemes. Could the same happen with suprasegmental signs?

Consider pitch. Sememic pitch (intonation) is familiar in English. An example is the melody signalled in conventional orthography by the question mark. Phonemic pitch (tone) is familiar in the so-called tone languages, like Mandarin.

Not a great deal is known about the origins of phonemic tone. Phonologisation of a high/low distinction, originally induced by neighbouring voiced or voiceless consonants (voiced is low, voiceless is high) is the most familiar process. But perhaps there are others.

The analogue to segmental double articulation would be the creation of phonemic tone from an originally morphological use of tone – the "degeneration" of intonation into, first, a grammatical marker, and then into phonemic tone through repetition. Are there plausible cases of this?

Or consider amplitude. As a sememe, amplitude is an icon of focus. As a phoneme, it is meaningless. Are there cases where the second derives from a reduction of the first? If languages assigned predictable word ictus to the same position within the word as they assigned to focus position within the utterance, this would provide suggestive evidence in favour of my hypothesis concerning the origins of double articulation.

In neither case do I know of any evidence regarding origins, so these remarks are totally speculative.

The Act of Direct Quotation
Part of the driving mechanism which reduces words to meaningless sounds is erosion through repeated utterance. In fact, *direct* quotation itself (essentially nothing more than the repetition of an utterance) does this kind of work through a single act: in saying *I quote* (or *I repeat*), the speaker is at least in principle disavowing a personal interest in the meaning of what he or she utters, and *imitating* what may well for the speaker be meaningless sounds. The same point is made by Quine

(1956:26, emphasis supplied) in his many discussions of the use/mention distinction, among them the following:

> From the standpoint of logical analysis, each whole quotation must be regarded as a single word or sign, whose parts count for no more than serifs or syllables. A quotation is not a description but a hieroglyph: it designates its object not by describing it in terms of other objects, but by picturing it. *The meaning of the whole does not depend upon the meanings of the constituent words.*

Quine could have been describing double articulation in this passage. That the internal structure of a quotation is not in itself significant, since it is the mere accurate imitation of the original which counts, is also an implicit insight of all programming languages like Pascal and LISP which distinguish fixed strings (in quotes) from concatenations of *interpretable* and manipulable symbols.

Double Articulation in Clichés
The insight that repetition drains meaning from words, converting them into phonemes, is also implicit in the use by many authors of hyphens to indicate *cliché phrases* which are reduced to the status of words (whose component words are thereby reduced to the status of Quine's "serifs or syllables," or phonemes):

> But now those Democrats can find easy cover in the weak-kneed *it's-just-not-politically-feasible* argument.
> (David Corn, *The Nation*, 1989)

> "Nuts with that *ruining-me-in-this-town* stuff," I said.
> (Budd Schulberg, *What Makes Sammy Run?*)

> – Show business is a *dog-eat-dog* world.
> – No, it s worse. It's a *dog-doesn't-return-the-other-dog's-phone-calls* world.   (Woody Allen, *Crimes and Misdemeanors*)

> Moreover, when she loses at mah-jongg, she takes it like a sport, *not-like-the-others-whose-names-she-could-mention-but-she-won't-not-even-Tilly-Hochman-it's-just-too-petty-to-even-talk-about-let's-just-forget-she-ever-brought-it-up.*   (Philip Roth, *Portnoy's Complaint*)

The essence of this orthographic insight is that all direct quotation (whether of the single utterance or of the oft-repeated cliché) is an act of *repetition*. It differs profoundly from the act of indirect quotation, which is essentially an intelligent act of *translation*: shifting from one code to another a message whose meaning is preserved. A parrot may directly quote an utterance in an unkown language, but indirect quotation is beyond its powers.

It is notable that the rather recherché practice of rendering clichés with dashes parallels a more widespread practice, which is encountered in written representations of the act of "spelling out:" one spells *lawyers* *L-A-W-Y-E-R-S*. To spell out a word, of course, is to represent it in its phonological articulation: again, the components between the dashes are understood to be themselves meaningless. And what makes them meaningless (I contend) is that they have been repeated.

ASPECTS OF LINGUISTIC EMANCIPATION

Phonologisation
In the sound articulation of language, *phonologisation* is a well-understood example of codification. Originally automatic or random fluctuations become phonologised (that is, both distinctive and uniform) when they are *emancipated* from their conditioning environments.

Owing to some imprecision in their formulation, some of the classic discussions of phonologisation leave the erroneous impression that the process is *caused* by the loss of the original conditioning environment. Thus à propos the phonologisation of umlaut in Middle High German, Twaddell (1938[1957:87]) states that "the phonetic differences are phonologised... when the environmental differentiation is eliminated." Jakobson (1931[1972:136]) says that "the loss of the reduced vowels (weak "jers") in the Slavic languages brought about [*sic*] a correlation of phonologisation for consonants." A moment's reflection will show that the loss of the conditioning environment does not cause phonologisation: it only demonstrates that phonologisation has indeed occurred. Consider Twaddell's schematisation of Old High German umlaut, for example (where 'U' represents the original phoneme /u/, with allophones [u] and [y], 'x' represents a consonant (cluster) over which umlaut could occur, and 'xx' represents a cluster over which umlaut was inhibited). In Old High German, the umlaut rule (U → y/___xi), yielded the phonetic results of "stage 1", while in Middle High German, after the operation of a merger (a,i → ə), "we have" the phonetic results of "stage 2":

Inherited Form	Stage 1	Stage 2
Uxi	yxi	yxə
Uxxi	uxxi	uxxə
Uxa	uxa	uxə

The question is, how do "we have" the latter results? Obviously, not by virtue of the umlaut rule, which by stage 2 has nothing to apply to. The inescapable conclusion is that already in stage 1, *before the conditioning environment has disappeared*, the contrast [u] vs. [y] has been established as something that can be maintained. Emancipation from the phonetic stimulus precedes loss of the stimulus itself.

From Connotation to Denotation
In discussions of "cognitive" vs. "emotive" meaning, the primacy of the former is generally agreed upon (cf. Lyons 1968:449). It is denotation, not connotation, which is the business of the grammarian (just as it is culture, not individual personality, which is the business of the anthropologist). But ontologically, in the documented cases of ritualisation, it seems to be connotation which came first. Together with behaviourists like Pavlov and Russell, we might say that *denotation is emancipated connotation*. As Russell puts it, "signs depend, as a rule, upon habits learnt by experience ... We say that A is a 'sign' of B if it promotes behaviour that B would promote, but that has no appropriateness to A alone" (Russell 1940:11).

Schematically: a symptomatic gesture or fidget (let us say, a cry of pain like [aaaa]) accompanies a psychological state. That is, originally the gesture *connotes* the state. It becomes a signal which still *connotes* that state once it is recognised and responded to by some other animal. Finally, it becomes a sign (say, the English word *ouch*) which *denotes* the state only once it is emancipated both from the stimulus which produced it originally, and from the motivated state of which it served as a signal. Denotation, like ritualisation, occurs in consequence of this same process of emancipation. Mutatis mutandis, recall Pavlov's famous experiment; or, recall the story of the dancing fly.

That emancipation from its referent or "abstractness" is a crucial and defining property of a linguistic sign is wittily illustrated in Umberto Eco's essay 'Sugli specchi'. A reflection, he argues, cannot be a sign, because it is *never* emancipated from the stimulus which produces it. Since a mirror can never show anything other than what is in front of it, it is also incapable of providing significance through contrast.

Ritualisation of Stress: Compound Stress
Consider the familiar contrast between *black bird* and *blackbird*. The latter, clearly a ritualised form (note that the incorporated morpheme *black-* has typically undergone the semantic bleaching characteristic of gram- maticalised forms), is treated for stress purposes as a single word. The former is treated as two. It is misleadingly reductionist to characterise the

difference as one between compound stress (stress on the first syllable) and nuclear stress (stress on the last syllable). The essential difference is between a single word whose predictable grammaticalised ictus is automatically on the first syllable, and between a string of two words either one of which may be stressed at the will of the speaker. The phrase *black bird* can be uttered *black BIRD* or *BLACK bird*.

Ritualisation of Intonation: Singsong

A frequently observed property of ritual or play activity is its stylisation: the originally instrumental act when ritualised is rhythmically repeated, or its component parts exaggerated (Morris 1956; Blest 1963:110; Loizos 1966:7; Miller 1973:89; Moore & Myerhoff 1977:7). How do analogues look in human language?

Uncoded natural signs (or symptoms) of anger, boredom, disgust, or excitement are universal (cf. Fónagy 1971a,b for some pioneering studies). But they are not ritualised: Sebeok (1962:431) suggests that they are "codified" in analogue terms, while other "rational" aspects of existence are codified in digital terms. What Jakobson called the "ars obligatoria" of Grammar (ritual or codification in our sense) begins formally, as we all seem to agree, with digitisation. Digitisation is perhaps necessary for intersubjectivity and replicability: it may be what distinguishes movable type from personal handwriting, linguistic from paralinguistic verbal behaviour or, more generally, what distinguishes culture from personality. It is certainly one of the features which distinguishes ritual from spontaneous instrumental behaviour. A number of ethologists have commented (as we have already seen) on the feature of *typical intensity*: the tendency for a ritual gesture to remain constant irrespective of the force (or even of the presence) of the stimulus which produced it. Ipso facto, rituals are insincere (Manning 1967:138):

> Postures or movements which have a typical intensity are more easily recognised *but correspondingly convey less information about the signaller's motivational state.*

Conceptually, the ritualisation of such symptoms occurs when the "exuded expressions" over which the speaker has no control are replaced by "standardised vocal comments on circumstances that are not, or no longer, beyond emotional or physical control" (Goffman 1983:100, 107). It occurs, in other words, where the universal symptomatic expression of pain, for example, is replaced by language-specific digitised coded signs like *ouch*. Language begins, ritual begins, where etiquette begins, at the point where it becomes possible for the speaker to lie. For what is lying but another kind of emancipation: from correspondence with the external world? (In associating ritual with lying, I take issue with Gombrich [1966:398], who declares that "animals lack that distinctively human achievement, the lie," insofar as animal communication through ritualisation of gestures with a typical intensity is possible, to this extent animals communicate something other than the way they feel.)

For the view from a great linguist (if not yet the view from linguistics), Bolinger's remarks (1975:20) are very apposite:

> A sign of adulthood is the "insincerity" of originally autonomous actions. A smile is no longer the betrayal of a feeling but a purposive act intended to please. The hollow laugh and the crocodile tear are instinctive gestures that have become part of etiquette.

So, too, the courtship ritual of the male balloon fly: pure etiquette.

As a theory of language origins, the historical change from the personal involuntary *aaaaargh* to the codified *ouch* seems suspect, if only because involuntary expressions are controlled by different portions of the brain than human language: citing a recent dissertation, Bolinger (1975:315) suggests that:

> Whereas language and tool using are related in the brain, language and primitive cries are not. In man, an electrical stimulus on the cortex – the region of highest organisation – will cause vocalisation; in animals the stimulus generally has to be applied below the cortex. This makes it highly unlikely that there was any direct transition from emotional noises to propositional language.

Bolinger's hesitation may be overcautious. Throughout the animal kingdom, ritualisation is often marked precisely by "the transfer of the signal function from one set of effectors to another" (Blest 1963:110-111 enumerates some spectacular examples). More to the point, even higher level and demonstrably recent functions such as reading in humans take place in different brain locations, depending on whether the act is one of processing unfamiliar letter strings or the ritualised one of recognizing familiar vocabulary (cf. Givón & Gernsbacher [ms.], and the numerous references there).

Almost completely lacking a palaeontology of language, as of most other behaviour, we should treat comparative observations of this sort as some of the best data we can build our speculations on. But not the only data.

With insignificant exceptions like *ouch* and *boo-hoo*, we cannot observe how words developed out of non-words: however far back we go, it seems that all our etymologies of words trace back to nothing but other, older words. But, we may be able to observe the genesis of codification in the stereotyping of intonation, which, as has often been noted, lies at the border between paralinguistic and linguistic behaviour. Although there is much stereotyping (codification) in this realm, it is inherently less digitally coded than morphosyntax, more inherently iconic (cf. Bolinger 1986), and more subject to personal variation.

The quintessentially ritualised or stereotyped intonation is the array of singsong chants (cf. Liberman 1979) which signal clichés (cf. Ladd 1978, Fónagy et al. 1983). For reasons which we will get to in a moment, the ritual in the case of (M)HL, (Mid) High Low, is something uttered playfully, or whose informative meaning is not attended to.

A good locus of singsong intonation cross-linguistically is in the self-conscious repetition of phrases that are felt to be clichés. Among these are:

(a) stale proverbs which the speaker feels to be irrelevant or dull;

(b) clichés of greeting, etc. (cf. Fónagy et al. 1983);

(c) rote speeches of instruction, greeting, etc. uttered by those whose sad business it is to deliver them *repeatedly* (auctioneers, bus drivers, receptionists, telephone operators, clerks, airline stewardesses: cf. Justice [ms.], Kuiper & Haggo 1984).

It also occurs (relatively infrequently, but with impeccable semantic motivation, cf. Almansi 1984:35, Haiman 1989b, 1990) in

(d) utterances which are intended playfully or sarcastically. Examples of clichés so uttered with the (L)HM melody with which most of us are highly familiar include *Too bad, Never mind, Thank you, Sorr-eee* or *Oh boy*, uttered to the tune of *Ho-hum* (Bolinger 1986:230) or *Bo-ring*.

A more complex example of the same (L)HM melody occurs at one point in Jonathan Demme's film, *Married to the Mob*, where the philandering villain, in a nightmare, is confronted by his homicidally jealous wife. Aiming a rifle at his groin she smiles sweetly and chants:

L   H M
"Kiss it good-by-eee"

The (L)HM is not the only ritualised or stylised intonation in English, of course. Another is LH, which is similarly ironic when used for stylised expressions of congratulation:

L	H
Waita go,	*dad*
Good	*job*
Nice	*going*

What is most remarkable about singsong intonation not only in these examples, but in a variety of languages where I have observed it, is that it correlates with much the same range of (meta-)messages: one of these is what Bolinger (1986:231) calls the meta-message that "everybody knows." Another is predictability or boredom, the meta-message "here we go again" (cf. Ladd 1978:520, Kuiper & Haggo 1984:216). Another is playfulness or sarcasm, the meta-message "I don't mean this" or "this is play" (cf. Fónagy et al. 1983:157, 178). It is teasing playfulness, of course, which is signalled by the homicidal wife in *Married to the Mob*. Why is singsong never used to code anger, grief, shame, or ecstasy (to cite some paralinguistic and personal messages)? Why is it never used to code interrogation (to cite only the most impeccably "grammatical" message)?

Repetition alone is not enough to explain this restriction: people have been expressing emotions and asking questions for some time. But *self-conscious* repetition is something else. What is common to each of the meta-messages which singsong intonation can be used to code is precisely this: "I am repeating;" "I quote." ("And I know it. That is why I am bored, insincere, playful.") Here are some striking examples of the (L)HM chant, accompanied by commentaries from the speakers who produced them.

In American English: *bo-ring, too bad, sor-ree,* etc.

In Turkish: the expressions *seker çocuk* 'sweet child' or *zavallï çocuk* 'poor child' can be uttered in a singsong fashion. When so uttered, they are no longer expressions of compassion or appreciation, but of sarcastic denigration. One of my teachers suggests that the first can be addressed to a close friend (and only to such a friend: other people might take offence) who "did something wrong, but is acting innocent." The understood message is "I'm on to you, you hypocrite." To call someone's name on this same melody (HM) is "acceptable for women; for a man to do this is sarcastic, and equivalent to calling the person named a sissy." The expression *tabi, tabi* 'sure sure' uttered in normal form can be an expression of agreement. Chanted as a HM melody, it denotes sarcastic agreement, exactly as does English *sure, sure,* or *yeah, right.* The singsong melody of the lexical representation of weeping *y hy hy hy hy* conveys the same sarcasm. The expression *dikkat* 'watch out' uttered with this melody is similarly playful: "you might imagine 'warning' someone in this way who was about to get water dumped on him as he lay on the beach – as if to say 'you're gone'." Alternatively, it could be uttered in the same way as *oops*, "by a teacher to a student who got a wrong answer." In the same way that a schoolteacher's question is not a sincere question (inasmuch as the teacher knows the answer he or she is trying to elicit), the schoolteacher's warning is not a sincere warning: the frame of the classroom is far removed from the dangers of the real world.

In Korean: the expression *çusim he* 'watch out' is restricted to girls only. The reason given by my (female) consultant was that there was a connotation of non-seriousness.

In Literary Arabic: the expression *heðaaðim* 'big', when uttered in a singsong fashion, is sarcastic and means something like English *big deal*. A name called on this chanted melody connotes a teasing reproach to someone small who has done something wrong.

In Russian: the expression *konecno, konecno* 'sure, sure' has the same interpretation as the sarcastic *sure, sure* when it is uttered in a singsong chant.

In Berber: the expression *sm he jiij* 'excuse me' is meant sarcastically when the final syllable [jiij] 'me' is lengthened, and the melody is stylised.

Perhaps singsong is one means of marking an oft-repeated cliché. But another one (with much the same semantic force) may be the mimicry of the act of repetition itself.

Sarcastic Assent

> Lecturer: Thus, although it is possible in human language for two
> negatives to make a positive, the converse is never true.
> Heckler: Yeah, yeah.

The most plausible interpretation of repetition is an iconic one: if you say something once, maybe you mean it, but if you say it two or three times, you *really* mean it. Thus, reduplication, as often noted, typically has the vaguely iconic function of signalling plurality or intensification (Haiman 1980).

It is therefore remarkable that repetition of signs of assent, like *sure, right, of course*, or *yeah* signals not heartiness, but irony, as in the epigraph. Nor is this limited to colloquial American English. The same is noted by native language consultants for Turkish, Russian, Hungarian, and Oromo renditions of the expression 'of course.' To be sarcastic, the repeated words have to be pronounced in a weary deadpan way, of course: but for some reason, repetition helps to achieve this.

I suggest that a possible reason for the sarcastic flavour of repeated *yeah, yeah* is that speakers who repeat such expressions are themselves *mimicking the process* whereby these words, like any others, have lost their original meanings through repetition by other speakers. (It is notable that sarcastic repetitions are uttered not only in a more-or-less singsong fashion, but on a series of downstepped tones, HM(L), mimicking a fading of intensity over time.)

Ritual Language

If language is action emancipated from an instrumental function, ritual language is language which has been emancipated from even this derived semiotic function. Its formal properties and development are both accessible to investigation, and therefore of the highest interest.

At the very heart of Goffman's *Frame Analysis* (1974) lies the important idea that any given event may be viewed through what he calls "successive laminations" or frames. If a "frame" is a code, then successive laminations are *codes within codes*. Ritualisation may be thought of as a potentially repeated process of codification, lamination – or emancipation – from brute reality. We can illustrate this with respect to the familiar (expressive, referential, directive, metalinguistic, aesthetic, etc.) functions of language.

As human acts (like expressive cries of rage, wonder, and pain) become emancipated from the laws of nature, they become what Goffman calls stereotyped "willed doings" – cultural facts. As cultural acts become in their turn liberated from functional or instrumental purposes, they become "symbolic" or magical communicative gestures – of these, the most important are the gestures which comprise spoken language, and the most instrumental function of language is to make others do one's bidding (cf. Russell's insight that the most primitive use of language is to command, 1940:24). As language becomes liberated from its instrumental (magical) function, it becomes referential. As referential language becomes liberated from even this abstract communicative function, it becomes *ritual* (either ludic or phatic): grammaticalised as phatic communication or as ritual, language and culture reach their highest degree of playfulness, abstraction, or liberation from the natural world of brute reality (cf. Tambiah 1968:179; Wheelock 1982:57).

Phatic language stands in the same relationship to language in general as money stands to shoes and ships and sealing wax. The original use function of both has been totally supplanted by their exchange function.

A marvellously compact demonstration of the transformation of the originally expressive language of obscenity into purely ritual or phatic communication is afforded by the interchange between Dilbert and the mechanic:

Dilbert / By Scott Adams

The endlessly instructive F--- word, originally expressive, is here a ritual sign of blue-collar bonding. At the service station, as in the armed forces, it is the verbal equivalent of a handshake.

How do these "successive laminations," this emancipation, this stereotyping, occur in ritualised behaviour? Margaret Mead (1973:90) suggests the obvious answer: "It is of the essence of ritual that those who participate in it have participated before." One may, of course, participate in a ritual for the first time. But it *is* essential that those who participate are following a model that has been established (perhaps by others) who *have* participated before: if not in that exact ritual, then in others that are similar. (This is true even of invented rituals or rituals of "junction" [Moore & Myerhoff 1977:7], which celebrate unique events. It is arguably even true of unprecedented acts whose onlookers spontaneously realise that "something sacred has happened here," their recognition depending largely on whether they have rehearsed the ritual in their heads.)

Gombrich (1966:399) makes a similar point, but in a rather less respectful way, when he says that:

> It may have been liberating for Jackson Pollock to break all bonds and pour his paint on the canvas, but once everybody does it, it becomes a ritual in the modern sense of the term, a mere trick that can be learned and gone through without emotion.

That is, acts are not only *invested with* meaning through repetition: they may be *emancipated from* (among other things) meaning by the same process. Ritual is born (at least in part) through repetition. In the same way, ritual language is born from repetition of ordinary language. If ritual language develops from ordinary language through repetition of the latter, we can account for a remarkable but really puzzling fact: ritual language does (often) resemble ordinary language (cf. Wheelock 1982:60, who remarks that this is "obvious"). The Lord's Prayer, for example, is made up of phrases in English that can be understood by speakers of English and translated into phrases of any other language. Previous investigators have understandably chosen to emphasise ways in which ritual speech is keyed to be understood as distinct from ordinary language, but the first fact which requires explanation is that ritual language in cases of this sort *is* recognizably pretty much the same as the "real life" language from which it stands apart. (So, too, ethologists like Tinbergen have typically succeeded in showing how ritualised communicative behaviour can be recognised as deriving from similar autochthonous non-communicative behaviour. So too, students of bureaucracy point out that all bureaucratic organisations once had functions other than the maximisation of their budgets.) In saying that ritualised language comes from repeated ordinary language, we have accounted for this (very familiar) similarity. Otherwise, a resemblance which we can and should dismiss as both obvious and banal would have to be treated as an intriguing and inexplicable coincidence.

Even more striking than the similarity between ritual and everyday language are some of the recurrent differences between them, admirably summarised in DuBois 1986. Two of the distinctive features of ritual or formulaic language which DuBois enumerates are already familiar from our earlier discussion of superficially unrelated speech genres. Among them are *stylised intonation* (for example: Quiche "stylised intonation contour," Seneca "short staccato phrases with a final rising tone, followed by a closing phrase with a fixed falling melody;" Cuna "chanted intonation;" Kiriwina "singsong"); and what DuBois calls *gestalt form* (for example: Kiriwinan magicians as a rule cannot repeat spells slowly or piecemeal; Mojave informants apparently experience great difficulty in slowing down the sequence of memorised texts). The latter we recognise as the double articulation characteristic even of the orthography of the oft-repeated cliché.

CREATIVITY, AUTONOMY AND REPETITION

It is virtually a cliché in all the arts that formulaicity and arbitrariness are most established in the *smallest* units. Kiparsky (1966:93) does no more than echo this common idea in his discussion of oral poetry. Within words, derivational morphology is more arbitrary than inflectional morphology; words are more formulaic than phrases (e.g., the order of morphemes in a word is fixed, cf. Perlmutter 1971:100); phrases are more rigid than sentences; sentences, more structured than paragraphs; paragraphs, more fixed than themes.

This cliché itself requires explanation. Granted, perhaps, formulaicity is the same as ritualisation. Why, then, are the smallest units the ones in which ritualisation has proceeded the furthest? Because the smallest units are the ones which are the most often repeated. (Note that this is true whether smallness allows more repetition on a simply statistical basis or whether, as Zipf proposed in 1935, repetition of a given form results in its erosion.) Either way, *ritualisation comes with repetition.*

REPETITION, CREATOR OF CREATIVITY

The infinite creativity of language is a given of current theoretical approaches (so much so that paeans in its praise have come, paradoxically, to typify the very opposite). There can be no denying the fundamental fact that finite linguistic codes are adapted for conveying an infinite number of possible messages. When, however, we look at what *makes* these codes finite – design features like digitisation and double articulation – it seems likely that they arose precisely through repetition and the stylisation of form and habituated response that repetition gives rise to. And when we look at what makes these codes change over time – and formal reduction through grammaticalisation is certainly one of the universal changes which all languages undergo – then again it seems likely that repetition is the motor which drives this very basic process.

Unquestionably, the uniqueness of human language seems to deride evolutionary theories of its origin. Nevertheless, the biological evolutionary genesis and decay of signs in the animal kingdom exhibits intriguing formal parallels with the social and psychological genesis of ritual in humans (cf. Moynihan 1970). And, while the physiology of ritualisation in human beings is unknown, it seems overwhelmingly likely that repetition plays an important and insufficiently appreciated part in its development.

REPETITION, CREATOR OF AUTONOMY

> The analysis of bureaucracy by Merton... can be translated into a theory of reification. An organisation of a social system is altered in such a way that its means are changed and become autonomous goals.   (Israel 1971:59)

The sheer dysfunctionality of many putative syntactic universals is used by generativists as one of their strongest arguments for the innateness of grammar, and against functionalism in general. (A very strong statement of this position is found in the closing lines of Koster 1987.) Even granting the apparent uselessness, not to mention the correctness, of such universals as the Empty Category Principle, innateness is not the only explanation for dysfunction or the vaunted "radical autonomy of syntax." Or rather, if we wished to claim this, we would have to say that red tape, no less than the Empty Category Principle, is hardwired into the genetic structure of the human species.

On the contrary, I believe we can show that the process of emancipation, like every universal law, operates in every corner of its proper realm. To restrict ourselves merely to the development of human institutions, we see ritualisation and routinisation – the genesis of autonomy – at work in the development of money, bureaucracies, and the six o'clock news, as well as in the development of language.

Like the white silk bundle of the dancing fly, these constructs have cut free of their empirical moorings and taken on a life of their own.

NOTE

Thanks for insightful suggestions to Dwight Bolinger, Talmy Givón, Michael Kac, Bill Pagliucca, Joseph Stemberger, Sandra A. Thompson, Chuck Torrey and Anna Wierzbicka.

Thanks also to the John Simon Guggenheim Foundation, for partial financial support during the writing of this essay.

Thanks, finally, to John Finlay, for giving bureaucracy a good name.

REFERENCES

Almansi, G. 1984. *Amica ironia*. Milan: Garzanti.

Andersen, H. 1972. Diphthongization. *Language* 48:11-50.

Barthes, R. 1972. Structure of the *fait-divers*. *Critical Essays*, R. Howard, tr. Evanston, Illinois: Northwestern University Press.

Bassett, M., & L. Warne. 1919. On the Lapse of Verbal Meaning with Repetition. *American Journal of Psychology* 30:415-418.

Beetham, D. 1987. *Bureaucracy*. Minneapolis: University of Minnesota Press.

Blest, A. 1963. The Concept of "Ritualization." W. Thorpe & O. Zangwill eds., *Current Problems in Animal Behaviour*, 102-125. Cambridge: Cambridge University Press.

Bolinger, D. 1975. *Aspects of Language*, 2nd ed. New York: Harcourt Brace Jovanovich.

—. 1986. *Intonation and its Parts*. Stanford: Stanford University Press.

Boorstin, D. 1962. *The Image*. New York: Atheneum.

Brophy, J., & E. Partridge. 1931. *Songs and Slang of the British Soldier: 1914-1918*. 3rd ed. London: Routledge & Kegan Paul.

Bryan, W., & N. Harter. 1899. Studies on the Telegraphic Language: The Acquisition of a Hierarchy of Habits. *Psychological Review* 6:345-375.

DuBois, J. 1986. Self-evidence and Ritual Speech. W. Chafe & J. Nichols, eds., *Evidentials: The Linguistic Coding of Epistemology*, 313-333. Norwood, New Jersey: Ablex.

Fónagy, I. 1971a. The Functions of Vocal Style. S. Chatman, ed., *Literary Style: A Symposium*, 159-76. London: Oxford University Press.

—. 1971b. Synthèse de l'ironie. *Phonetica* 23:42-51.

— et al. 1983. Clichés mélodiques. *Folia Linguistica* 17:153-185.

Firth, R. 1972. Verbal and Bodily Rituals of Greeting. J. LaFontaine, ed., *The Interpretation of Ritual*, 1-38. London: Tavistock.

Givón, T. 1970. The Resolution of Gender Conflicts in Bantu Conjunction. *Papers of the Chicago Linguistic Society* 6:250-261.

—. 1976. Topic, Pronoun, and Grammatical Agreement. C. Li, ed., *Subject and Topic*, 149-188. New York: Academic Press.

—. 1979. *On Understanding Grammar*. New York: Academic Press.

—, & M. Gernsbacher. (ms.) The Processing of Second Language Vocabulary: From Attended to Automated Word-recognition.

Gleitman, H. 1986. *Psychology*, 2nd ed. New York: Norton.

Goffman, E. 1974. *Frame Analysis*. New York: Harper.

—. 1983. Response Cries. *Forms of talk*, 2nd ed., 78-123. Philadelphia: University of Pennsylvania Press.

Gombrich, E.H. 1966. Ritualized Gesture and Expression in Art. J. Huxley. ed., *A Discussion on Ritualization of Behaviour in Animals and Men*, 393-401. Philosophical Transactions of the Royal Society of London, series B, 251.

Haiman, J. 1980. The Iconicity of Grammar. *Language* 56:515-540.

—. 1989a. From V/2 to verb agreement. B. Heine & E. Traugott, eds., *Grammaticalization*. Amsterdam: John Benjamins.

—. 1989b. Alienation in Grammar. *Studies in Language* 13:129-170.

—. 1990. Sarcasm as Theater. *Cognitive Linguistics* 2:186-209.

—, & P. Benincà. 1991. *The Rhaeto-Romance Languages*. London: Routledge.

Hopper, P. 1990. Phonogenesis. G. Davies et al., eds., *Explanation in Historical Linguistics*. Amsterdam: John Benjamins.

Israel, J. 1971. *Alienation*. Boston: Allyn & Bacon.

Jakobson, R. 1931. Principles of Historical Phonology. [reprinted in A. Keiler, ed., *A Reader in Historical Linguistics*, 121-138, New York: Holt Rinehart & Winston, 1972]

Justice, D. (ms.) Etiology of a Prosodic Shift: Enallage Ictus.

Karsten, A. 1928. Psychische Sättigung. *Psychologische Forschungen* 10:142-254.

Kessel, E. 1955. The Mating Activity of Balloon Flies. *Journal of Systematic Zoology* 4:97-104.

Kiparsky, P. 1966. Oral Poetry: Some Linguistic and Typological Considerations. B.A. Stolz & R. Shannon, eds., *Oral Literature and the Formula*, 73-125. Ann Arbor: Center for the Coordination of Ancient and Modern Studies, University of Michigan.

Koster, J. 1987. *Domains and Dynasties*. Dordrecht: Foris.

Kuiper, K. & D. Haggo. 1984. Livestock Auctions, Oral Poetry, and Ordinary Language. *Language in Society* 13:205-234.

Ladd, R. 1978. Stylized Intonation. *Language* 54:517-540.

Lambert, W., & L. Jakobovitz. 1960. Verbal Satiation and Changes in the Intensity of Meaning. *Journal of Experimental Psychology* 60:376-383.

Liberman, M. 1979. The Intonational System of English. Bloomington, Indiana: Indiana University Linguistics Club.

Loizos, C. 1966. Play in Mammals. P.A. Jewell & C. Loizos, eds., *Play, Exploration, and Territoriality in Mammals*, 1-9. (Symposia of the Zoological Society of London, 18). London: Academic Press.

Lyons, J. 1968. *An Introduction to Theoretical Linguistics*. Cambridge: Cambridge University Press.

Manning, A. 1967. *An Introduction to Animal Behaviour*. New York: Addison-Wesley.

Mead, M. 1973. Ritual and Social Crisis. J. Shaughnessy, ed., *The Roots of Ritual*, 87-101. Grand Rapids: Eerdmans.

Meinhof, C. 1936. *Die Entstehung flektierender Sprachen*. Berlin: Reimer.

Merton, R. 1968. *Social Theory and Social Structure*. New York: Free Press.

Miller, S. 1973. Ends, Means, and Galumphing. *American Anthropologist* 75:87-98.

Moore, S., & B. Myerhoff. 1977. Introduction. S. Moore & B. Meyerhoff, eds., *Secular Ritual*, 3-24. Amsterdam: van Gorcum.

Morris, D. 1956. Typical Intensity and its Relation to the Problem of Ritualization. *Behaviour* 11:1-12.

Moynihan, M. 1970. Control, Suppression, Decay, Disappearance, and Replacement of Displays. *Journal of Theoretical Biology* 29:85-112.

Mumford, L. 1960. *Art and Technics*. New York: Columbia University Press.

Ochs, E. 1983. Making it Last. E. Ochs & B. Schieffelin eds., *Acquiring Conversational Competence*, 26-39. London: Routledge & Kegan Paul.

Perlmutter, D. 1971. *Deep and Surface Structure Constraints in Syntax*. New York: Holt Rinehart & Winston.

Plooij, F.X. 1978. Traits of Language in Wild Chimpanzees? A. Lock, ed., *Action, Gesture, and Symbol*, 111-132. London: Academic Press.

Quine, W. 1965. *Mathematical Logic*. Cambridge: Harvard University Press.

Russell, B. 1940. *An Inquiry into Meaning and Truth*. London: Allen & Unwin.

Sebeok, T.A. 1962. Coding in the Evolution of Signalling Behavior. *Behavioral Science* 7(4):30-42.

Smith, D., & A. Raygor. 1956. Verbal Satiation and Personality. *Journal of Abnormal and Social Psychology* 52:323-326.

Smith, J. 1966. *The Theory of Evolution*, 2nd ed. Harmondsworth: Penguin.

Tambiah, E.S. 1968. The Magical Power of Words. *Man* n.s. 3(2):175-208.

Tinbergen N. 1952. "Derived" Activities: Their Causation, Biological Significance, Origin, and Emancipation During Evolution. *Quarterly Review of Biology* 27:1-32.

Twaddell, W.F. 1938. A Note on Old High German Umlaut. [reprinted in M. Joos, ed., *Readings in Linguistics*, 85-88, Chicago: University of Chicago Press, 1957]

Wescott, R. 1967. The Evolution of Language: Reopening a Closed Subject. *Studies in Linguistics* 19:67-81.

Wheelock, W. 1982. The Problem of Ritual Language: From Information to Situation. *Journal of the American Academy of Religion* 50:49-71.

Zipf, G.K. 1935. *The Psychobiology of Language*. Boston: Houghton.

Levels of Conjunction in Tauya

Lorna A. MacDonald

One of the most striking typological features of the Papuan languages of Papua New Guinea is the existence of medial verb constructions. These languages lack independent words equivalent to English conjunctions such as *and*, *then*, etc., for conjoining clauses. Instead, conjunction is effected through the use of MEDIAL VERB forms: in a series of conjoined clauses, the verbs in the non-final clauses occur in a special medial verb form; and only the verb in the final clause occurs as a FINAL VERB. The sentence in (1) illustrates both:

(1) *mei   fofe -   i - te   nen - yau - e - 'a.*
     here come   3p MED   3p   see   1s IND
     'They came here and I saw them.'

In (1), the medial verb consists of the verb stem *fofe-*, the third-person plural subject suffix *-i-*, and a medial verb suffix *-te*; the final verb consists of the verb stem *yau-*, a prefixed object marker, a subject suffix, and the indicative mood suffix *-'a*.

Medial and final verb forms differ both morphologically, in their potential for inflection, and syntactically. In Tauya, the primary morphological distinction is that only medial verbs include a medial verb suffix, whereas only final verbs include inflections for mood. Syntactically, the primary distinction between the two kinds of verbal constructions is their ability to occur alone. Clauses which include final verbs may occur in isolation as complete, grammatical sentences:

(2) *nen - yau - e -'a.*
     3p   see   1s IND
     'I saw them.'

Clauses which include medial verbs, on the other hand, cannot occur as independent sentences:

(3) * *mei fofe - i - te*
     here come 3p MED
     (not * 'They came here and')

As suggested by the English translation in (3), medial verb forms in isolation are ungrammatical (here marked by an asterisk) because they are interpreted as parts of conjunctions.

In Tauya, there are several different kinds of medial verb constructions, which express different kinds of relationships which may hold between the medial and following clauses. These medial verb forms are as follows:

medial verbs	subordinate		
	coordinate		
		same-subject	
			pa construction
			ti construction
			zero construction
		different-subject	

The first distinction is between SUBORDINATE medial verbs, used in clauses which stand in a subordinate relationship to the following clause, and COORDINATE medial verbs, used in clauses which stand in a coordinate relationship to the following clause. Subordinate medial verb forms will not be discussed here; for their forms and functions see MacDonald 1990.

For coordinate medial verbs, the primary distinction is between same-subject and different-subject medial verb forms. That is, these verbs indicate whether or not the subject of the medial clause is the same as the subject of the following clause; this is known as a SWITCH-REFERENCE system. If the subjects are identical, as in (4), the medial verb occurs as a SAME-SUBJECT (SS) medial verb form; if the subjects are not identical, as in (5) (and in (1), above), the medial verb occurs as a DIFFERENT-SUBJECT (DS) medial verb:

(4)   *yate - pa ni -   e - 'a.*
       go   SS eat   1s IND
       'I went and ate.'

(5)   *yate - e - te   ni -   a -'a.*
       go   1s DS   eat   3s IND
       'I went and he ate.'

There is only one construction used in Tauya to coordinate DS medial verbs, i.e., the construction illustrated in (1) and (5). This construction has the following form:

DS: (OBJECT) + STEM (+ASPECT) (+HABITUAL) + SUBJECT + *te*

That is, DS medial verb forms obligatorily include a verb stem, a suffix marking the subject of the medial clause, and the DS medial verb suffix *-te*. They may also include a prefix indicating the object, various auxiliary verbs to mark aspect, and the habitual auxiliary.

However, three different constructions are used to coordinate SS medial verbs. These are referred to here as the *pa*, *ti*, and zero constructions, according to the phonological shapes of the medial suffixes they include. These three constructions have the following forms:

pa construction:
   (OBJECT) + STEM (+ASPECT) + *pa*

(6)   *nen - tu - fe -   pa yate - e - 'a.*
      3p   give PERF SS go   1s IND
      'I gave [it] to them and went.'

ti construction:
   (OBJECT) + STEM + *ti*

(7)   *ya - 'amai - ti mepi -   a -   'a.*
      1s   carry   SS come down 3s   IND
      'He carried me and came down.'

zero construction:
   STEM

(8)   *mepi   ya - tu - i - 'a.*
      come down 1s   give 3p IND
      'They came down and gave [it] to me.'

Note that all three constructions can be translated into English as simple conjunctions. However, they are morphologically distinct: they differ with respect to the possibility of including various inflectional categories, and they also differ with respect to the presence, and the phonological shapes, of medial suffixes. The question to be addressed in the following sections is: Do these morphological distinctions reflect any fundamental syntactic distinctions among the three constructions?

2. LEVELS OF STRUCTURE

Following Foley & Van Valin (1984) and Foley & Olson (1985), it is assumed that clauses consist of various levels of structure. At each level, there is a set of OPERATORS which apply to the constituents at that particular level.

The lowest level of structure is the NUCLEUS, i.e., the verb stem; the most common class of operators at this level is aspect. The intermediate level of structure is the CORE, which consists of the nucleus and all of its core arguments, i.e., normally subject and object. Operators at the core level are rare, but may include, for example, certain manner adverbials (Foley & Olson 1985:35). The highest level of structure is the PERIPHERY, which includes the nucleus, the core, and all of the non-core arguments, such as those expressing spatial/temporal orientation. There are a variety of operators at the peripheral level, including tense and mood (or 'illocutionary force'). Clause structure can thus be represented as follows where $NP_{n\text{-}c}$ represents non-core argument(s):

[$NP_{n\text{-}c}$ [NP_{Sbj} (NP_{Obj}) [Verb Stem] Nucleus] Core] Periphery

In this framework, junction may apply at each level; it functions to join two tokens of the same level. For example, a nucleus can be joined to another nucleus. In anticipation of the discussion of junction levels in Tauya, reference should be made here to a particular feature of both core and peripheral level junction. According to the descriptions of the three levels of structure given above, nuclear level conjuncts will share all core level arguments, i.e., subject and object. Conjuncts at the core level, on the other hand, may include independent specification for core arguments, as may peripheral level conjuncts, since each peripheral conjunct includes its own core. However, in serial, or 'dependent', verb constructions, there is often a requirement that all of the conjuncts share one core argument (Foley & Van Valin 1984:189). In Tauya, all SS medial verb constructions share the same subject, regardless of the level at which junction occurs. Thus, in the following sections, where reference is made to Tauya core arguments, only the status of the object will be considered.

Three different kinds of junction may occur: SUBORDINATION, COORDINATION, and CO-SUBORDINATION. Subordination represents an embedded construction, in which one constituent is embedded within the other. This kind of junction does not apply to any of the Tauya SS medial verb constructions examined here, and thus will not be considered further.

Coordination and co-subordination differ with respect to the scope of the operators. In a coordinate junction, each conjunct may be independently specified for the operators at that level. For example, in a nuclear coordinate junction, each nucleus can be independently specified for aspect. In a co-subordinate junction, on the other hand, the conjuncts must share the operators that apply at that level. Thus, in a nuclear co-subordinate junction, aspect will be shared by both nuclei.

coordinate junction: [conjunct]   +   [conjunct]
                              ↑   ↑
                          operators   operators

co-subordinate junction: [conjunct]   +   [conjunct]
                                        ↖   ↗
                                      operators

This framework provides a useful model for determining the kinds of syntactic distinctions which may exist among the three SS medial verb constructions found in Tauya. That is, nine different junctions are distinguished, according to junction level and type, and clear diagnostic criteria are provided for the identification of particular instances of junction. The question addressed in the following sections is: Do the three different SS medial verb constructions in Tauya differ in terms of the kinds of junctions they represent?

3. TAUYA CLAUSE STRUCTURE

Clauses in Tauya are verb-final. Since most clause constituents are represented in the verb phrase via inflections, a complete, grammatical sentence may consist simply of a fully inflected, or final, verb form. Fully inflected verbs have the following structure (the numbers are used to indicate inflectional positions, and are referred to in subsequent sections):

$(OBJECT_1 +)$ STEM $(+ ASPECT_2) (+ HABITUAL_3) (+ AVOLITIONAL_4)$
$+ SUBJECT/TENSE_5 (+ DUBITATIVE_6) + MOOD_7$

For example:

(9)   nen - tu -   'afe - a -   rafo - 'a.
      3p   give   PROG 3s   DUB   IND
      'Maybe he's giving [it] to them.'

(10) tepau -   fe -   'ate - a -   'a.
      break   PERF   AVOL 3s   IND
      'It would be bad if he broke it.'

Clauses may also include a variety of noun phrases representing both core and non-core arguments:

(11) 'e   nono -   ni   sema tepau -   fe -   'ate - a -   'a.
      DEM   child   ERG   pot   break   PERF   AVOL 3s   IND
      'It would be bad if that child broke the pot.'

(12) *Towe -   sou   Bramani   yate - e - 'a.*
           COM   go   1s IND
      'I went to Brahman with Towe.'

Other clause constituents include a variety of adverbial modifiers and the
negative morpheme.

4. TAUYA JUNCTIONS

4.1 THE *pa* CONSTRUCTION

There are no lexical restrictions upon medial verbs in the *pa* construction;
it may include any verb stem which is found in Tauya.

  Medial verbs in this construction, as is indicated in the formula given
in section 1, may not be inflected for the affixes in positions 3 to 7 of the
verb phrase; the verbs obligatorily share these inflections with the
following verb. Examples (13)-(15) demonstrate the shared statuses of the
habitual, avolitional and dubitative inflections:

(13) *mei   fofe - pa ni -   pope - a -   'a.*
      here   come SS eat   HAB   3s   IND
      'He always comes here and eats.'
      (not 'He comes here and always eats.')

(14) *pomu -   pa mei - 'ate - a -   'a.*
      fall   SS cry   AVOL 3s   IND
      'It would be bad if he fell and cried.'
      (not 'He fell and it would be bad if he cried.')

(15) *Bramani yate - pa 'ufiya neri - a -   rafo - 'a.*
              go   SS food buy   3s   DUB IND
      'Maybe he went to Brahman and bought food.'
      (not 'He went to Brahman and may have bought food.')

Medial verbs in the *pa* construction may also share the mood marked on
the following verb:

(16) *pomu -   pa mei - e - nae?*
      fall   SS cry   2s Q
      'Did you fall and cry?'

(17) *yate - pa ni -   a -   e!*
      go   SS eat   2sFut IMP
      'Go and eat!'

In Tauya, tense is marked on the verb by the subject inflection: one set
of subject suffixes is used in the aorist tense, and a second set is used in
the future tense. Medial verbs in the *pa* construction do not include

subject inflection; thus, they are not marked for tense, but are interpreted as sharing the tense marked on the following verb:

(18) *yate - pa ni -   e - 'a.*
      go   SS eat   1s IND
      'I went and ate.'

(19) *yate - pa ni -   amu - 'a.*
      go   SS eat   1sFut IND
      'I will go and eat.'

The shared inflections described above, i.e., habitual, avolitional, tense, dubitative and mood, can be defined as peripheral level operators. Both tense and mood are by definition peripheral operators (Foley & Van Valin 1984:209, 220). Although habitual inflection is often classed as an aspect inflection, Givón (1984:273) points out that it may be identified as a tense inflection. Inflections which express the speaker's attitude towards an event are also generally classed as peripheral operators (Foley & Olson 1985:37), and the Tauya avolitional suffix, which indicates that the speaker views the event expressed in the clause as unfavourable, falls within this class. According to Foley & Van Valin (1984:213), another class of peripheral operators is status inflection, i.e., inflections which refer to the likelihood of an event being realised, and the dubitative suffix in Tauya clearly falls within this class.

Thus, conjuncts in the *pa* construction share peripheral level operators. However, these conjuncts may be independently specified for those arguments which are introduced at the peripheral level of the clause, i.e., non-core arguments. Thus, in (20), each conjunct is associated with its own locative noun phrase:

(20) *Bramani yate - ti -   pa Tauya - sa   etite -   e -'a.*
               go   PERF SS   ADESS   return   1s IND
      'I went to Brahman and returned to Tauya.'

Conjuncts in the *pa* construction are also independently specified for all clause constituents which are introduced below the peripheral level. They are independently specified for objects, which are core-level arguments:

(21) *wesiwesi   tei -   poru -   te -   pa mopamo ne -pi*
      grass REDUP touch pull   get   SS brother   3s GEN

      ni'iti -   'ai   momune -   fe -   pa ai   ne -   pi
      root   ADESS   sit   TR   SS brother 3s   GEN

      'asu   parete -   pa ...
      knife carve   SS

'[The older brother] pulled out a lot of grass and sat his younger brother down at the root [of a tree] and the older brother carved a knife and he...'

In (21), there are three medial verbs in the *pa* construction, and each is associated with its own object noun phrase.

Conjuncts in the *pa* construction are also independently specified for aspect, which is a nuclear level operator:

(22) *ni - 'afe - pa yau - a -   'a.*
     eat   PROG SS see   3s   IND
     'He was eating and he saw her.'

(23) *'ini - mene -   pa a'e yau - a -   'a.*
     sleep STAT   SS dream 3s   IND
     'He was asleep, and he had a dream.'

The examples given above indicate that the *pa* construction represents junction at the peripheral level, since each conjunct may include its own set of non-core arguments, and each may be independently specified for clause constituents below the peripheral level. Since the conjuncts in this construction obligatorily share all of the peripheral level operators, the junction can be identified as one of co-subordination, i.e.,

   pa construction: [periphery] + [periphery]

                              ↖   ↗
                             operators

According to Foley & Van Valin (1984:257), medial verb constructions in the Papuan languages frequently represent this kind of structure.

4.2 THE *ti* CONSTRUCTION

Medial verbs in the *ti* construction are subject to lexical restrictions, although these restrictions are minimal: the first conjunct in this construction may not be one of the four basic verbs of motion, i.e., *yate-* 'go', *fofe-* 'come', *mai-* 'come up' or *mepi-* 'come down.' All other verbs stems may occur as the first conjunct, and there are no lexical restrictions on the second conjunct in this construction. However, despite the fact that lexical restrictions on this construction are minimal, it is attested infrequently in texts, in comparison to the *pa* and zero constructions, and is only rarely volunteered in elicitation.

Medial verbs in the *ti* construction may not include any of the inflections in positions 3 to 7 of the verb phrase. Like verbs in the *pa* construction, they obligatorily share these peripheral level operators with the following verb:

(24) *tou - ti ni - amu - rafo - 'a.*
      pick SS eat 1sFut DUB IND
      'Maybe I'll pick and eat it.'
      (not 'I picked it and maybe I'll eat it.')

However, unlike verbs in the *pa* construction, conjuncts in the *ti* construction obligatorily share all non-core, or peripheral level, arguments. Thus, the locative noun phrases in (25) and (26) describe the locations of the events referred to in both of the conjuncts:

(25) *Tei - sa   nen - 'amai - ti mepi -   a -'a.*
             ADESS   3p   carry   SS come down 3s IND
      'He carried them down to Teri.'
      (not 'He carried them and (then) came down to Teri.')

(26) *mei   ni - ti firo - 'afe - a -   'a.*
      here eat SS roam PROG 3s   IND
      'He is eating and roaming around here.'
      (not 'He is eating here and roaming around.')

That conjuncts in the *ti* construction obligatorily share their temporal orientation is suggested by the kind of interpretations given to this construction by Tauya speakers. Compare the interpretations provided for (27), which includes the *ti* construction, and (28), which includes the *pa* construction:

(27) *ni - ti firo - e - 'a.*
      eat SS roam 1s IND
      'I roamed around eating.'

(28) *ni - pa firo - e - 'a.*
      eat SS roam 1s IND
      'I ate and/and then roamed around.'

That is, the *ti* construction is interpreted as representing simultaneous actions, whereas the *pa* construction may represent either simultaneous or sequential actions.

Since conjuncts in the *ti* construction obligatorily share all of the peripheral level arguments, this construction must represent junction below the peripheral level. There is additional support for this conclusion: the *ti* construction is occasionally used to increase the valence of verb stems. Generally, valence is increased in Tauya by the following construction:

STEM   OBJECT + *fe* + ...

That is, the verb stem occurs in an uninflected form and is followed by the transitivising auxiliary *fe*, which takes all verbal inflections. For example:

(29)   'umu -   a - 'a.   →   'umu fei -   fe -   a -   'a.
       die   3s IND   die   3s   TR   3s   IND
       'He died.'   'He killed him.'

(30)   wate   e'i -   a - 'a.   →   wate   e'i   ne -   fe -   e - 'a.
       house   make 3s IND   house   make   2s   TR   1s IND
       'I built a house.'   'I built a house for you.'

However, even though the verb stem in this construction generally occurs in an uninflected form, it is occasionally attested with the medial verb suffix *ti*:

(31)   sifi -   ti fei -   fe -   e - 'a.
       dress SS 3s   TR   1s IND
       'I dressed him.'

(32)   o'o   'utu - ti nen - fe -   a -   te...
       fire   heal SS 3p   TR   3s   IND
       'The fire died on them and...'

The constructions with and without *ti* appear to be in free variation, that is, although the construction without *ti* is attested much more frequently than the one which includes it, the distributions of the two constructions are not lexically determined.

Constructions which increase the valence of a verb stem are clearly not motivated at the peripheral level, since their function is to permit the inclusion of additional core arguments. Furthermore, the transitivising construction in Tauya cannot be identified as a peripheral level junction, since the transitive auxiliary cannot serve as an independent clause nucleus. Therefore, the *ti* construction must represent junction at the core and/or nuclear level.

Medial verbs in the *ti* construction may not include inflection for aspect, i.e., any inflections which occur in position 2 of the verb phrase. Instead, they obligatorily share the aspect marked on the following verb:

(33)   'ufiya   fei -   ti ya -   tu -   'afe - a -   'a.
       sweet potato   boil SS 1s   give   PROG 3s   IND
       'She is cooking sweet potatoes and giving them to me.'
       (not 'She cooked sweet potatoes and is giving them to me.')

(34) *epi - ti yate - we - a -   'a.*
      stand SS go   CON 3s   IND
      'He tried to stand up and go.'
      (not 'He stood up and tried to go.')

Example (36) is relevant in this context: in Tauya there is a rarely attested aspect auxiliary, *-wa'ase-*, which implies that the event specified by the verb nearly happened. For example:

(35) *pomu -   wa'ase - e - 'a.*
      fall   nearly   1s IND
      'I nearly fell.'

In (36), this aspect morpheme does not occur as a verbal auxiliary, but as an independent verb stem; the verb to which the aspect applies occurs in the *ti* construction:

(36) *ou - ti wa'ase - fe - a -   te...*
      shoot SS nearly   TR   3s   DS
      'He nearly shot her and...'

Since medial verbs in this construction obligatorily share aspect inflection, and aspect is a nuclear level operator, the construction appears to represent co-subordination at the nuclear level, i.e.,

    ti construction: [nucleus]   + [nucleus]

                                  ↖   ↗

                           operators

According to Foley & Van Valin (1984:262), co-subordination is the most common kind of junction found at the nuclear level. However, if, as is argued here, the *ti* construction in Tauya represents this kind of junction, it does not manifest many of the characteristics typically associated with it. Nuclear junctions, which are essentially verb compounds, usually lack any overt coordinators; in the *ti* construction, *ti* functions as a coordinator. In nuclear junction, there are frequently lexical restrictions on the conjuncts; in the *ti* construction, lexical restrictions are minimal. Finally, in nuclear junction, the junction is often lexicalised, such that the meaning of the complex nucleus is not always predictable from the meanings of the stems involved; in the *ti* construction, the meanings are fully predictable.

There are in Tauya constructions which are typical examples of nuclear co-subordination. For example:

(37) *'ou*   'bite' + *topi* 'cut'   → *'outopi-* bite off'
      fai   'cut' + *'asou* 'cover'   → *fai'asou-* 'cut all'
                                              (e.g., trees from garden site)
      su'u 'start' + *tu*   'give'   → *su'utu-* 'ask'

Similarly, the transitivising construction without *ti*, described above, is a prototypical example of nuclear co-subordination. In contrast, the *ti* construction resembles, in terms of its morphological form, lexical selection and transparent semantic interpretation, a junction at the peripheral level. An explanation is required for this apparent inconsistency; one is suggested in section 5.

4.3 THE ZERO CONSTRUCTION

In terms of both morphological form and lexical restrictions, the zero construction is a likely candidate for nuclear level junction. The initial conjunct in this construction occurs as an uninflected stem. For example:

(38) *mai*   *yau - a -   'a.*
      come up see   3s   IND
      'He came up and looked.'

There are rigid lexical restrictions imposed upon the first conjunct in this construction, that is, only the four basic verbs of motion identified in section 4.2 can occur in this position; there are no lexical restrictions on the second conjunct. Note that these lexical restrictions result in complementary distribution between the *ti* and zero constructions: the former cannot include the basic verbs of motion as the first conjunct.

The initial conjunct in the zero construction cannot include object prefixes, i.e., inflections in position 1 in the verb phrase. However, this restriction does not derive from the syntactic nature of the construction, but rather from the verb stems involved, i.e., only intransitive verbs occur in this position.

Like the *pa* and *ti* constructions, the first conjunct in the zero construction cannot include inflections in positions 3 to 7 of the verb phrase. These peripheral level operators are obligatorily shared with the following verb:

(39) *yate*   *yau - 'e -   rafo - 'a.*
      go   see   3sFut DUB IND
      'Maybe she'll go and see [it].'
      (not 'She went and maybe she'll see it.')

Verb stems in the zero construction also share all non-core arguments. Although these arguments can intervene between the conjuncts, as in (40), in all of the attested examples of this construction, these arguments can be interpreted as including both conjuncts within their scope:

(40) mai   amo tupu -   'ai   momune - pa...
      come up tree log   ADESS   sit   SS
      'She came up (to) and sat on a log...'

(41) ene   ya'e yate epi - i - na...
      floor water go   stand 3p SUB
      'They went to and stood (in) the Ramu River (lit., 'floor water')...'

The fact that conjuncts in the zero construction are associated with a single set of peripheral level arguments suggests that this construction, like the *ti* construction, represents a junction below the peripheral level.

The first conjunct in the zero construction, like that in the *ti* construction, cannot be marked for aspect. However, in contrast to the *ti* construction, this conjunct does not share the aspect marked on the following verb. For example:

(42) yate 'ufei - mene - a - te...
      go   watch   STAT   3s   DS
      'He went and was watching it...'

In (42), the stem *yate-* cannot share the aspect marked on the following verb. Although the verbs of motion can occur with the stative auxiliary, they do so only where the verb refers to a state, as in (43), rather than to an activity, as in (42):

(43) 'e   sa   Bramani yate - mene - a - 'a.
      DEM   road   go   STAT   3s   IND
      'That road goes to Brahman.'

Similarly, the progressive aspect marked on the second conjunct in (44) does not apply to the preceding verb:

(44) mei   fofe ni - 'afe - a - 'a.
      here come eat   PROG 3s   IND
      'He came here and was eating.'

In order to mark the progressive aspect on the first verb, it must occur in the *pa* construction.

Since the conjuncts in the zero construction do not share aspect, which is a nuclear level operator, this construction must represent either coordination at the nuclear level, i.e.,

zero construction: [nucleus]   +   [nucleus]
                          ↑   ↑
                      operators   operators

or junction at the core level. There is evidence that the second alternative is most likely. First, coordination at the nuclear level is rare (although it does occur in at least two Papuan languages; Foley & Van Valin 1984:248). Second, there is evidence that the conjuncts in the zero construction do not share all core level arguments; in particular, they do not obligatorily share an object noun phrase (or an object complement). For example:

(45) wa'a nono - ra   yate   ate   aniyamo 'ati - fe -   a -'a.
      girl   TOP   go   woman   mother   say   TR   3s IND
      'The girl went and told [her] mother.'

(46) mai   "ate -   ya"   o -   a -   'a.
      come up woman   VOC   say   3s   IND
      'He came up and said "Woman!" '

(47) yate   i'emo   sa'ama   'afa   omai -   te -   a -   na...
      go   mountain   small   INDEF climb   get   3s   SUB
      'He went and climbed a small mountain...'

Moreover, occasional examples of the zero construction are attested in which the conjuncts do not even share the same subject:

(48) 'esami   pu - i - na   yate   yate   yate   wa'a nono
      then   run   3p SUB   go   go   go   girl

      ne -   pi -   ra   'emamo   mai -   a -   te...
      3s   GEN   TOP   stomach come up 3s   DS
      '[A boy and his sister] ran, they went and went and went, and his sister was out of breath [lit., 'his sister's stomach came up']...'

In (48), the subject of the verb in the zero construction, yate-, is the two children; the subject of the following verb is is 'emamo.

Since the conjuncts in the zero construction do not obligatorily share core level arguments, this construction appears to effect core level junction, even though, in its morphological form and lexical restrictions, it superficially resembles nuclear level junction. Whether this junction can be identified as coordinate or co-subordinate depends upon the scope of the core level operators. Unfortunately, operators at this level are rare and, as yet, none have been found in Tauya.

There is some additional evidence that conjuncts in the zero construction are less tightly knit syntactically than those in the ti construction, such that they represent junction at a higher level. In section

4.2, the *ti* construction was identified as effecting nuclear level junction. In this construction, the only constituents which are permitted to intervene between the two conjuncts, aside from the coordinator *ti* itself, are object prefixes added to the second stem. Thus, whereas (49) is acceptable, (50), in which an object noun phrase intervenes between the conjuncts, is not:

(49) *'ufiya*   *fei -   ti ya -   tu -   a -   'a.*
      sweet potato boil SS 1s   give 3s   IND
      'She cooked sweet potatoes and gave them to me.'

(50) * *'ufiya fei -   ti towe tu -   a -   'a*
      ('She cooked sweet potatoes and gave them to Towe.')

The same tightly knit form is required of the two other constructions identified in section 4.2 as effecting nuclear junction, i.e., the transitivising construction (both with and without *ti*) and the verb compounds. However, as was illustrated above in examples (40) and (45)-(48), a variety of noun phrases, representing both core and peripheral arguments, can intervene between the conjuncts in the zero construction.

5. THE DIACHRONIC DEVELOPMENT OF JUNCTION

The examples and discussions presented above suggest that the three SS medial verb constructions in Tauya do, in fact, represent junctions at various levels of structure. However, neither the *ti* construction nor the zero construction manifests all of the characteristics generally associated with its junction type. In this section, a possible diachronic explanation is suggested for the aberrant form of the *ti* construction.

In section 4.2, this construction was identified as effecting nuclear-level co-subordination, although it has some characteristics normally associated with peripheral level junction. These characteristics may arise from the possibility that, historically, the *ti* construction effected junction at this higher level.

In Tauya, as was demonstrated in section 4.1, peripheral level co-subordination is effected synchronically by the *pa* construction, when the conjuncts share the same subject. If, on the other hand, the conjuncts do not share the same subject, the DS medial verb construction is used, i.e.,

(OBJECT +) STEM (+ ASPECT) (+ HABITUAL) + SUBJECT + *te*

where *te* is a DS medial verb suffix. In this construction, as in the *pa* construction, conjuncts obligatorily share all peripheral level operators (with the exception of the habitual auxiliary), but may be independently specified for non-core arguments. Thus, both constructions are of the same syntactic type; they differ morphologically only with respect to the presence vs. the absence of subject inflection, and the phonological shapes of the medial verb suffixes.

According to a typology of switch-reference systems developed by Haiman (1983:108), this system of switch-reference marking is an exemplar of the GAPPING MODEL:

DS = VERB + SUBJECT
SS = VERB

That is, DS and SS medial verbs differ only with respect to the inclusion of inflection for the subject. However, as Haiman points out, few Papuan languages manifest this model exactly; in most, the SS medial verb form includes a suffix marking the temporal relation between the medial and final clauses, usually distinguishing simultaneous and sequential actions.

In Tauya, not only do SS medial verb forms require a medial verb suffix, but DS medial verbs require a medial suffix as well, i.e.,

DS = VERB + SUBJECT + *te*
SS = VERB + *pa*

The medial suffixes *pa* and *te* do not have any semantic content, i.e., they do not distinguish different temporal relations between the conjuncts; they simply serve as coordinators. An obvious question is: Why should the coordinators in DS and SS medial verb constructions be distinct, since they make no semantic contributions to the constructions, and the DS/SS distinction is already manifested by gapping, i.e., the presence vs. the absence of subject inflection?

In addressing this question, it is useful to compare the basic morphological form of the DS construction with that of the *ti* construction:

DS =   VERB + SUBJECT + *te*
ti (SS) =   VERB + *ti*

Again, both the DS and SS medial verb constructions require medial suffixes, but here these suffixes are possible cognates, both deriving from **te*. The vowel change *e* > *i* is attested elsewhere in Tauya synchronically (see below). In fact, Haiman (1987:16) suggests that **tV* can be reconstructed as a coordinating conjunction in the Gorokan family of Papuan languages, which are related, albeit distantly, to Tauya.

The morphological similarities between the DS and *ti* constructions may derive from the fact that, historically, they were both used to effect the same junction that the DS construction represents synchronically, i.e., peripheral level co-subordination. The constructions would have the following forms:

DS = VERB + SUBJECT + *te
SS = VERB + *te

where *te represents a simple coordinator. This hypothesis would explain the idiosyncratic features that the *ti* construction has synchronically, i.e., it shares some characteristics with peripheral level junctions because it has developed from just such a junction. Over time, the conjuncts in the SS construction have become more and more closely linked syntactically, such that the construction is now used to effect junction at the nuclear level. This kind of reanalysis may have been motivated by the co-existence of the *ti* and *pa* constructions, i.e., two constructions which (for reasons as yet unknown) came to have exactly the same function, such that one was subsequently reanalyzed as representing a different kind of junction.

As was indicated above, the proposed vowel change, *e* > *i*, is attested synchronically in Tauya. It occurs in several different environments, and one such environment has interesting implications for the change *te* > *ti* in SS medial verb constructions. This rule applies synchronically to stem final *e* of verb stems, the personal pronouns, and the deictics. For example, (51) illustrates the application of this rule to a verb stem, and (52) illustrates its application to a pronoun:

(51) /yate -fe-/   → [yati -fe-]
     go   TR   'make X go'

(52) /ne - 0/   → [ni]
     3s   ABS   'he' (absolutive case)

Generally, as in the examples above, raising applies in word-final position. However, this is not the only environment which conditions this rule: it also applies to verb stems which are followed by an aspect auxiliary. For example:

(53) /yate - 'afe-/   → [yati'afe-]
     go   PROG   'be going'

     /yate - we-/   → [yatiwe-]
     go CON   'try to go'

However, none of the peripheral level operators which can occur as inflections on verb stems condition this rule:

(54) /yate - pope-/   → [yatepope-]
     go   HAB   'always go'

(55) /yate - 'ate-/   → [yata'ate-] (by assimilation)
     AVOL   'it would be bad if X went'

It is perhaps significant that the aspect auxiliaries, i.e., nuclear level operators, which are syntactically very closely bound to the stem, condition the raising rule, whereas the peripheral level operators, which are much more loosely associated with the stem, do not. This provides a precedent for the vowel change proposed here for the coordinator *te, where it occurs in SS constructions. That is, as these conjuncts were reinterpreted as being more tightly bound together syntactically, the raising rule was applied to the coordinator in the same way that it applies synchronically to tightly bound constituents elsewhere in the verb phrase. On the other hand, in the DS construction, the conjuncts remained loosely bound, such that the raising rule did not apply.

That the *ti* construction is a junction in transition is synchronically suggested by the fact that it occasionally occurs in constructions which are given an interpretation almost exactly parallel to that given to the corresponding *pa* construction. For example:

(56) 'ipai   *feti - pa*   *tu - a - te* 'ipai   *aniyamo sa'ama*
      arrow   carve SS   give 3s   DS arrow   mother small

      kʷanesa'ama -   piya   feti - ti tu - a - te ...
      small   INTEN   carve SS give 3s   DS
      'She carved an arrow and gave it to him, and she carved a very tiny bow and gave it to him...'

There may be slight differences in interpretation between the *pa* and *ti* constructions in (56), but these differences are not at all obvious in the context. On the other hand, the *ti* construction is also used in constructions which are given interpretations exactly parallel to constructions which clearly represent nuclear level junction, i.e., in the transitivising constructions with and without *ti* as described in section 4.2. That is, there is evidence that the *ti* construction in some instances has a peripheral-like interpretation, and in others, a nuclear-like interpretation.

The explanation for the aberrant features of the *ti* construction presented here, if correct, has some implications for the diachronic development of junction. In particular, it suggests that syntactic change, i.e., the reanalysis of junction level, may precede both morphological and lexical reanalysis. Thus, the *ti* construction represents a nuclear level junction syntactically, but in terms of its morphological structure, i.e., the presence of an overt coordinator, and lexical selection, i.e., the fact that its lexical restrictions are minimal, it retains the characteristics of its original, peripheral level function.

6. SUMMARY

The examples and discussions presented in section 4 suggest that the three Tauya ss medial verb constructions do, in fact, represent different syntactic structures, that is, they represent junctions at different levels of structure. The *pa* construction effects co-subordination at the peripheral level; the *ti* construction effects co-subordination at the nuclear level; and the zero construction effects junction at the core level. However, it is also clear that these constructions, in particular the *ti* and zero constructions, do not consistently manifest the characteristics which are typically associated with these different junction levels. In section 5, it is suggested that the inconsistencies related to the *ti* construction may have a historical explanation. However, it must be stressed that the analysis and identification of Tauya junctions presented here is merely preliminary, and must be tested with additional data.

NOTE

Tauya is spoken in Madang Province, Papua New Guinea (cf. MacDonald 1990). The field work on which the present study is based was financially supported by the Social Sciences and Research Council of Canada. I would like to thank Dick Carter for his help in clarifying theoretical issues; however, any errors or inconsistencies in the analysis presented here are my own.

REFERENCES

Foley, William A. 1986. *The Papuan Languages of New Guinea*. Cambridge: Cambridge University Press.
—, & Van Valin, Jr., Robert D. 1984. *Functional Syntax and Universal Grammar*. Cambridge: Cambridge University Press.
—, & Mike Olson. 1985. Clausehood and Verb Serialization. J. Nichols & A.C. Woodbury, eds., *Grammar Inside and Outside the Clause*, 17-60. Cambridge: Cambridge University Press.
Givón, Talmy. 1984. *Syntax: A Functional-typological Introduction, 1*. Amsterdam: John Benjamins.

Haiman, John. 1983. On Some Origins of Switch-Reference Marking. J. Haiman & P. Munro, eds., *Switch-Reference and Universal Grammar*, 105-128. Amsterdam: John Benjamins.

—. 1987. Proto-Gorokan Syllable Structure. *Language and Linguistics in Melanesia* 16(1/2):1-22.

MacDonald, Lorna A. 1990. *A Grammar of Tauya*. Berlin: Mouton de Gruyter.

Language Planning Goals in Contemporary Hebrew

Moshe Nahir

Language planning may be defined as an organised attempt at affecting the linguistic or sociolinguistic status or the development of a language. The revival of Hebrew at the turn of the century and its development since have attracted the attention of practitioners and theoreticians because it is the only recorded case of a language which, after having ceased to exist in spoken form, was later restored or "revived" as a community's vernacular. Language planners have sought to study both the revival itself and the means by which the Hebrew speech community in Israel (and, prior to 1948, in Palestine) has coped with the overwhelming difficulties of turning a liturgical language into a modern, spoken language.

The language planning goals which commissions and committees have pursued ever since the Italian and French academies made their first attempts at language modification in 1582 and 1635, respectively, may be classified as follows (cf. Nahir 1984): (1) language purification (internal or external), (2) language (or speech) revival, (3) language reform, (4) language standardisation, (5) language spread, (6) lexical modernisation, (7) terminology unification, (8) stylistic simplification, (9) interlingual communication (worldwide or regional), (10) language maintenance (dominant or ethnic), (11) auxiliary-code standardisation. Planning agencies may pursue several of these goals simultaneously; as circumstances change, moreover, they may be replaced by others, abandoned, or shifted from major to minor status or vice versa.

The development of Modern Hebrew may be divided into three periods defined by the prevalence of one or more language planning goals: (1) 1890-1916, speech revival; (2) 1916-1948, language standardisation and language spread; (3) since 1948, lexical modernisation. The first and, to a lesser extent, the second of these periods have been investigated in some depth (e.g., Bachi 1956; Bar-Adon 1977; Ben-Asher 1977; Blanc 1954; Fellman 1973; Haramati 1979; Hofman & Fisherman 1971; Nahir 1977a, 1978a, 1983, 1988; St. John 1952; Saulson 1979;

Tur-Sinai 1960). The present study concentrates on the third period in which, as will be shown, lexical modernisation is the major goal of the agencies involved, although several minor goals (terminology, unification, language purification and reform) are being pursued as well.

The discussion will follow Kloss' useful and by now well established distinction (1969) between status planning and corpus planning. While the former is primarily concerned with language policies and their formulation, the latter deals with the codification of language, including the adoption (or adaptation) of a writing system (Ferguson 1968), the formulation of a "correct" grammar and the selection of an appropriate lexicon (Haugen 1966, 1983). Thus, codification activities have typically attempted to produce prescriptive orthographies, grammars and dictionaries.

This study, then, will review both status planning and corpus planning in Hebrew in the current stage of its development (since 1948). However, different goals call for different ratios of status and corpus planning. Unlike the major goals pursued in the two previous periods, lexical modernisation largely requires corpus planning since most of the problems predictably involve the further adaptation of the language to modern times. In fact, it will be seen that even activities related to the minor goals (purification, reform, and terminology unification) in this period involve the corpus rather than the status of the language.

THE LEXICAL MODERNISATION OF HEBREW

Lexical modernisation may be defined as "word creation or adaptation as a way to assist developed, standard languages (sometimes labelled 'mature') that have borrowed concepts too fast for their natural development to accommodate" (Nahir 1984: 307). A standard language, in other words, needs to keep up with modern life, especially when it is faced with an "invasion" of terms or expressions from an outside speech community. It ought to be noted that lexical modernisation as defined here is a goal, not an activity, and must accordingly be distinguished from lexical and terminological activities; the latter may constitute part of the process of codification, which is the second of Haugen's four language planning processes carried out in pursuit of a given language planning goal (Haugen 1983). In the case of developing or growing (sometimes labelled "immature") languages, the lexicon needs to be expanded to incorporate technological and scientific terms. The lexical and terminological work of the Hebrew Language Committee (since 1953, the Academy), for example, had language revival (in the first period) and language spread and standardisation (in the second) as its goals. In the current period, lexical modernisation is the dominant language planning goal for Hebrew.

FROM LANGUAGE SPREAD AND STANDARDISATION
TO LEXICAL MODERNISATION

Despite an eightfold increase in the Jewish population during the second period (1916-1948), by the beginning of the third the proportion of speakers of Hebrew as an "only or major language" had grown from 40% to 71.3%: in a Jewish population of 716,500 (Bachi 1956) there were 511,000 speakers of Hebrew aged two or over. The creation of the State of Israel in 1948 was immediately followed by new, huge waves of immigration; these resulted from the removal of the British-imposed ban on immigration by the Jewish survivors of World War II and, following the Arab-Israeli war of 1948, from the transfer to Israel of entire Jewish communities from the Middle East and North Africa. Nevertheless, the proportion of the Hebrew-speaking segment of the Jewish population continued to grow. According to the 1961 census, in the four-and-a-half decades since the previous census (1916) and the end of Ottoman rule (1917), the Jewish population had increased more than twenty-fold, from 85,000 to 1,847,860, while the number of Hebrew speakers had increased fortyfold, from 34,000 to 1,360,180 (or 73.6% of the Jewish population).

By 1948 Hebrew had spread sufficiently to become the community's vernacular and national language and, together with Arabic, the language of the minority, one of the country's two official languages. On the whole, those who do not speak Hebrew are now recent arrivals who have yet to acquire it. It is the native and, except among immigrants' offspring, the only language of those born or grown up in Israel. Societal bilingualism or multilingualism, so dominant in the community and in the country as a whole only a few decades earlier, has virtually disappeared; other than at the peripheries, where some contact exists between the otherwise mostly separate Jewish and Arab societies, and except for a few small ultra-orthodox groups where Hebrew-Yiddish diglossia[1] has prevailed for decades, bilingualism in the Jewish population, where it still exists, is strictly individual.

The goal of language standardisation was largely achieved (Nahir 1978a, 1987) concurrently with the spread of the language. By the beginning of the third period, therefore, Hebrew had developed into a fully "mature" standard language. The codification work of the Hebrew Language Committee and of numerous individuals had coincided with the practical need to use, in all areas, a language which was the only means of communication for the majority. By 1959, Morag (1959:258, 261) could summarise the situation as follows:

> Very acute at the early stages of the Revival, the problem of the vocabulary has by now lost its prominence. Today Modern Hebrew, both in its spoken and written forms, possesses a sufficient number of words to function normally.

It had, in fact, become,

> the national tongue of the State of Israel, [while] its vitality and ability to serve both as a means of every-day communication and a vehicle of literacy and scientific expression are doubted no longer.

At the same time, new concepts are constantly being formed and, consciously or otherwise, assigned names – in Hebrew as in all languages. Similarly, new concepts are continually borrowed from other speech communities (in this third period mainly from English). With the rate and intensity of modern technology transfer and with advanced communication, however, the natural, self-adjusting mechanism inducing lexical formation is frequently unable to keep pace with concept borrowing. Such a situation often results in the formal establishment of a language planning agency, and this is what occurred in the case of Hebrew.

Early in the third period, in 1953, the Israeli Knesset (Parliament) debated whether Hebrew should be left to adjust on its own or if, instead, the Hebrew Language Committee, formed just before the turn of the century to lead the linguistic revival,[2] should be charged with the task of "assisting" this process. Concerns were raised as to the feasibility or wisdom of attempting artificially to guide the natural development of the language. Yizhar Smilansky (a highly respected author and then member of the Knesset), for example, feared that the Language Committee, if endowed with legal authority, might become a mere "word factory;" its rôle ought to be limited to recording what would develop "naturally," and it should be left to "the people" to create new words. Representing the majority view, however, B. Dinor (also a renowned scholar and author, and then Minister of Education) insisted that there was a need for a specialised language planning agency: "This work ought not to be done exclusively by [people in the arts and creative craftsmen] when they are in a creative mood. [It] should be approved by professionals... We cannot accept that every [government] office should have its own scientists, language experts, linguists and experts on writing... There is now a need for a leading scientific institution to direct the natural development of the Hebrew language."[3]   The lengthy, often heated discussions concluded in a bill which transformed the Hebrew Language Committee into the Hebrew Language Academy.

THE HEBREW LANGUAGE ACADEMY

According to the Hebrew Language Academy Act (1953), the Academy was to consist of twenty-three members. In addition, it could appoint twenty-three "advisory members," to be drawn from among Hebrew scholars and writers, and further elect "honorary members." Its decisions would be binding on all government departments and agencies and government-affiliated educational and scientific institutions, including all primary and secondary schools. The Academy's objectives, published in 1954, were similar to those of its predecessor, the Hebrew Language Committee. They were, briefly:

(1) to gather data on all the periods of the Hebrew language;
(2) to investigate the structure and history of Hebrew;
(3) to guide the development of Hebrew in vocabulary, grammar, orthography, and script.

Despite the puristic tendencies evident in these objectives, in the Knesset debate that led to the Academy's creation and in the Academy's plenary meetings (for details, cf. Nahir 1974), the lexical modernisation of Hebrew has become the Academy's major focus.

The Academy consists of four levels: the Plenum, which includes all members and advisory members, meets bi-monthly to decide on the proposals of the Executive Board and the Supervisory Committees and to appoint members to all its committees, with its minutes published annually in the *Records of the Hebrew Language Academy*. The Executive Board, elected regularly by the Plenum and including the President and Vice-President and the chairmen of the Supervisory Committees, has responsibility for the Academy's day-to-day work. The Supervisory Committees, elected biennially by the Plenum and consisting of three members each, are responsible for Grammar, Terminology, the Historical Dictionary of the Hebrew Language, Publications, and Finance. The Subcommittees (the Terminology Committees of the former Hebrew Language Committee), made up of two or more Academy members and, where required, outside specialists, prepare reports for their respective Supervisory Committees which then submit them to the Plenum for approval.

The Academy's lexical work is delegated to its Terminology Committee which, in turn, appoints subcommittees to deal with specific areas of terminology; each committee is assisted by a scientific secretary. The procedure followed by these terminology subcommittees, which disband once their work has been completed, consists of six steps:

(1) Preparing lists of foreign terms in the committee's field (e.g., chemistry, cooking, transportation), defining them in case of doubt or ambiguity, and suggesting for them Hebrew terms collected from earlier sources or current usage.

(2) First Reading: discussion in committee.

(3) Inviting the comments of all Academy members and of outside specialists on the lists which now include (a) words already in use; (b) newly created words on which the committee is in agreement; and (c) concepts for which the committee could not agree on satisfactory Hebrew terms; as a rule, the latter two lists are the shortest.

(4) Second Reading: considering the comments received following (3).

(5) Circulating the committee's decisions to all Academy members, drawing attention to (a) the changes between the final and previous lists; (b) terms involving special difficulties, to be resolved by the Plenum.

(6) The Plenary session: the items in (5b) are discussed and voted on together with the entire list (3).

Lists approved by the Plenum, like all its other decisions, are proclaimed by the Minister of Education and Culture in the *Official Gazette* and are thus binding on all government and government-affiliated agencies, including all television and radio stations and the government-funded school system.

In recent decades this procedure has been followed by virtually all terminology subcommittees, whether formed by the Terminology Committee or at the request of an outside body such as the Law Society, the Psychological Association, the Electric Company, etc. In a pioneering study, Fellman & Fishman (1977) have compared two terminology subcommittees (librarianship and inorganic chemistry) representing these two types – consumer- and committee-initiated. Their study explores how terminology committees actually operate, their composition, work cycle and procedures. One of the major questions faced by the Academy's general Terminology Committee was whether the subcommittees should attempt to translate *all* foreign terms in their areas, or only those needed by Israeli librarians and chemists; following lengthy discussion it was decided that "even if only one person in the world needed a complete Hebrew terminology in librarianship or chemistry, that was reason enough for preparing such a list" (Fellman & Fishman 1977:6). It also turned out that the problem of "indigenousness/internationalness of terminology" is much more severe in one field than in the other although both sought to avoid adoption of foreign terms. Fellman & Fishman further found that the two committees were alike in their operation and attitudes and differed only in their formation and composition: on the consumer-initiated librarianship subcommittee, the outside experts were appointed by the requesting body, not by the Academy. Such a difference may be more significant than it seems, as it may well affect the level of loyalty of the outside specialists to earlier Academy rulings. There is, of course, an Academy tradition which affects the members' attitudes on such issues as borrowing, purism, etc. and their votes as members of the terminology committees.

EXTRA-ACADEMY LEXICAL MODERNISATION

Although lexical modernisation is its major *raison d'être*, the Academy has not been the only agency engaged in this task. Other bodies, whose major functions are non-linguistic, have also been active in what may be termed extra-Academy lexical modernisation (Nahir 1979). The military, the Communications Ministry, the Institute of Productivity, the Institute of Standards and the Technion carry out their own terminological work; in accordance with the Academy Act, each includes a representative of the Academy (whose advice, however, is not necessarily followed). It is remarkable that the work of these "auxiliary language planning agencies" (Nahir 1979) has greater continuity and permanence than that of the Academy's terminology subcommittees, which disband as soon as their work has been completed.

For the first three decades of the third period, the military was the most active of the auxiliary language planning agencies. Local terminology committees in all the branches translated foreign technical literature into Hebrew and also drew up lists of foreign terms without Hebrew equivalent, which would then be turned over to a Higher Terminology Committee; in this way, thousands of terms in technology, electronics, and military hardware, tactics and strategy were created, disseminated and ultimately, published in a *Dictionary of Military Terminology* (1957), now in its third edition, the product of what may be called "codification maintenance."

When the Academy realised that the Plenum could no longer, as required by law, approve terminological innovations individually, it formulated the concept of *hora'at ša'a* 'temporary regulation' which allowed the delegation of this power to a lower authority, such as its representative on a terminology subcommittee. This new flexibility greatly enhanced the effectiveness of the military's Higher Terminology Committee. The military's new terminologies, which were entirely user-initiated and user-oriented, have also been accepted by the Academy and have been included in its specialised dictionaries (for seafaring, engineering, soil science, metallurgy, etc.).

When the Communications and Electronics Council set up a Committee for Terminologies in Communications and Electronics in collaboration with the Academy, the two agencies agreed that the committee would be made up of "individuals of appropriate background and education" recommended by the Academy and the government ministries represented on the Council; in the event, several relevant industries and the military were also represented. The Council's work was published in 1970 in the *Dictionary for Terminologies in Communications and Electronics*, and more recent work on terminologies in radio communications and in microelectronics resulted in a revised edition with a total of 9,000 terms.

The Technion (Israel Institute of Technology), by its very nature a constant "consumer" of technological and scientific terminologies, also formed a Central Committee for Terms in Technology. This lexically influential standing committee has published (jointly with the Academy) dictionaries in such areas as telephone communication, welding, hydraulics, measurement theory in metals, sewage and sanitary installation, soil science, dams, strength of materials, photography, concrete, seamanship, hydrology, joinery, casting, physics (mechanics), sea waves and currents, work analysis, drafting, pumps and office equipment (Nahir 1979).

The auxiliary language planning agencies differ from the Academy's terminology subcommittees not only by their history and organisational structure but, more significantly, by the fact that they have been strictly user-oriented. Theirs has been a case of corpus planning by and for the "consumer."

MINOR LANGUAGE PLANNING GOALS

Although the major goal of the various agencies has been modernisation, several minor goals have also been pursued, albeit not all with equal vigour or success: terminology unification (championed by the Israel Institute of Standards) and, in the Academy's own domain, language reform and purification. In terms of more normative motivation, the first and the last of these goals represent opposing extremes.

TERMINOLOGY UNIFICATION

"Establishing unified terminologies, mostly technical, by clarifying and defining them, in order to reduce communicative ambiguity in the technological and scientific domains" (Nahir 1984:308) is an obvious necessity. An extreme example of such ambiguity, though in a non-technical area, is the existence in Hebrew as in other languages of words with directly opposing meanings, such as *hig'il* 'to cause to be dirty' and 'to clean'; *kiles* 'to scorn' and 'to praise'; *nifkad* 'to be counted in a census or roll call' and 'to be absent or missing'; *na'ana* 'to receive a reply' and 'to reply or respond'.

Terminology unification in Hebrew has been practised almost exclusively by the Israel Institute of Standards; the Institute also coins terms, yet it does so only when the Academy's subcommittees fail to provide it with the terms required. As a rule, the Institute does not merely find Hebrew equivalents for foreign terms, which is usually done by the Academy and the other auxiliary language planning agencies, but attempts to provide definitions and to establish the relationships between them.

The lexical work of the Institute is carried out on two levels. When standards are being prepared, terms which are used are defined by the committee which works on the standard (and subsequently examined by a language editor); they apply only to the standards in which they occur.

Large groups of terms are also defined and then published specifically as standards. Such definitions, now standards in their own right, apply to the respective terms in all Israeli standards. They are usually based on translations from foreign standards, e.g., the standards of term definitions of the International Standards Organisation, or the International Electronics Commission; in the Institute's publications, Hebrew terms are followed by their English equivalents, and by definitions. The committees preparing these standards include a representative of the Hebrew Language Academy in addition to the Institute's technical personnel and a language editor. Although many of the terms defined by the Institute are supplied by the Academy, the Institute has tended to accept existing usage where it has been seen to be well entrenched. Standards of term definitions have been published, for example, for screw-threads, textiles, electronics, sampling, printed circuits, fluid engineering, rubber, welding, public broadcasts and automated data processing (Nahir 1979).

HEBREW SCRIPT AND SPELLING

For centuries, language reform has been attempted in many parts of the world. It may be defined as "deliberate change in specific aspects of language, intended to facilitate its use, [usually involving] changes in, or simplification of, orthography, spelling, lexicon, or grammar" (Nahir 1984:302). Obviously, the term *reform* is used here in its narrow sense, or it would be at least partially synonymous with *language planning* as a whole, and specific language planning goals would remain indistinct.

The major problem faced by readers and writers of both Modern and pre-Modern Hebrew has undoubtedly been the absence of vowel letters in Hebrew orthography. For centuries, a system of diacritics has been used to indicate vowel quality. This system, consisting of marks above, below, and beside consonant letters, has been used almost exclusively for printing Bibles, prayerbooks, poetry, and books or magazines for young children and learners of Hebrew as a second language. Employing it universally would result in great practical difficulties, prohibitively high printing costs and extra time spent in writing. In most situations, therefore, no vowels are indicated. Although speakers of Hebrew usually overcome this difficulty without apparent effort, errors and difficulties in reading and even the odd miscommunication do occur. The absence of vowel letters has also rendered the learning of Hebrew reading by children and newcomers a lengthier task than it would otherwise be. Consequently, two consonant letters have been increasingly utilised – as they were in fact prior to the development of the present diacritic system over a millennium ago – in an auxiliary capacity to indicate certain vowels: *y* ("yod") for /i/ or, less commonly, for /e/; and *v* ("vav") for /o/ and /u/. This is termed *ktiv male* 'full [plene] spelling' in contrast with *ktiv xaser* 'defective spelling', which is used when vowel diacritics are employed. Since the traditional rules of Hebrew grammar frequently do not allow the use of these two letters, and since most Hebrew speakers are not sufficiently familiar with the highly complex system of rules, usage of the 'full' spelling has been erratic.

This deficiency results in numerous problems (cf. Rabin 1971): the existence of a double spelling system; a lack of regularity in the more commonly used 'full' spelling; misreading, miscommunication, and over-dependence on context (without vowel indication, countless words can be read in numerous ways); children's dependence on reading materials with vowels indicated by diacritics; dependence of learners of Hebrew as a second language on some prior speaking proficiency for reading.

The problems of Hebrew orthography have been under discussion at least since a Hebrew Language Committee meeting in 1913. Following decades of unsuccessful attempts by several Academy committees to produce a reformed spelling system that would be acceptable to a majority of its members and to the public, the Academy in 1968 adopted one which had been proposed in 1948 already. This decision provides for the use of either 'full' (plene) or 'defective' spelling, but with the qualification that the 'defective' system be used only with vowel diacritics (or "pointing") fully applied, and that all indication of vowels be omitted in 'full' spelling. In rejecting extreme proposals, this functional approach has, in effect, accepted an approximation of what is common practice. The Academy has thus given legitimacy to the (eventual) complete dichotomy between 'full' spelling (i.e., where vowel diacritics are not applied) in most situations, and the use of the 'defective' spelling (in which vowels are indicated by diacritics and auxiliary letters are therefore neither needed nor used).

In reaching its decision on spelling reform, the Academy actually signalled that it was unable to reach a consensus and therefore had to opt for a less than desirable decision rather than reach no decision at all. According to Chaim Rabin, a linguist and Academy member, the status quo was the Academy's only choice: "It was proved that the existing spelling – simply by the fact that it existed even if its use was restricted – was able to rally a clear majority" (1971:115). In comparing the Academy's unimpressive accomplishment in spelling reform with its success in the lexical modernisation of Hebrew, Rabin attributes the latter to two factors: (1) it had met the real need of a well-defined group willing to accept normative rulings; (2) these had come in small units, more easily digested. The spelling reform, on the other hand, would "affect all at once the entire web of communication [and] require an immediate willingness to change habits" (1971:118). A thorough spelling reform would also require large-scale investments in printing, in typewriters, in reprinting books, etc. Further, differences in target population also affect the rate of acceptance of Academy rulings. Finally, Rabin compares the Hebrew spelling reform with other, successful spelling reforms which concerned single orthographic features (in Germany, Holland and Norway). He concludes that "the feature that makes spelling reforms so much more arduous to agree on than other areas of language planning is its systematic character" (1971:120). This certainly reconfirms the notion that, like status planning, corpus planning and its implementation activities must be geared to their user communities if they are to make a difference.

PURIFICATION

Language purification is a common planning goal throughout the world. The two types delineated, external and internal purification, have also been among the goals of Israel's language planners, albeit in minor status.

In recent decades, the former has been concerned primarily with the status of English.

External purification may be defined as "prescription of language usage in order to preserve the 'purity' of a language and protect it from foreign influences" (Nahir 1984:299). In the case of Hebrew, the foreign influence most noticed and feared is in the lexical domain, although Israel's language contacts with Europe and the U.S.A. are reflected in some grammatical and, in the Revival period, phonological changes as well. In the lexical domain, the ever-increasing rate of concept borrowing and subsequent lexical borrowing has led to fears in many circles that Hebrew may be swamped by the "donor" languages and eventually lose its linguistic identity.

As in numerous other speech communities in recent decades, the language from which Hebrew has been borrowing most is clearly English, due to the worldwide popularity of this language as a *lingua franca* and also to the close and many faceted ties between Israel and the U.S.A. with its large Jewish community. In fact, British rule over Palestine (1917-1948) also resulted in massive lexical borrowing from British English, particularly in areas where contact with the administration was closest, such as the legal system, security, etc.

The widespread lexical borrowing from English has thus for many decades been an issue of concern for Academy (and previously Committee) members and other purists. More recently, there has also been increasing scholarly interest in the community's exposure to English.

Nadel & Fishman (1977), for example, have studied the impact of English upon the Hebrew-speaking majority (99% spoke Hebrew and 83% read it in 1972) in Israel. In the school system all students are required to take English from the fifth grade through secondary school for four hours a week. English programs on Israel's radio which, like television, is government-funded and publicly administered, take about one-and-a-half hours of air time daily; this is similar to the time assigned to French and Russian programs and more than that assigned to all other foreign languages. Yet while the latter are broadcast for the benefit of immigrants, it is obvious that, with less than 1% of the population being native speakers of English, "the function of English [radio] for Israelis is not the same as that of the immigrant languages per se" (1977:150). (In fact, many more English radio broadcasts are available to Israelis externally, particularly from the BBC and the Voice of America which have daily programs beamed at the Middle East twenty-four and twelve hours each day, respectively.)

Virtually all non-Hebrew and non-Arabic material on Israel's two-channel (until recently, single-channel) television is in English. It is estimated that about 60% of all films screened in theatres are in English (with Hebrew subtitles; 4% are in Hebrew). While English plays are almost never shown in Israeli theatres, many Hebrew productions are translations from English, which undoubtedly also affects Hebrew usage.

Although the great majority of books published in Israel are in Hebrew, the number of local English publications – including the daily *Jerusalem Post* – has been growing steadily and exceeds that in all other foreign languages; English language magazines and newspapers are imported at double the rate for any other language, and there is clearly a "positive attitude toward English... and the language's special status relative to all other foreign languages in Israel" (1977:159). While in public libraries English titles made up only six percent of the total in 1973, over 50% of all books in specialised libraries, e.g., in museums, universities, and hospitals, were in English (84% in medical libraries) (1977:162f).

The privileged status of English in Israel is further evident in the rapid growth in signs carrying English words, or English names written in Hebrew letters (Gold 1981).

Despite the increase in their exposure to English, particularly through the education system and the mass media, most Israelis do not seem opposed to it, because Hebrew, the national language, retains complete dominance internally; a clear distinction exists between the internal and external functions of language in the community – and locally, Hebrew has no rival. Nadel & Fishman's prediction that Jewish Israelis may "become increasingly bilingual in Hebrew and English only" (1977:165) seems to be based on an overly broad view of bilingualism. There seems to be no indication at all that English, with all its prestige, will in the foreseeable future be other than a second language studied in school by most students, actually acquired as a second language by a smaller number, and mastered with reasonable spoken and written fluency by fewer still. Despite decades of close contact with the English language and compulsory English study (from the fifth grade on), only 36% of the 18-24 age category (which was the highest of all categories, with an average for the total population of 24%) "self-reported" that they could "speak, read and write" English (1977:146) – and 43.1% failed their (secondary school) English language matriculation examination (1977:144). The use of English, therefore, seems (Gold 1981:50)

instrumental rather than internally integrative or symbolic, and it seems that it will always remain a second language, never becoming nativised or ever acquiring major functions in domestic life. The only integrative rôle played by English is an external one (linking Israel with the non-Israeli world) and its only symbolic rôle is seen in the injection of bits and scraps of English by Hebrew-speakers who are actually not very adept in using it (*sori*, *aym-veri-sori*, etc.)

Although the pattern of English loans has not yet been seriously investigated, there is some concern that the extent to which English is used and its growing prestige are bound to affect the corpus of the Hebrew language, if not its status, severely. With the status of Hebrew completely entrenched, the threat has been perceived almost exclusively as aimed at the corpus – excessive borrowing, particularly from English, in lexicon and, to a much lesser degree, in syntax. (With the exception of Ben-Yehuda and his associates[4] there has always been at last some willingness to accept foreign words where suitable equivalents could not be found or coined, or where foreign words were already entrenched in Hebrew.)

As long ago as 1966, the Academy reacted to such concerns by holding a plenary session on the issue of purism.[5] The dilemma is obvious when one reads "of the flood of foreign elements" in a speech which includes such loan-words as *aktuali* 'up to date', *demagogya* 'demagoguery', *mexani* 'mechanical', *texni* 'technical', *organi* 'organic, living', and *telegrama* 'telegram' (a borrowing competing with the already dominant *mivrak*), and two until then entirely foreign terms, *realistika* (probably) 'realism' and *bravura* (probably) 'courage, bravery'.

But the puristic attitudes of the majority are only in part reflected in the Academy's lexical work. It is evident that the more technologically or scientifically specialised terminology subcommittees have tended to be more liberal in their acceptance of borrowings than the Plenum (Nahir 1974). Realising that there is no longer a threat to the survival and identity of the language, and that they must compromise if they are to have any impact on usage, Academy members have in recent years approved phonemically acceptable, established loan-words on a much larger scale than in the two previous periods.

Internal purification may be defined as " 'protection' of the accepted standard code as it exists at a given time against deviation that occurs from *within* in the form of non-normative, 'incorrect' usage in a language" (Nahir 1984:301). As in the case of external purification, there has been some softening of the Academy's attitudes to internal purification, but to a lesser extent, since there have been no pressing lexical needs.

The Academy's approach to language in general and to Hebrew in particular is unmistakably normative. Even Chaim Rabin, representing the Academy's least normative wing, agreed in 1966 that "one of the main functions of the [Academy] is normative..., which endows it with state authority;" accordingly, the Academy ought not to approve of deviation from "accepted grammar and syntax [but] use its authority for the sake of retaining the status quo, [which] is what the public is actually striving for." Bestsellers such as *Proper Hebrew* (Y. Perets), *Be Correct!* (Bahat & Ron) and *Compendium of the Language* (Y. Avineri) and the decade-long popularity of language columns in the press, advising readers on correct usage, reflect the same normative attitude.[6]

The majority at the Plenum was even more authoritative; in the words of A. Mirsky, "The language needs overall regulating, to correct its style and spirit and to straighten its ways." In the matter of correcting style, he went further than most in order to avoid "a division between us and the style of the Bible..., the Mishna, the Midrash, the Talmud, Rashi, and Maimonides, the foundations of Hebrew culture."

Despite its legal authority and normative tendencies, the Academy has exerted little pressure to have its position accepted; it prefers implementation to be carried out by other bodies, limiting its own rôle mostly to the process of codification. One of the few exceptions has been the publication of specialised dictionaries and word-lists.

The Academy also has a language consultant on the Broadcasting Authority which administers radio and television. As the Academy's watchdog, this representative sees to it that broadcasters use only "good Hebrew." For decades, this "Good Hebrew" policy has resulted in a forced spoken variety of the language which, while thoroughly comprehensible to Hebrew speakers, is restricted to these media and has been referred to as *Ivrit šel haradyo* 'radio Hebrew'. What little research has been done on broadcast Hebrew suggests that it has virtually no impact even on the formal speech variety of the educated (Nahir 1978b). A further attempt at implementing Academy decisions is made through a daily five-minute "correct language" programme on radio ("A Moment of Hebrew"), also without demonstrable results.

Then there is the monthly distribution, since 1962, to all schools, government offices, etc., of the Academy's poster series, *Lemad Lešonxa* 'Learn your language', each listing two or three dozen newly coined or approved terms and a few "correct Hebrew" forms.   Finally, the Academy also exerts some control over language in school texts since by law these need approval by the Ministry of Education which, in turn, is required to follow Academy rulings.

Voluntary activities include *Lešonenu La'am* [Our Language for the People], the more scholarly *Lešonenu* [Our Language] and *Zixronot Ha'akademya Lalašon Ha'ivrit* [Records of the Hebrew Language Academy], which often include articles in synchronic and historical Hebrew linguistics. Finally, as in many speech communities where purification is a language planning goal (e.g., in Sweden; see Jernud 1977), "correct language" columns in the press are still popular though not as much as in the past when the desire to protect the language from excessive internal change was almost a national preoccupation.

ATTITUDES TOWARDS HEBREW AND ITS PLANNING

The crucial rôle language attitudes play in language behaviour has been recognised, even before the advent of language planning, in various case-studies (e.g., Labov 1963, 1966; Lambert et al. 1965). Soon after, the theoretical and methodological investigation of language attitudes also began to take shape both in macro- and micro-sociolinguistics (e.g., Shuy & Fasold 1973; Cooper & Danet 1980; Williams 1974).

For Hebrew, Hofman & Fisherman (1971:205), for example, found that the "motives" have changed since the Revival "from one in which values (beliefs, ideology) dominated ... to one in which function (instrumentality, private need) dominates ... today." While Hebrew is still viewed by the majority of Israelis as "a value worthy of nurture and care," this is so "more perhaps because of its having become a norm than for any of the sort of philosophical arguments that used to be advanced in its favor."

Hofman (1974a) focusses more specifically on chemists' knowledge and use of terms approved by the Academy, and their attitudes towards them. Specifically, he attempts to assess the relative weight of non-attitudinal factors (such as personal background, language history and claimed language proficiency) and attitudinal factors in predicting criteria for success in language planning. The predictors he identifies include attitudinal ones, and Hofman offers encouragement to language planners "who must feel a bit too far from the madding crowd." The forces they help set in motion "are not at all devoid of lawfulness, predictability, and explainability; and hence not at all beyond their ability to influence language behavior significantly" (Hofman 1974a:60). In another study on the predictability of the use of Hebrew terms among Israeli psychologists, Hofman (1974b) attempts to replicate some of the major findings of his earlier study, and here, too, speakers' attitudes to the language serve as an important variable. Hofman's studies offer valuable models for the study of language attitudes both in Hebrew and in the field at large.

Language attitudes also constitute one of the variables investigated by Alloni-Fainberg (1974), who seeks to determine the extent to which the public uses Academy-coined terms pertaining to the car. While the older subjects in her study show a markedly positive attitude towards Academy terms, in actual use they tend to prefer, perhaps out of habit, competing terms not approved by the Academy.

The language attitudes of Israeli students and teachers and their opinions ábout certain aspects of Modern Hebrew are the primary focus of Seckbach 1974. However, the questions used in this study (e.g., about journalists who the subjects thought were "users of good Hebrew;" a specific place in Israel where they thought poor Hebrew was spoken, etc.) were such that many subjects ignored some questions (no question was answered by even 50% of the students), that the respondents showed a "general lack of interest in these language issues," and that they "were also information-poor in areas requiring specific answers, such as titles or authors of grammars" (Seckbach 1974:123). Further, since the author failed to justify the choice of variables, and in the absence of any theoretical framework, the significance of the findings remains unknown.

Focussing directly on attitudes towards the Hebrew Language Academy, Fellman (1977:155) attempts to "analyze how the Israeli public has viewed [it]." An interesting question, yet the study consists merely of a brief review of "certain relevant articles which have appeared in Israeli newspapers and literary journals." The conclusion, therefore, that "the Israeli public viewed the Academy as both fulfilling an ideal function on the institutional level (the revival of the language...) and realising and implementing specific language tasks on the practical level" (1977:156) may at best be true of the Israeli press's view of the Academy, not the public's.

Most research on language attitudes in Hebrew has so far been speaker-oriented. In directing attention to the "product" of language planning, Nir (1982) asked university students and graduates to guess the meanings of Academy-coined words which they claimed were unknown to them. He found that one of the factors determining the acceptance of such words was the measure of their "linguistic transparency" which is defined as "a relativistic morpho-semantic feature, [whose] assessment depends on the lexical competence of a specific speaker or of a defined group of speakers" (1982:21). Although limited in scope, this study introduces a crucial question and a sound approach to its investigation. Its findings, albeit rather limited, also indicate the need to consider psycholinguistic factors such as transparency in the process of coining new terms.

Despite deficiencies in research methodology, then, the beginnings of a trend to investigate the planning agencies, their "product" and its acceptance by the community are evident. Recent work on the theoretical aspects of language attitudes promises progress on the Hebrew scene as well.

SUMMARY

Based on a classification of language planning goals and a survey of the development of Modern Hebrew according to the major goal dominant in each of the three periods delineated, this study is concerned with the third period (since 1948) and the goals pursued in it. While lexical modernisation as been the dominant goal of the Academy and the other agencies, three minor goals have also been pursued, namely terminology unification, reform and purification (both external and internal) – involving corpus rather than status planning and pursued mostly, though not exclusively, by the Academy. This discussion reaffirms the notion that, as in other areas, language planners must have the interest of the "consumers" as their principal motivation if they are to have any impact on the development either of the status or the corpus of the language they attempt to plan.

NOTES

[1]   First used in English by Ferguson (1959), the term *diglossia* may now be defined as the use of a community's highly valued language or dialect (learned consciously, usually through formal education) in relatively formal situations and the use of a less valued language or dialect (learned as a native variety, with no conscious effort) in relatively informal situations.

[2]   On the formation and the contributions of the Hebrew Language Academy see Fellman (1974) and Nahir (1974). For an evaluation of the work of Eliezer Ben-Yehuda, one of its founders and a leader in the Revival, see Fellman (1973) and Nahir (1978c).

[3]   Cited after *Lešonenu* 18(3/4):229ff., 1953; all translations in this essay are by the author.

[4]   Ben-Yehuda was probably the only Hebrew language planner to propose (in 1914) the creation of new *roots* from which new words could be derived where none existed or to replace borrowings (cf. Ben-Asher 1977); these proposals were never adopted or even considered in earnest.

⁵ *Zixronot Ha'akademya Lalašon Ha'ivrit* [Records of the Hebrew Language Academy] 16, 1966 includes a full record of the debate; it is summarised and discussed in Nahir (1974) from which all the passages here cited are drawn.
⁶ For the effectiveness of such texts, used by over a generation of Israeli secondary-school students, see Nahir 1978b, an empirical study of normative vs. educated speech.

REFERENCES

Alloni-Fainberg, Yafa. 1974. Official Hebrew Terms for Parts of the Car: A Study of Knowledge, Usage and Attitudes. *International Journal of the Sociology of Language* 1:67-94.

Bachi, Roberto. 1956. A Statistical Analysis of the Revival of Hebrew in Israel (and Palestine). *Scripta Hierosolymitana* 3:179-247.

Bar-Adon, Aaron. 1977. On the Nativization of Modern Hebrew and the Role of Children in the Process. P.J. Hopper, ed., *Studies in Descriptive and Historical Linguistics: Festschrift for Winfred P. Lehmann*. Amsterdam: John Benjamins.

Ben-Asher, Mordechai. 1977. [Traditionalists versus innovators in the revival of Hebrew.] *Balšanut Šimušit* 1:7-20. [in Hebrew]

Blanc, Haim. 1954. The Growth of Israeli Hebrew. *Middle Eastern Affairs* 5:385-392.

Cooper, Robert L., & Brenda Danet. 1980. Language in the Melting Pot: The Sociolinguistic Context for Language Planning in Israel. *Language Problems and Language Planning* 4:1-28.

Fellman, Jack. 1973. *The Revival of a Classical Tongue: Eliezer Ben-Yehuda and the Modern Hebrew Language*. The Hague: Mouton.

—. 1974. The Academy of the Hebrew Language: Its History, Structure and Function. *International Journal of the Sociology of Language* 1:95-103.

—. 1977. Hebrew Language Planning and the Public. J. Rubin et al., eds., *Language Planning Processes*, 151-156. The Hague: Mouton.

—, & Joshua A. Fishman. 1977. Language Planning in Israel: Solving Terminological Problems. J. Rubin et al., eds., *Language Planning Processes*. The Hague: Mouton.

Ferguson, Charles A. 1959. Diglossia. *Word* 15:325-340.

—. 1968. Language Development. J.A. Fishman et al. eds., *Language Problems of Developing Nations*, 27-36. New York: Wiley.

—. 1978. Language and Global Interdependence. E.M. Gerli et al., eds., *Language in American Life*, 23-31. Washington, D.C.: Georgetown University Press.

Gold, David L. 1981. An Introduction to English in Israel. *Language Problems and Language Planning* 5:11-56.

Haramati, Shlomo. 1979. *[The rôle of the Hebrew teacher in reviving the Hebrew language: 1882-1914.]* Jerusalem: Rubin Mass. [in Hebrew]

Haugen, Einar. 1966. Linguistics and Language Planning. W. Bright, ed., *Sociolinguistics*, 50-71. The Hague: Mouton.

—. 1983. The Implementation of Corpus Planning: Theory and Practice. J. Cobarrubias & J.A. Fishman, eds., *Progress in Language Planning*, 269-289. The Hague: Mouton.

—. 1987. *Blessing of Babel: Bilingualism and Language Planning*. Berlin: Mouton de Gruyter.

Hofman, John E. 1974a. The Prediction of Success in Language Planning: The Case of Chemists in Israel. *International Journal of Sociology of Language* 1:39-65.

—. 1974b. Predicting the Use of Hebrew Terms among Israeli Psychologists. *International Journal of the Sociology of Language* 3:53-65.

–, & Haya Fisherman. 1971. Language Shift and Maintenance in Israel. *International Migration Review* 5:204-226.

Jernudd, Björn H. 1977. Thee Language Planning Agencies and Three Swedish Newspapers. J. Rubin et al., eds., *Language Planning Processes*, 143-149. The Hague: Mouton.

Kloss, Heinz. 1969. *Research Possibilities on Group Bilingualism: A Report*. Québec: International Centre for Research on Bilingualism.

Labov, William. 1963. The Social Motivation of a Sound Change. *Word* 19:273-309.

—. 1966. *The Social Stratification of English in New York City*. Washington, D.C.: Center for Applied Linguistics.

Lambert, Wallace E., M. Anisfeld & G. Yeni-Komshian. 1965. Evaluational Reactions of Jewish and Arab Adolescents to Dialect and Language Variations. *Journal of Personality and Social Psychology* 2:84-90.

Morag, Shlomo. 1959. Planned and Unplanned Developments in Modern Hebrew. *Lingua* 8:247-263.

Nadel, Elizabeth, & Joshua A. Fishman. 1977. English in Israel: A Sociolinguistic Study. J.A. Fishman et al., eds., *The Spread of English: The Sociology of English as an Additional Language*, 137-167. Rowley, Massachusetts: Newbury House.

Nahir, Moshe. 1974. *Language Academies, Language Planning, and the Case of the Hebrew Revival*. Ph.D. dissertation, University of Pittsburgh.

—. 1977a. Language Revival versus Speech Revival: A Question of Terminology. *Language Planning Newsletter* 3(4):7.

—. 1977b. The Five Aspects of Language Planning: A Classification. *Language Problems and Language Planning* 1:107-123.

—. 1978a. Language Planning Functions in Modern Hebrew. *Language Problems and Language Planning* 2:89-102.

—. 1978b. Normativism and Educated Speech in Modern Hebrew. *International Journal of the Sociology of Language* 18:49-67.

—. 1978c. Review of *The Revival of a Classical Tongue: Eliezer Ben-Yehuda and the Modern Hebrew Language,* by Jack Fellman. *Language Problems and Language Planning* 2:177-181.

—. 1979. Lexical Modernization in Hebrew and the Extra Academy Contribution. R.E. Wood, ed., *National Language Planning and Treatment,* 105-116. [special issue, *Word* 30(1)]

—. 1983. Sociocultural Factors in the Revival of Hebrew. *Language Problems and Language Planning* 7:263-284.

—. 1984. Language Planning Goals: A Classification. *Language Problems and Language Planning* 8:294-327.

—. 1987. L'aménagement de l'hébreu moderne. J. Maurais, ed., *Politique et aménagement linguistiques,* 239-316. Québec: Conseil de la langue française.

—. 1988. Language Planning and Language Acquisition: The 'Great Leap' in the Hebrew Revival. C.B. Paulston, ed., *International Handbook of Bilingualism and Bilingual Education,* 275-295. Westport, Connecticut: Greenwood Press.

Nir, Raphael. 1982. [Linguistic transparency of neologisms coined by the Hebrew Language Academy.] *Hebrew Computational Linguistics* 19:20-33. [in Hebrew]

Rabin, Chaim. 1971. Spelling Reform – Israel 1968. J. Rubin & B.H. Jernudd, eds., *Can Language be Planned?,* 95-121. Honolulu: University Press of Hawaii.

Rubin, Joan, & Björn H. Jernudd, eds. 1971. *Can Language be Planned?* Honolulu: University Press of Hawaii.

St. John, Robert. 1952. *Tongue of the Prophets: The Life Story of Elizer Ben-Yehuda.* New York.

Saulson, S.B. 1979. *Institutionalized Language Planning: Documents and Analysis of the Revival of Hebrew.* The Hague: Mouton.

Seckbach, Fern. 1974. Attitudes and Opinions of Israeli Teachers and Students about Aspects of Modern Hebrew. *International Journal of the Sociology of Language* 1:105-124.

Shuy, Roger, & Ralph W. Fasold, eds. 1973. *Language Attitudes: Current Trends and Prospects*. Washington, D.C.: Georgetown University Press.

Tur-Sinai, N.H. 1960. *The Revival of the Hebrew Language*. Jerusalem: Hacohen Press.

Weinberg, Werner. 1985. *The History of Hebrew Plene Spelling*. Cincinnati: Hebrew Union College Press.

Williams, Frederick. 1974. The Identification of Linguistic Attitudes. *International Journal of the Sociology of Language*. 3:21-32.

"Chant to the Fire-fly":
A Philological Problem in Ojibwe

John D. Nichols

The "Chant to the Fire-fly" is a song text collected by the ethnologist Henry Rowe Schoolcraft from Ojibwe children at Sault Ste. Marie. In the briefest of three translations given by Schoolcraft of the Ojibwe original:

> Fire-fly, fire-fly, light me to bed.
> Come, come, little insect of light,
> You are my candle, and light me to go.
>
> (1851-57, 5:564)

Its charm is enhanced by the story he tells of its collection, placing us at the Sault:

> In the hot summer evenings, the children of the Chippewa Algonquins, along the shores of the upper lakes and in the northern latitudes, frequently assemble before their parents' lodges, and amuse themselves by little chants of various kinds, with shouts and wild dancing. Attracted by such shouts of merriment and gambols, I walked out one evening, to a green lawn skirting the edge of the St. Mary's river, with the fall in full view, to get hold of the meaning of some of these chants. The air and the plain were literally sparkling with the phosphorescent light of the fire-fly. By dint of attention, repeated on one or two occasions, the following succession of words was caught. They were addressed to this insect. (1845:61)

While no one has claimed great literary merit for its few lines, this was perhaps the most well-known Native American poem to readers in the nineteenth century through the original Ojibwe texts and translations published by Schoolcraft and through its full-blown literary expansion by Henry Wadsworth Longfellow in "Hiawatha":

> At the door on Summer evenings
> Sat the little Hiawatha;
> . . . .
> Saw the fire-fly, Wah-wah-taysee,
> Flitting through the dusk of evening,

With the twinkle of its candle
Lighting up the brakes and bushes,
And he sang the song of children,
Sang the song Nokomis taught him:
"Wah-wah-taysee, little fire-fly,
Little, flitting white-fire insect,
Little, dancing, white-fire creature,
Light me with your little candle,
Ere upon my bed I lay me,
Ere in sleep I close my eyelids!"

(Longfellow 1855, Canto III)

Its fame continues in the twentieth century through reprintings of the Schoolcraft and Longfellow versions in numerous anthologies of Native American song and poetry; through re-expressions, often called new translations; and, through discussions of the problems of the translation and presentation of Native American poetry which use it as a case study. I am responding here to Dell Hymes, who after observing inconsistencies between the apparent structure of the Ojibwe text and the translations, called for the philological study of the text:

> Most of us, despite Schoolcraft's eminence as a pioneer ethnologist, would wish for a specialist in Algonquian languages, if not in Ojibwa (Chippewa) itself, to analyze the original text. Even better would be to have the text heard by an informant and redictated and retranscribed, a procedure that has been followed in the case of nineteenth-century Delaware (another Algonquian language) by Voegelin, for Kalapuya (a language of Oregon) by Jacobs, and increasingly by contemporary specialists in such cases, where knowledge of the language, but not of certain valued texts, survives. By such a procedure, the defects of earlier materials in form can be remedied. By ascertaining the actual phonological, grammatical and lexical structure of the texts, modern techniques bring out the full value of earlier enterprise in collection, something like the restoration of older paintings. (1965:320)

LOCATION OF THE TEXT

The first task in the restoration of "Chant to the Fire-fly" is to locate the earliest Ojibwe text and translation. Hymes himself does not cite Schoolcraft, but rather A. Grove Days's study and anthology *The Sky Clears: Poetry of the American Indian* (1951:27-28). Day there cites Schoolcraft's monumental six-volume *Historical and Statistical Information*

Respecting the History, Condition, and Prospects of the Indian Tribes of the United States (1851-57) but without volume or page number. While serendipitous navigation in Schoolcraft's jumbled compendium always reveals items of interest, specific items are most easily located in the index prepared by Frances S. Nichols (1954). An Ojibwe text and a translation of "Chant to the Fire-fly" with the attribution "By the Indian Children" appear in the fifth volume, published in 1855 (Schoolcraft 1851-57, 5:564), but neither the text nor the translation is identical with any of those cited by Day and, following Day, Hymes. This text will be referred to here as the 1855 text.

Older anthologies give no specific source in Schoolcraft's publications for the translations they print (Judson 1914:140; Cronyn 1918:12). Two recent anthologies work from Day's presentation but acknowledge only *Historical and Statistical Information*, again without volume or page number (Brandon 1971:97; Sanders & Peek 1973:104-107). Petrone (1983:50) acknowledges Schoolcraft but actually cites Day as a source.

Only John Greenway and John Robert Colombo correctly cite sources in Schoolcraft's publications for the versions they print. Greenway (1964: 13-14) cites page 230 of Schoolcraft's *Western Scenes and Reminiscences* (1853), one of the many pirated editions of his *Oneóta, or the Red Race of America*, which first appeared in book form under that title in 1845 – and in ten additional editions under five different titles between 1847 and 1853, all from the same plates but with some pages reordered (Freeman 1959). Colombo (1983, 1:40, 111-113) cites page 61 of the 1845 edition of *Oneóta*. There appears the Ojibwe text and the translations erroneously cited by Day as being in *Historical and Statistical Information*. This text will be referred to here as the 1845 text.

Day and, following him, Hymes, Sanders & Peek and Petrone, made one copying error and introduced three silent emendations to the Ojibwe text. The Ojibwe text given by Greenway has three independent and equally silent emendations. Only Colombo presents an Ojibwe text exactly as printed by Schoolcraft.

THE FORMS OF THE TEXT

The 1845 and 1855 Ojibwe texts of Schoolcraft differ in details of transcription, grouping of syllables, punctuation, arrangement of lines, and repetition of words:

1845 Text (from *Oneóta*, p. 61)

Wau wau tay see!
Wau wau tay see!
E mow e shin
Tshe bwau ne baun-e wee!
Be eghaun—be eghaun—ewee!
Wa Wau tay see!
Wa wau tay see!
Was sa koon ain je gun
Was sa koon ain je gun.

1855 Text (from *Historical and Statistical Information*, 5:564)

Wau wau taisee, wau wau taisee,
Emow e shin tsche bwau ne baun e we,
Be-ezhaun, be-ezhaun e wee,
Wau wau taisee, wau wau taisee,
Wassa koonain djeegan.

In 1973, the texts were read to the late Selam Ross of Cass Lake, Minnesota and to Maude Kegg of Vineland, Minnesota, speakers of Ojibwe dialects quite close to the Lake Superior dialect recorded by Schoolcraft. The text resulting from the redictation and the resulting analysis is presented in a contemporary orthography, a description of which is available in Nichols & Nyholm (1979).

Reconstructed Text

waawaatesi waawaatese'amawishin
   ji-bwaa-nibaayaan E WEE.
   bi-izhaan! bi-izhaan! E WEE.
   waawaatesi, waawaatesi,
waasakonenjigan, waasakonenjigan.

The only apparent dialect differences between the words of Schoolcraft's texts and those given by the Minnesota speakers are in the variation between *waawaatesi* and *wewaatesi* 'firefly' given by Maude Kegg and in the replacement of the *s* by *z* in *waasakonenjigan* 'candle, lantern' in the Minnesota dialects due to a rule of dissimilation. The reconstructed text maintains Schoolcraft's forms. The vocable syllables E WEE have been left as spelled by Schoolcraft (with syllable division normalised) due to the difficulty of interpreting his transcriptions of non-lexical material. In the discussion of the texts, forms in their original spelling are enclosed in guillemets; all forms in the contemporary orthography are italicised.

VARIATION IN SCHOOLCRAFT'S TEXTS

Schoolcraft's transcriptions reflect Ojibwe accurately enough to allow us to recover the Ojibwe words. The inconsistencies of transcription within each version and between them are not sufficiently significant to warrant discussion here. (The carelessness, however, with which later editors treated the text is nothing new, for the 1845 version by Schoolcraft also has an error, probably introduced by the typesetter. Both instances of *bi-izhaan* 'come here!' are spelled with «gh» for the correct «zh» (for lenis [š]), which does appear in the 1855 text. Schoolcraft did not use «gh» in any of his other transcriptions of Ojibwe, and his handwritten «z» closely resembles his «g».)

Of more interest are the differences between the two texts in the division of the song into lines and in the repetitions of words. In the 1845 text Schoolcraft divided the text roughly into syllables. He used line division to indicate word division, except the fourth line where a hyphen separates *ji-bwaa-nibaayaan* 'before I sleep' from the vocable syllables «e wee» and the fifth line where *bi-izhaan* 'come here!' appears twice, with an intervening dash, followed by a dash and the vocables «ewee». In the 1855 text, some syllables were written together and each line was set to contain two words, except for the last, a single word not repeated as it had been in the 1845 text.

THE CHITTENDEN-BAKER TEXT

No performance of the "Chant to the Fire-fly" has been recorded directly from the oral tradition other than by Schoolcraft, and the Ojibwe speakers to whom his texts were presented did not recognise them. A musical setting of a variant Ojibwe text was given by Theodor Baker in his pioneering study of Native American music (1882:74), without mention of Schoolcraft, but rather with an acknowledgement to Professor T.W. Chittenden of Appleton, Wisconsin. If the Chittenden-Baker version is authentic, it would allow a comparison of the structures of the music and the text. The text resembles the 1855 version as it lacks the repetition of the last line characteristic of the 1845 version. It is given in a transcription differing from both of Schoolcraft's, but directly analogous to them. It has *bi-izhaan* 'come' with a «g» apparently borrowed from the erroneous «gh» of the 1845 version, omits the inflectional ending also omitted by Schoolcraft from *nibaayaan* 'that I sleep', and it follows the 1845 text in making an unusual division between the third and fourth syllables of *waasakonenjigan* 'candle, lantern': «was sa kun ēn dji gŭn» (Baker 1882), «Was sa koon ain je gun» (Schoolcraft 1845). Although his retranscription shows that Chittenden may have been familiar with Ojibwe, these three features derive from Schoolcraft's published texts, not from the direct transcription of sung or spoken Ojibwe. The Chittenden-Baker text thus appears to be a conflation of the two Schoolcraft texts.

According to the leading student of Ojibwe music, Thomas Vennum, Jr., the music presented by Baker is very unlikely to be of Ojibwe origin; in melodic direction, use of C# as a leading tone, tonal patterns, and use of paired phrases it is typical of European song (Vennum, letter to the author, 9 January 1978). Thus neither the text nor the music of the 1882 Chittenden-Baker version offers any new evidence for the reconstruction of "Chant to the Fire-fly".

OJIBWE SYLLABIC VERSE

Neither of Schoolcraft's Ojibwe text versions represents well the verse structure. Schoolcraft, though aware of the syllable-counting nature of much Ojibwe verse, failed to observe it here and made a major error in word division which limited the possible line arrangements available to him.

Intensely interested in what he termed "oral composition," Schoolcraft searched in vain for signs of English metrics in Ojibwe song texts. Even as he remarks on the lack of metre in the English sense, he acknowledges that the verse appears in regulated lines with "syllabical quantity:"

> It is certain that the Indian ear is exact in noting musical sounds, and in marking and beating time. But little observation at their dances, will be sufficient to establish this fact. Nor is it less certain, by attention to the philology of their language, that they are exact in their laws of euphony, and syllabical quantity. (1845:45)

He observed two main patterns of syllabic verse:

> Most of the graver pieces, which have been written out, are arranged in meters of sixes, sevens, and eights. The lighter chants are in threes or fours... (1845:45)

Many Ojibwe song texts have lines with an equal number of syllables. The line divisions always occur at a word boundary and, when the line is long enough to contain several words, also at a grammatical phrase boundary. Numerous examples can be quoted from Schoolcraft and from the collections of Frederick Burton and Frances Densmore.

Like Schoolcraft, Burton did not consider Ojibwe song texts to be metrical. Of verse in Ojibwe song texts, he noted that "it is vague; it lacks form, that is, nothing is there that corresponds to rhyme, there is seldom a suggestion of corresponding or contrasting phrases, and it is only by good fortune, apparently, that it ever assumes a metrical aspect" (1909: 153). However, song texts he transcribed often have regulated length. In the following text there are seven distinct lines, some of which are repeated, each exactly eight syllables long. The dots at the ends of lines mark the extension of the syllable to correspond to the length of tied notes in the musical setting:

> Ne-ne-mo-shayn ne-wah-ne-ah,.........
> ne-ne-mo-shayn ne-wah-ne-ah,........
> Me-go-be-nish gay-ze-wah-bung,.....
> me-go-be-nish gay-ze-wah bung,....
> Kah-ne-wah-bung ne-wah-bun-dan......
> E-ge-wiz nin-ge wah-shen-ay,........
> guay-che-gizh-o ne-ne-mo-shayn....
> a-ny wah wah sah bo-ye-zud,......
> Mahng o doog-win nind-en-en-dam.........
> a-ny-wah wah-sah bo-ye-zud.......

(Burton 1909:98)

The examples below from Densmore have been retranscribed, in some cases from the recordings of the performances, and the glosses supplied. The syllable count is given in front of each line.

> On the Bank of a Stream
>
> (7) *agaami-ziibiiwishenh*   across the stream
> (7) *endanaajimigooyaan.*   where I am said to be
>
> (Odjïb'we, in Densmore 1913:81, no. 9)

The following is of one of the "lighter chants":

> I Have Lost My Sweetheart
>
> (4) *geyaabi go*   still
> (4) *niwani'aa*   I have lost him/her
> (4) *niinimoshenh.*   my sweetheart
>
> (Ki'miwûn, in Densmore 1913:280, no. 157)

VOCABLES

Non-lexical syllables in Native American songs are called vocables; many contemporary Ojibwe song texts consist entirely of vocables. In songs with texts containing words, vocables may have multiple functions, one of which is to extend the length of a line to match a preferred number of syllables, whether required to adjust the text to the length of a musical phrase or to another line. The vocables are usually inserted at the end of a line and so function as line markers; less commonly they appear at the beginning of a line or between words in a line.

Schoolcraft observed the use of vocables, which he termed the "chorus":

> Increments of the chorus are not infrequently interspersed, in the body of the line, which would otherwise appear deficient in quantity ... (1845:45).

In the following examples the vocables are written in capitals and left in the spelling of the original source due to the difficulty of interpreting impressionistic transcriptions of non-lexical material. The lines match in the number of syllables when the vocatives are counted:

An Eagle Feather I See

(9)	*giniwigwan niwaabamaa* WE.	eagle feather / I see it
(9)	*ogichidaa nindebibinaa.*	warrior / I catch him
(9)	*giniwigwan niwaabamaa* WE.	eagle feather / I see it
(9)	*ogichidaa ninawadinaa.*	warrior / I grab him

(Odjîb'we in Densmore 1913:72, no. 3, transcription from recording)

The Song of the Butterfly

(7)	*bi-gizhaate giizhig* E	its heat comes / day
(7)	*ji-bi-naaniibawiyaan.*	that I stand about here

(Mec'kawiga'bau in Densmore 1913:179, no. 80)

Song of the Sentry

(7)	*gaye niin mistadimong*	as for / me / on a horse
(7)	*babaamoomigoyaan* E.	I'm riding around

(Ĕ'niwûb'e in Densmore 1913:186, no. 82)

VARIATION IN LINE LENGTH IN SYLLABIC VERSE

Many transcribed song texts in the collections fail to show such regular syllabic structure. In at least some cases, this is due to the preference of the collectors for obtaining what they felt to be the underlying text, rather than transcribing full performances in which word order and stock are varied, vocables are inserted, and words and lines are repeated. (The actual structure of such orally composed texts in performances can be partially recovered from the surviving cylinder recordings made by Densmore; for Schoolcraft and Burton such recordings are not available.

Unfortunately, the performances recorded by Densmore do not necessarily represent normal performances. In order to squeeze as much onto each cylinder as possible, she controlled the length of songs recorded, possibly distorting both music and text form (Vennum 1980:56-57).)

Other song texts show less than perfect regularity in line length. Variation of one syllable seems common, and Schoolcraft noted performance techniques other than the insertion of vocables which can shorten or extend lines. In the following text, a couplet with one line of seven syllables and a second line of eight syllables appears against the background of a repeated eight syllable refrain:

I Feel No Fear

gaawiin ninzhaagwenimosii	not / I feel no fear
gaawiin ninzhaagwenimosii	not / I feel no fear
gaawiin ninzhaagwenimosii	not / I feel no fear
gichi-ziibiiwinini	man of the Mississippi band
nibowin wayaawiindangin	death/whenever he speaks of it
gaawiin ninzhaagwenimosii	not / I feel no fear
gaawiin ninzhaagwenimosii	not / I feel no fear
gaawiin ninzhaagwenimosii	not / I feel no fear
gaawiin ninzhaagwenimosii	not / I feel no fear

(Odjīb'we Densmore 1913:89, no. 13)

This overall pattern of the contrast of a figure (the couplet) against the ground (the repeated refrain) is common in performance, but rarely recorded in writing by the collectors.

A less prominent pattern of contrast may be seen in song texts where a set of lines of equal length (within the allowed margin of one syllable) is framed by non-refrain lines of a different length. This overall pattern occurs in the third section of a complex text which was performed for me in 1971 by Jim Littlewolf of the Mille Lacs Band of Minnesota (Vennum 1989, audio-recording). The structure of this text has been determined from the way it is related to the musical phrase structure, as well as on metrical and linguistic grounds. There are three sections: a couplet, the first line of eight syllables and the second of seven; five lines of eleven syllables, containing a couplet sandwiched between three repetitions of a refrain; three eleven-syllable lines sandwiched between two four-syllable lines.

My Short Sweetie

gii-ayaadog niinimoshenh,
wenjibaayaan goshaa niin.

niinimoshenh goshaa wiin gaa-takoozid.
gii-minwendam goshaa wiin gii-kanoonag.
niinimoshenh goshaa wiin gaa-takoozid.
ngii-minwendam goshaa wiin gii-kanoozhid.
niinimoshenh goshaa wiin gáa-takoozid.

wenjibaayaan,
gii-ayaadog goshaa wiin niinimoshenh.
aaniish wiin naa waa-wenda-waabamag,
ndaa-ojiimaa goshaa wiin waabamag wiin,
gaa-apiitenimag wiin niinimoshenh,
gaa-takoozid.

My sweetheart must be back,
Where I come from.

My short sweetie.
She was happy when I called her.
My short sweetie.
I was happy when she called me.
My short sweetie.

Where I come from,
That's where my sweetheart must be.
I want to see her so much,
I'd kiss her if I could see her,
That's how much I think of her, my sweetheart,
The shortie.

"CHANT TO THE FIRE-FLY": THE MIDDLE SECTION

Given the metrical nature of some Ojibwe song texts, we might expect to find it in the "Chant to the Fire-fly" despite Schoolcraft's disavowal: "Metre there was none, at least, of a regular character: they were the wild improvisations of children in a merry mood" (1845:61).

As demonstrated above, vocables often mark the end of lines. In the "Chant" two such lines are so marked, here quoted (with added glosses) from the 1845 version:

(6)   Tsche bwau ne baun-e wee!   before I sleep
(8)   Be eghaun—be eghaun—ewee!   come / come

The lines differ in the number of syllables; with vocables included, six in the first and eight in the second. The actual disparity, however, is within the one typically allowed in Ojibwe syllabic song texts, for the transcription of the first line omits a syllable. The final *aa* of the verb stem *nibaa-* 'sleep' and the first-person singular suffix *-yaan* have been run together. This may be a transcription or copying error, or it may be a reflection of the deletion of *y* between two occurrences of *aa* characteristic of a number of Ojibwe dialects. This results in an extra long vowel with a noticeable dip in the middle, but may have been heard by Schoolcraft simply as a long vowel. The restoration of this syllable brings the count closer:

(7)   *jibwaa-nibaayaan* E WEE.
(8)   *bi-izhaan! bi-izhaan!* E WEE.

If the two instances of *waawaatesi* 'firefly' which follow are treated as a single line, as in Schoolcraft's 1855 text (but not the 1845 text), the next line is eight syllables long, providing the model length for the preceding two lines, and thus accounting for the appearance of the vocables:

(7)   *jibwaa-nibaayaan* E WEE.
(8)   *bi-izhaan! bi-izhaan!* E WEE.
(8)   *waawaatesi, waawaatesi,*

"CHANT TO THE FIRE-FLY": THE FIRST SECTION

The first section of the text, if Schoolcraft's word division is followed, consists of three four-syllable words. However, Schoolcraft's word division is wrong. His third word unit, «E mow e shin» (1845) / «Emow e shin» (1855), separated from the preceding unit by punctuation and a line division in both versions of the text, is not a word but rather an incomplete stretch of derivational and inflectional suffixes: *-'-amaw-i-sh-(i)n*. Schoolcraft took it as a complete verb meaning 'light (for) me' and thus interpreted the unit preceding it as a repetition of 'firefly'. However, this unit is the underlying verb stem *waawaatese-* 'there is a flashing light' to which the derivational and inflectional affixes must be attached. It is not identical to the noun *waawaatesi* although it shares with it a further underlying verb stem *waawaate-*, attested in Northern Ojibwe (where it means 'Northern Lights'). The suffixes on the intransitive stem *waawaatese-* make it into a transitive and benefactive verb stem inflected as an imperative form with a second-person singular subject and a first-person singular object: *waawaatese'amawishin* 'flash light for me!'.

We have, therefore, a four-syllable word followed by an eight-syllable word, neither separately nor together forming a line of a length matching those of the middle section. This suggests that, if the "Chant" is a syllabic song text, it has a framing pattern, as described above for the last section of Littewolf's "My Short Sweetie". It is necessary then to turn to the last section of the "Chant" to see if it matches the initial section in length, either as a two-line unit of four followed by eight syllables or a single line of twelve syllables.

"CHANT TO THE FIRE-FLY": THE LAST SECTION

The remaining section is different in the two versions. The 1845 version has *waasakonenjigan* 'candle, lantern' repeated while the 1855 version gives it only once. A count of syllables not only reveals the line structure of the text but allows us to determine that the repetition of this word in the 1845 version is authentic.

The word *waasakonenjigan* is six syllables long. If the repetition in the 1845 version is correct, there is a clear framing structure in the text with an initial line of twelve syllables matched by a final line of twelve syllables. If the single occurrence of the 1855 text were correct, we would have a single line of six syllables not matching either of the possible line arrangements of the initial section of the text.

"CHANT TO THE FIRE-FLY" RECONSTRUCTED

The proposed reconstruction of the Ojibwe text thus follows the 1845 text, but is arranged in lines to reflect the syllabic structure.

(12)   *waawaatesi waawaatese'amawishin*
(7)   *ji-bwaa-nibaayaan* E WEE.
(8)   *bi-izhaan! bi-izhaan!* E WEE.
(8)   *waawaatesi, waawaatesi,*
(12)   *waasakonenjigan, waasakonenjigan.*

The translation I offer here, while no real improvement over the 1855 translation of Schoolcraft, follows the word repetitions in the Ojibwe text without adding others and attempts to mimic the syllabic structure of the Ojibwe text by using line lengths of six and four syllables, counting *fire* as monosyllabic:

Firefly, flash light for me
     Before I sleep.
     Come here, come here!
     Firefly, firefly,
A lantern, a lantern.

REFERENCES

Baker, Theodor. 1882. *Über die Musik der nordamerikanischen Wilden.* Leipzig: Breitkopf & Härtel.

Brandon, William, ed. 1971. *The Magic World: American Indian Songs and Poems.* New York: William Morrow.

Burton, Frederick R. 1909. *American Primitive Music, with Especial Attention to the Songs of the Ojibways.* New York: Moffat, Yard.

Colombo, John Robert, ed. 1983. *Songs of the Indians.* [n.p.]: Oberon.

Cronyn, George W. 1918. *The Path on the Rainbow: An Anthology of Songs and Chants from the Indians of North America.* New York: Boni & Liveright.

Day, A. Grove. 1951. *The Sky Clears: Poetry of the American Indians.* New York: Macmillan. Reprinted, 1964, Lincoln: University of Nebraska Press.

Densmore, Frances. 1910. *Chippewa Music.* Bureau of American Ethnology Bulletin 45. Washington.

—. 1913. *Chippewa Music—II.* Bureau of American Ethnology Bulletin 53. Washington.

Freeman, John Finley. 1959. Pirated editions of Schoolcraft's *Oneóta.* *Papers of the Bibliographic Society of America* 53:252-261.

Greenway, John. 1964. *Literature among the Primitives.* Hatboro, Pennsylvania: Folklore Associates.

Hymes, Dell. 1965. Some North Pacific Coast Poems: A Problem in Anthropological Philology. *American Anthropologist* 67:316-341.

Judson, Katharine B., ed. 1914. *Myths and Legends of the Mississippi Valley and the Great Lakes.* Chicago: McClurg.

Longfellow, Henry Wadsworth. 1855. *The Song of Hiawatha.* Boston: Ticknor & Fields.

Nichols, Frances S. 1954. *Index to Schoolcraft's "Indian Tribes of the United States".* Bureau of American Ethnology Bulletin 152. Washington.

Nichols, John D., & Earl Nyholm, eds. 1979. *Ojibwewi-Ikidowinan: An Ojibwe Word Resource Book.* Occasional Publications in Minnesota Anthropology 7. St. Paul: Minnesota Archaeological Society.

Petrone, Penny, ed. 1983. *First People, First Voices.* Toronto: University of Toronto Press.

Sanders, Thomas E., & Walter W. Peek. 1973. *Literature of the American Indian.* Beverley Hills: Glencoe.

Schoolcraft, Henry R. 1845. *Oneóta, or Characteristics of the Red Race of America. From Original Notes and Manuscripts.* New York: Wiley & Putnam.

—. 1853. *Western Scenes and Reminiscences: Together with Thrilling Legends and Traditions of the Red Men of the Forest. To Which is added Several Narratives of Adventures among the Indians.* Buffalo: Derby, Orton & Mulligan.

—. 1851-1857. *Historical and Statistical Information, Respecting the History, Conditions and Prospects of the Indian Tribes of the United States.* 6 vols. Philadelphia: Lippincott, Grambo.

Vennum, Thomas, Jr. 1980. A History of Ojibwa Song Form. *Selected Reports in Ethnomusicology* 3(2):43-75.

—. 1989. *Ojibway Music from Minnesota: A Century of Song for Voice and Drum*, Minnesota Musical Traditions [audio-recording]; *Ojibway Music from Minnesota: Continuity and Change* [accompanying booklet]. St. Paul: Minnesota Historical Society Press & Minnesota State Arts Board.

Henry Kelsey's Christmas Message, 1696

David H. Pentland

Three days after Christmas, 1696, Henry Kelsey inserted a brief note in Cree in his journal:

> Arrabeck or indian language of hudsons bay

> Cakiththa keeshquebbaujwahtchee j aihttee naunneewee Ne wee No tee / Squea wan Kescot nee Kiththee Chua quoaming Pee lanee ma Newa Wha / pimmok Kagi a Nee pa autta Meshs hee woan poos co Tabbiscanuza[a]

He certainly did not intend this passage (Kelsey 1929:60-61) to be read by others – on the facing page he added "A pleasant fancy of old time which made me write in an unknown tongue because counsel is kept best in one single Breast."

Kelsey is best known as the first European to see the Canadian plains, in 1690-92. K.G. Davies (1969:311) has suggested that this portion of *The Kelsey Papers* may be "a post-journal or draft or copy of one rather than a private document," since Kelsey is sometimes referred to in the third person and the journal describes events at York Factory even when he was absent. While Kelsey may have incorporated entries from the official journal kept by Governor Henry Baley, the existing version is more likely a copy (made by a clerk under Kelsey's supervision) of a private record that Kelsey made while third in command at York Factory in 1696-97: while it contains many innocent entries like "M[r] Kelsey wth 2 hands went up y[e] river in a Cannoe" (p. 46), it also mentions two disputes between the governor and one of his officers in which "the Governor turned him out of place and house" (pp. 60, 68), and of course it includes the Cree text which would have provoked a response from London whether it could be understood or not.

Doughty and Martin show little familiarity with the text they published as part of *The Kelsey Papers* – they misdate it by three days and describe it as "half a dozen lines of Indian dialect," when it is only three lines in addition to the title – and less confidence in the transcription supervised by J.F. Kenney: "Cree, or some related dialect, but the transliteration is so uncertain that translation cannot be attempted" (Kelsey 1929:xxiii). Actually, Kelsey's handwriting is quite easy to read, and the published transcription, except perhaps for the last three letters, is flawless. The dialect is unquestionably Woods Cree, and the only reason that Doughty and Martin could not attempt a translation is that neither knew any Cree. This is not to say that the text is free of problems, of course: there are several ambiguities, and some of the words are no longer current, but the general sense of the note can be made out, showing why Kelsey did not intend it to be read by others.

Even a casual inspection suggests the general tenor of the text: the first two words are 'Everyone is drunk', and the remainder seems to be Kelsey's longing for a woman (or women in general). The linguistic details are discussed in a separate section below; a provisional free translation follows:

> Everyone is drunk because of the celebrations. I'd like to fetch a
> woman (or, my woman). I always have trouble (?) sleeping. If only
> I could see her, I'd be able to sleep, even if I got into trouble the
> same night.

The first sentence needs little explanation: Christmas and other holidays were celebrated at the Hudson's Bay Company posts by an increased consumption of food and drink (Rich 1958:603). Kelsey's journal makes no reference to the holiday – on Christmas Eve an unnamed Indian died and was cremated, and on Christmas Day three of the local Indians came in to trade – but in later years enough alcohol was drunk to worry even an eighteenth-century Committee, especially after Moose Factory burned to the ground during the 1735 Christmas party, because, it was claimed, no one was sober enough to notice the fire (Rich 1958:546-547).

The remainder of the text is more difficult, in part because of inherent ambiguities in the Cree: Kelsey's spelling does not distinguish *nātiskwēwē-* 'fetch a woman' from *nōtiskwēwē-* 'court, chase women', and either word may also have meant 'commit adultery', to judge from the modern derivatives cited by Faries (1938). The two following words are unknown to my Plains Cree consultants, but probably have something to do with Kelsey's sleep (or lack of it). The remaining phrases are more or less intelligible in modern Cree, with only minor difficulties of transcription and interpretation. In any case, the paragraph was not something to be read either by Kelsey's superiors at York Factory or by the governing committee in London.

THE AUTHOR

By 1696 we are no longer dealing with "the Boy Henry Kelsey" of popular history, but with a man close to thirty years of age, third in the hierarchy of York Factory.

E.E. Rich (1946:124) denied that "Henry Kellseyes Indenture Dated 1676" in a 1683 inventory of HBC documents has anything to do with the explorer and fur trader, because our Kelsey "was reputed to be only six years of age in 1676." However, Alice Johnson has shown that payments were posted to Henry Kelsey's account following the expiration of a seven-year indenture beginning 15 March 1676/7 (Davies & Johnson 1965:376, 381), and K.G. Davies (1969:308) presents evidence that he was born "not later than the summer of 1667." Therefore, when George Geyer was told in 1688 to send "the Boy Henry Kelsey" to explore inland (Kelsey 1929:xiii), he was already at least 21, and Joseph Robson's later account of "a little boy" who ran off with the Indians (Robson 1752:72) is only a legend which he heard ten or twenty years after Kelsey's death. In 1682 John Nixon had recommended that the company send out "lykly country lads of 17 or 18 years of age" (Rich 1945:251); when Kelsey was "entertained in the Company's Service for 4 years as their Apprentice" (Rich 1946:232) in 1684 he would have been exactly the kind of material Nixon had sought.

But the legend dies hard. Although Kenney (1929:40) had already recognized that Kelsey was probably older than most apprentices – his agreement in 1684 was for only four years instead of the usual seven – most later writers still named 1670 as his year of birth. Rich (1958:296) suggested that he may have been "a poor relation of the 'Captain Kelsey' who had supplied the Committee with a dinner in 1669," but there is not a word of truth in Paul Thistle's description of Kelsey in 1690 as "a slight youth recently swept up from the mean streets of London, apprenticed to the HBC only six years earlier at the age of fourteen" (Thistle 1986:15).

KELSEY'S WIFE

Another part of the legend passed on by Joseph Robson (1752:72) was that when Kelsey returned from the plains in 1692,

> he came down with a party of Indians, dressed after their manner, and attended by a wife, who wanted to follow him into the factory. The governor opposed this; but upon Kelsey's telling him in English, that he would not go in himself if his wife was not suffered to go in, he knew him, and let them both enter.

There is no confirmation elsewhere of Robson's tale, but Jennifer Brown (1980:52-53) considers it plausible, even though it is the only recorded case before 1700 of an HBC employee taking an Indian wife. That the records do not mention a woman living with Kelsey is no mystery. As early as 1679, Governor Jóhn Nixon had complained about the "licentiousness" of HBC employees (Rich & Johnson 1948:xxxvi); in response the Committee (1948:40-41) wrote in 1682:

> We are very sensibly [sic] that the Indian Weoman resorting to our Factories are very prejudiciall to the Companies affaires... It is therefore our possitive order that you lay your strict Commands on every Cheife of each Factory upon forfiture of Wages not to Suffer any wooman to come within any of our Factories... and if not withstanding all this, there shall bee any refactory Persons that shall Presume to entertaine, any Weaman, let us have an account of them by the first Opertunity and wee will not faile to send for them home for we cannot never Expect good Servises from such, whome neither the Lawes of God or Man can restraine from Wickedness.

Similar instructions were issued almost every year for the next century, but with little effect – the Cree sought marriage ties with the traders (Van Kirk 1980:28-29), the Committee was far away, and men faced with a long term of residence on Hudson Bay would have had few qualms about disobeying the regulation if they could.

When in 1692 Governor Geyer refused to allow an Indian woman to enter the fort with Kelsey, he was simply following instructions; when he relented and let the couple in, he could be reasonably confident that unless he himself reported the incident London would never hear of it. Indeed, there may already have been other Indian women at York Factory when Kelsey arrived, including one in Geyer's quarters – certainly the men in charge of York Factory and Churchill a generation later (James Isham and Richard Norton) had such arrangements, and from John Nixon's complaints back in 1679 we know that they were far from the first to do so.

It is likely that by 1696 Kelsey's Indian wife was no longer at his side. A year after his return from the plains Kelsey sailed for England. He came back the following summer, but only two months later York Factory was captured by the French. After spending a hard winter in the woods Kelsey was sent to France with the other surviving prisoners; he did not return until the fort was retaken in September 1696. A year later York was surrendered a second time, ending Kelsey's "Tedious winter & tragical Journal," and he married Elizabeth Dix in his home town of East

Greenwich soon after his release from captivity (Davies 1969:311, 313). While the newly-married Kelsey was soon back in the Company's service, York Factory remained in French hands for the next seventeen years: not until 1714 did Kelsey return to his old haunts. During the winter of 1694-95 more than half of the English prisoners died of starvation (Whillans 1955:152). If Kelsey's companion was still with him, she may have had a similar fate; more likely she had already rejoined her own family or another group of Indians. The Cree text can be interpreted as suggesting that she was still alive and near the fort in December 1696, but not in Kelsey's quarters.

THE CREE TEXT

When he supervised the transcription of the manuscript (in the Public Record Office of Northern Ireland), J.F. Kenney assumed that the entire notebook was in Kelsey's handwriting, but later reached the conclusion that "the only part of Kelsey's book written by his own hand is the Indian entry" (Kenney 1929:39). It appears that when the clerk working under Kelsey's supervision came to this paragraph he wrote the title, then Kelsey himself copied out the Cree text.

The text requires little emendation to make sense of the Cree. Kelsey's «j» is the vowel «i», not a consonant, and his «l» is an uncrossed «t». The unusual combination «meshs» is probably a copying error for «meshe», and the following «hee» is then a misreading of «hoo». The last few letters are puzzling, and this is the only place I venture to disagree with Kenney's transcription.

The interpretation has been greatly assisted by the fact that of the thirteen words in the text, more than half appear in Kelsey's dictionary (1709), even though the dictionary is almost entirely restricted to words necessary for trading. Some entries are spelled exactly the same, and the others vary only within the relatively narrow limits of Kelsey's orthography. This impressive correspondence is especially important in the case of «Kescot»: Kelsey's is the only Cree vocabulary which lists the word, and it is unknown to modern speakers of the language.

LINGUISTIC COMMENTARY

«Arrabeck or indian language of hudsons bay» [title]. It is unclear whether «Arrabeck» is Kelsey's name for the Indian language of Hudson Bay (i.e., Cree) or, as far-fetched as it may seem, a misspelling of *Arabic* (with "Arabic-or-Indian" meaning little more than 'exotic'). If «Arrabeck» is a Cree word, it is probably to be phonemicized *aðāpēk*, but its meaning is obscure: it is not 'Cree language' (which would be *nēhiðawēwin* in

Woods Cree), nor is it the name of a well-known place or group of
Indians. The most curious feature of the word is its first consonant: there
was no *r* in the dialect Kelsey spoke. In the seventeenth century there
were two Cree dialects with *r*, one spoken in the district between Rupert
House and Moose Factory, the other on the Churchill River in Manitoba.
Kelsey could have picked up the name «Arrabeck» from either area: he
may have sailed to "the bottom of the bay" during his first
apprenticeship, and certainly knew men who had been posted there, and
he had very likely met speakers of the Manitoba *r*-dialect at Churchill.

«Cakiththa keeshquebbauj» *kahkiðaw kīškwēpēw* 'everyone is drunk'.
The combination «auj» is assumed to be equivalent to «ai», one of
Kelsey's usual spellings of Cree *ē*. Both words are in Kelsey's dictionary,
the first with exactly the same spelling («ca kith tha» 'all'), the second in
its stem form («kees squea bea» 'drunk', with incorrect «squ» for «shqu»).
In the text, as in his later dictionary, Kelsey omitted final *w* in both
words. In modern Plains Cree the verb would normally be plural, with
-wak rather than singular *-w*.

«wahtchee j aihttee naunneewee» *wēhci-ayēhtināniwik* (?) 'because of the
party, get-together'. The proposed interpretation requires the first «a» to
be interpreted as *ē*; alternatively, Kelsey may have intended *ohci-* (for
which «wahtchee» is a possible spelling), but its grammaticality is
questionable. The verb *ayēhtināniwi-* seems to be unattested: Kelsey's
spelling is unambiguous, but the nearest Plains Cree word my
consultants could suggest is *ayahtināniwi-* 'be a rendezvous, a place where
people gather'. If I have put the sentence together correctly the verb must
end in *-k*, but Kelsey often omits inflections.

«Ne wee Notee Squea wan» *niwī-nātiskwēwān* 'I'm going to, I'd like to
get a woman'. My translation is deliberately vague, because Kelsey's
orthography is ambiguous at the critical point: «not-» can represent either
nāt- or *nōt-*, and both roots are attested with the incorporated noun stem
-iskwēw- 'woman' («e squeaw» in Kelsey's dictionary). The most likely
verb is *nātiskwēwē-*, which can mean either 'fetch a woman' (Bloomfield
1984:170) or (to judge from its derivative *nātiskwēwāt-*, Faries 1938:353)
'commit adultery'. However, **nōtiskwēwē-* is historically expected beside
the attested *nōciskwēwē-* (and *nōcihiskwēwē-*) 'court women' (Bloomfield
1984:191), with derivatives again suggesting the alternative meaning
'commit adultery'. In modern Plains Cree the preverb *wī-* usually means
'going to', but eastern dialects still have the older meaning 'want, like to'.

«Kescot nee Kiththee Chua quoming» *kēskat nikiðiciwāhkwāmin* 'I
always [have trouble (?) getting to] sleep'. The first word is in Kelsey's
dictionary («kess cutt» 'always') but has not been found in any later Cree

vocabulary; however, the Montagnais cognate, *čēskat* 'often', is still current in the James Bay dialect (MacKenzie et al. 1987:278). The verb ends in *-in*: Kelsey's «-ing» is a hypercorrect spelling reflecting his pronunciation of the English suffix «-ing» as *-in*. The final element in the verb is almost certainly *-(ā)hkwāmi-* 'sleep', but the preceding part is unidentified, and the phonemic transcription is no more than a guess based on Kelsey's spelling of other words. The context demands a word meaning 'I have trouble sleeping' (Plains Cree *nikoskohkwāmin*) or 'I pretend to sleep' (Plains Cree *ninipēhkāson*), but the most similar forms that can be invented are **nikiðakihkwāmin* 'I itch while sleeping' and **nikiðāskihkwāmin* 'I lie about sleeping, pretend to sleep'.

«Pee lanee ma Newa Wha pimmok» *pitanima wā-wāpamak* 'if only I could see him'. The manuscript has a clear «l» in «Pee lanee ma», but there is no *l* in Woods Cree. An emendation to «Pee tanee ma» gives a recognizable word, *pitanima* 'if only, would that', and there are other examples of «l» for «t» in Kelsey's dictionary:

«Squil tay wau boe» 'brandy'	*iškotēwāpōw* 'liquor';
«Miss sitt» "fool"	*misit* 'a foot'.

In Kelsey's dictionary the entry is «pit taun ny mau» 'wish', showing that while his spellings are usually unambiguous they are far from consistent. The following verb is undoubtedly *wāpam-* 'see', but it must be emended either to *niwā-wāpamik* 'he sees me' (independent, with the vowels of the last two syllables accidentally reversed) or *wā-wāpamak* 'that I see him' (conjunct, with *ni-* erroneously added by analogy with the corresponding independent form, *niwā-wāpamāw* 'I see him'). The second reading is preferred by the Cree speakers I have consulted, despite its requiring us to ignore the entire syllable «Ne-», and it fits the context better. Since the Cree gender system contrasts animate and inanimate rather than masculine, feminine and neuter, the phrase can equally well be translated 'if only I could see her'.

«Kagi a Nee pa» *nika-kī-nipā* 'I would be able to sleep'. Although the syllable «a» is very clearly written, there is no way to fit it into the transcription: it is probably just a false start that Kelsey forgot to cross out. The verb appears twice in Kelsey's dictionary, as «ne paou» 'asleep' (i.e., *nipāw* 'he sleeps') and «ne pan» 'sleep' (i.e., {*ni*}*nipān* 'I sleep') with the dictionary's usual omission of the first-person prefix; the transcription assumes that Kelsey similarly omitted the prefix *ni-* before *ka-kī-* 'be able'.

«autta meshs hee woan» *āta mēšihowān* 'even if I get into trouble'. If «meshs hee» is a copying error for «meshe hoo», Kelsey's spelling would correspond perfectly with the proposed interpretation. The ending *-wān* is not attested elsewhere in Cree, though the eastern dialects have the longer ending *-wānē* in the conjunct dubitative paradigm. In Ojibwa (as in Proto-Algonquian), *-wān* is part of the negative verb paradigm. Alternatively, Kelsey may have intended *mēšihoyān*, with the ordinary conjunct suffix *-yān*, but his spelling would then be defective.

«poos co Tabbiscanuza^a» *pōsko-tipisk(āw?)* 'the same night'. Both words are in Kelsey's dictionary, as «pose co» 'some' and «ta bis cau» 'night' respectively. In all modern Cree dialects the particle meaning 'night' is *tipisk*, but Old Woods Cree may have had *tapisk* or *tapiskāw* – Kelsey twice gives «ta-», and James Isham (1949:6, 49, 56) consistently wrote «to-». The real mystery lies in the last three syllables, whether we follow Kenney in reading «-anura^d» or read «-anuza^a»: no such suffixes occur in modern Cree. Kelsey may have miscopied «Tabbiscauw» *tapiskāw* 'it is night', reading «u» as «n» and «w» as «ur» or «uz», with a final flourish being taken as «a^a».

KELSEY'S COMPETENCE IN CREE

In 1696, despite more than twenty-five years' contact with the Cree, the Hudson's Bay Company still did not have more than two or three employees who could understand any Indian language. James Knight was the governor at Albany, and Henry Kelsey was third in command at York Factory, under two ship-captains, Henry Baley and his deputy Nicholas Smithsend (Rich & Johnson 1967:283). Twenty years later only one additional man who could speak Cree had been added to the roster at York Factory, when in August 1717 James Knight sent William Stewart "to be Assistant to my Dep^ty In case he Should doo otherways than well, their not being a Man their [except, of course, the deputy governor, Henry Kelsey] as Understandeth one Word of Indian" (Kenney 1932:170).

Even a limited Cree vocabulary was a rare and valuable accomplishment among the early employees of the HBC: some of the men put in charge of posts no doubt knew no more than a few phrases, the numbers, and the names of trade goods. Only two of the traders recorded enough Cree to permit an assessment of their fluency in the language – Henry Kelsey and James Isham. Isham, chief at York Factory and Churchill from 1737 to 1761, included a lengthy vocabulary in his *Observations on Hudsons Bay, 1743* (1949). Isham's spelling – of English as well as the various Indian languages represented in the vocabulary – is very shaky, but he seems to have known a respectable number of Cree words. His 'Discourses upon different subjects of English & Indian', however, reveal a weak command of Cree grammar, with verbs often failing to agree with their subjects or objects, and other gross violations of Cree syntax.

Kelsey's competence in Cree was probably somewhat greater than Isham's, and he was a better speller. Unfortunately, we do not have any sentences other than this little text to show whether Kelsey understood such complexities of Cree grammar as the animate/inanimate gender system (and hence the AI/II and TA/TI distinctions in verbs), obviation, and the use of the conjunct. Probably neither Kelsey nor Isham could speak Cree free of basic grammatical errors on a consistent basis – some sentences would have been correct and idiomatic, either by luck or from having heard a similar sentence from a fluent speaker, but others would have suffered from inappropriate word choices, lack of concord (e.g., an inanimate noun with an animate verb, as in Isham's *nama kēkwān niwāpamāw* 'I didn't see anything', for *nama kēkwān niwāpahtēn*), or an incorrect selection of verb inflections (like Isham's *kimāham* for *kimāhēn* 'you came down the river'). However, the Indians probably understood the traders' Cree well enough, and that was sufficient for successful business dealings.

Certainly the governing committee of the HBC was satisfied with Kelsey's command of the language. In 1710 they wrote "you doe well to Educate the men in Literature but Especially in the Language that in time wee may send them to Travell If wee see it Convenient" (HBCA A.6/3, fo. 101v), and they printed up his little dictionary "that you may the Better Instruct the young Ladds with you, in ye Indian Language" (ibid., fo. 102). Of course the committee had no way to judge Kelsey's fluency – all they knew was that he spoke Cree better than their other employees, and for twenty years had been able to communicate with monolingual Indians.

The text contains several phrases whose grammaticality is in doubt. In modern Cree *kahkiðaw* 'all' usually takes a plural verb, but Kelsey uses a singular in 'everyone is drunk'; this may be just a dialect difference rather than an error, but the verb in the following phrase definitely requires an ending, probably -*k*. The phrase 'if only I could see her' has an impossible combination of the independent order first-person prefix *ni*- and the conjunct order suffix -*ak*, or else is a misspelling of 'if only she could see me', with a less likely form of the verb following *pitanima*. As mentioned in the linguistic commentary above, the final three syllables of the text are either miscopied or an ending unknown to speakers of modern Cree.

Kelsey's dictionary contains only one short paragraph on a grammatical topic, the formation of possessed nouns, but that is a curious mixture of accurate and wildly inaccurate information. He gives the following paradigm:

Noos ka jick	'my awl'
Koos ka jick	'thine awl'
Woos ka jick	'their [sic] or his awl'
Ne thaun Noos ka jick coom	'our awl'
Ke tha woa koos ka jick coom	'your awl'
We thaw woa oos ka jick coom	'their awl'

The singulars are correct, or nearly so: *nōskācik* (or *nōskācikom?*) 'my awl', etc. But the plurals are entirely wrong, with the independent personal pronouns substituted for the required possessive suffixes: *nīðān nōskācikom* for *nōskācikominān* 'our awl', etc. If this is a fair sample of Kelsey's Cree, he had only a beginner's knowledge of nominal inflections; how he coped with the thousand or more verbal inflections we can only guess.

As an example of early Cree prose Kelsey's Christmas message leaves much to be desired. We have far longer (and more easily interpreted) specimens from James Isham, and a better sample of Kelsey's own vocabulary range in his dictionary. But this little text has an importance all its own, as the earliest surviving example of fur-trader Cree, as the first written text composed in any Indian language in what is now western Canada, and as the only contemporary record of Henry Kelsey's private feelings during the long winter nights of December 1696.

NOTE

The decipherment of Kelsey's text could not have been attempted without the assistance of George J. Jimmy and Freda Ahenakew. When I first worked on the text more than fifteen years ago I managed to identify only half a dozen unconnected words: they have filled in the gaps, explained the syntax, and provided translations which made for a much less uncertain interpretation. *Ninanāskomāwak.*

REFERENCES

Bloomfield, Leonard. 1984. *Cree-English Lexicon*. New Haven, Connecticut: Human Relations Area Files.

Brown, Jennifer S.H. 1980. *Strangers in Blood: Fur Trade Company Families in Indian Country*. Vancouver & London: University of British Columbia Press.

Davies, K.G. 1969. Henry Kelsey. *Dictionary of Canadian Biography* 2: 307-315.

—, & A.M. Johnson, eds. 1965. *Letters from Hudson Bay 1703-40*. Publications of the Hudson's Bay Record Society, 25. London.

Faries, Richard, ed. 1938. *A Dictionary of the Cree Language as Spoken by the Indians in the Provinces of Quebec, Ontario, Manitoba, Saskatchewan and Alberta*. Toronto: General Synod of the Church of England in Canada.

Hudson's Bay Company Archives (HBCA), Winnipeg. A.6/3. London correspondence outwards.

Isham, James. 1949. *Observations on Hudsons Bay, 1743*. E.E. Rich & A.M. Johnson, eds., Publications of the Champlain Society, Hudson's Bay Company series, 12. Toronto.

Kelsey, Henry. [1709]. *A Dictionary of the Hudson's-Bay Indian Language*. [London].

—. 1929. *The Kelsey Papers*. A.G. Doughty & C. Martin, eds. Ottawa: Public Archives of Canada / Public Record Office of Northern Ireland.

Kenney, James F. 1929. The Career of Henry Kelsey. *Transactions of the Royal Society of Canada*, 3rd series, v. 23, section II, 37-71.

—, ed. 1932. *The Founding of Churchill; Being the Journal of Captain James Knight … 1717*. Toronto, London & Vancouver: J. M. Dent & Sons.

MacKenzie, Marguerite, et al. 1987. *Cree Lexicon, Eastern James Bay Dialects*. Baie-de-la-Poste, Mistassini Lake, Quebec: Cree School Board.

Rich, E.E., ed. 1945-46. *Minutes of the Hudson's Bay Company 1679-1684*. Publications of the Champlain Society, Hudson's Bay Company series, 8-9. Toronto.

—. 1958-59. *The History of the Hudson's Bay Company 1670-1870*. Publications of the Hudson's Bay Record Society, 21-22. London.

—, & A.M. Johnson, eds. 1948. *Copy-book of Letters Outward &c* [1679-94]. Publications of the Champlain Society, Hudson's Bay Company series, 11. Toronto.

—, & A.M. Johnson, eds. 1957. *Hudson's Bay Copy Booke of Letters Commissions Instructions Outward 1688-1696*. Publications of the Hudson's Bay Record Society, 20. London.

Robson, Joseph. 1752. *An Account of Six Years Residence in Hudson's-Bay, from 1733 to 1736, and 1744 to 1747*. London.

Thistle, Paul C. 1986. *Indian-European Trade Relations in the Lower Saskatchewan River Region to 1840*. Winnipeg: University of Manitoba Press.

Van Kirk, Sylvia. 1980. *"Many Tender Ties": Women in Fur-trade Society in Western Canada, 1670-1870*. Winnipeg: Watson & Dwyer.

Whillans, James W. 1955. *First in the West: The Story of Henry Kelsey, Discoverer of Canadian Prairies*. Edmonton: Applied Art Products.

The Syllabification of Verb Prefixes in Halfway River Beaver

Tiina Randoja

Linguists believe that language is rule-governed; that is, in looking at any aspect of language (phonology, morphology, syntax, discourse, etc.), linguists expect to find patterns that can be characterised by some degree of logic, naturalness and simplicity, qualities which are often summarised in the term "elegance." Often, one encounters language data in which patterns of any kind are not immediately discernible; sometimes, patterns elude discovery even after painstaking analysis. It is possible to conclude in such a case that the data constitute a true exception to the expected systematic character of language. It is equally possible, however, that the apparent bizarreness of the data is an indication of the inadequacy of the theoretical eyeglasses used to perceive and analyse the facts. In the latter circumstance, complex data serve the valuable function of challenging existing theories and encouraging new perspectives. In this study, morphophonemic alternations in verb prefixes in Halfway River Beaver constitute the complex data referred to, which indeed appear unsystematic when analysed within the theory of linear phonology, but which reveal an inherent logic and predictability when reanalysed within the prosodic theory of syllabification as articulated by Itô (1986, 1989).

Halfway River Beaver (HRB) is a Northern Athapaskan language spoken in northern British Columbia; it shares general phonological and morphological properties with neighbouring languages, particularly the Sekani language spoken at McLeod Lake, as documented by Hargus (1988). The alternation facts are presented first, with rules drawn from earlier accounts of similar phenomena. In the next section, these alternations receive a straightforward explanation when viewed in terms of mapping a syllable template. This new analysis requires us to allow extraprosodicity to be defined on an internal prefix domain, which is an apparent violation of the Peripherality Condition (Hayes 1981). Finally, we discuss the motivation for this aspect of the analysis, which is based on a view of verb formation found in Randoja (1990a) among others.

As a background to the data presented below, (1) gives a schematic representation of surface verb structure, where 12 prefix positions, numbered 0 to 11 by convention, are identified:

(1)

Prefix position:	0 1 2 3 4	#	[5 6 7 8 9 10]	11 stem
	Disjunct		Conjunct	

0 oblique object + postposition (pp)	6 deictic subject (dc S)
1 adverbial (adv)	7 derivational (der)
2 incorporated stem (inc st)	8 conjugation (cnj)
3 customary/reversative (rev)	9 mode (m)
4 distributive (dist)	10 subject (S)
5 (direct) object (O, DO)	11 classifier/voice (cl)

Determining the identity of some of the positions is not straightforward, especially when prefixes are obscured by complex morphophonemic alternations; the labelling chosen in (1) follows many of the assumptions of Hargus (1988) and Rice (1989) with respect to position identification. The labels DISJUNCT and CONJUNCT found beneath the numbers distinguish sets of prefixes with differing phonological characteristics. Some of these differing characteristics derive from the fact that disjunct prefixes were historically separate adverbial-type stems, later incorporated into the verb, in contrast with conjunct prefixes, which have always been part of the verb (cf. Li 1933, Kari 1975).

CONJUNCT PREFIX ALTERNATIONS

The data to be analysed consist of alternations in the conjunct domain where the shape of certain prefixes varies between CV and C; when surfacing as C, the prefix is either a coda or an onset. (2) is an example of the 2sS agreement prefix of position 10 undergoing some of these alternations.

(2)   (Note: ən]$_\sigma$ → i)

(a)   (i)   danəle   'you sg. hang it up (meat)'
          = [da -   [nə] -   le]
             1   10   stem
             adv   2sS   'handle pl.Ø'

      (ii)   nəȷ̃in   'you sg. sing'
          = [[nə] -   ȷ̃in]
             10   stem
             2sS   'sing'

(b)   (i)   zị̢xił   'you sg. kill sg.Ø'
       = [[zə -   n̲] -   xił]
           7   10   stem
           der   2sS   'kill sg.Ø'

       (ii)   ʔ ə nị̢ʔị̢   'you sg. steal Ø'
       = [[ʔə -   nə -   n̲] -   ị̢]
           5   7   10   stem
           0   der   2sS   'steal Ø'

In these representations, plain square brackets enclose the word, and boldface square brackets enclose the conjunct domain. The alternating prefix is underlined. The (a) examples show the prefix having the shape *nə* while the (b) examples show the prefix having the shape *n*-coda, which surfaces as ị̢ (nasalised *i*). The ən]$_\sigma$ in the parenthesised note on the first line of (2) explains that this ị̢ is derived from a rime consisting of schwa and *n*, so that the (b) alternant is really the coalescence of the vowel of the preceding prefix and the 2sS prefix having the shape *n*-coda. That is, in (b*i*), the schwa of position 7 *zə* coalesces with position 10 *n* and surfaces as ị̢.

Similar alternations in Navajo (Kari 1975), Sarcee (Cook 1984) and Sekani (Hargus 1988) have been noted and accounted for by linear rules such as that in (3):

(3)

ə → Ø / # ...Vn ___   (# = disjunct boundary)

This rule of 'nə-Absorption' (Hargus 1988) assumes that the 2sS prefix is underlyingly /nə/, and schwa is deleted whenever there is another conjunct vowel preceding *n*. This is indicated by the use of the disjunct boundary in (3).

One of the shortcomings of this approach to the alternation is that it accounts for the deletion of schwa in only a limited set of cases; other deletion rules, in addition to (3), are required to delete the same vowel, schwa. Thus, another deletion rule in (4) is posited to account for the alternations in (5), (6) and (7), and a further ə-deletion rule in (8) is posited to account for the alternations in (9), (10) and (11). (All of these rules were formulated for Sekani, but work equally well for the HRB data.)

(4)

$$\text{ə} \rightarrow \text{Ø} \,/\, \# \,...\text{V} \begin{Bmatrix} s \\ n \\ gh \end{Bmatrix} \underline{\qquad} \, [_1 \qquad \begin{array}{l} \# = \text{disjunct boundary} \\ [_1 = \text{stem boundary} \end{array}$$

$$\begin{Bmatrix} [\text{+cnj}] \\ [\text{+m }] \end{Bmatrix}$$

(5)

(a) (i)   səda   's/he sits'
= [[sə] -   da]
    8   stem
    cnj   'sit'

   (ii)   tusəkwən   's/he has a fever'
= [tu -   [sə] - kwən]
    1   8   stem
    adv   cnj   'be hot'

(b) (i)   tadèsła   's/he lost Ø'
= [ta -   [dè - s] -   ła]
    1   7   8   stem
    adv   der   cnj   'handle Ø'

   (ii)   sònawədèskał   's/he yawns'
= [sòna -   [wə -   dè -   s] -   kał]
    1   5   7   8   stem
    adv   Ø   der   cnj   'yawn'

(6)

(a) (i)   ts'enəssəts   'I get up'
= [ts'e -   [nə   -s]   -səts]
    1   8   10   stem
    adv   cnj   1sS   'get up'

   (ii)   ts'ewùnəsʔàʔ   'I wake them up'
= [ts'e -   [wù - nə -   s] -   ʔàʔ]
    1   5   8   10   stem
    adv   3pØ   cnj   1sS   'wake up Ø'

(b) (*i*)   ts'esį̀ʔàʔ   's/he wakes me up'

= [ts'e -   [sə̀ -   n̲] -   ʔàʔ]
    1   5   8   stem
   adv   1sØ   cnj   'wake up Ø'

(*ii*)   ts'esəghį̀ʔàʔ   'they wake me up'

= [tṣ'e -   [sə -   ghə -   n̲] -   ʔàʔ]
   1   5   6   8   stem
  adv   1sØ   3pS   cnj   'wake up Ø'

(7)

(a)   ʔəghəstı̀ts   'I ate Ø'

= [[ʔə -   ghə -   s]   tsı̀ts]
   5   8   10   stem
   Ø   cnj   1sS   'eat Ø'

(b)   ʔatsı̀ts   's/he ate Ø'

= [[ʔə -   gh̲] -   tsı̀ts]
   5   8   stem
   Ø   cnj   'eat Ø'

(8)

ə → Ø / _____ V

(9)

(a)   yàsəya   's/he swam across'

= [yà -   [sə̲] -   ya
   1   8   stem
  adv   cnj   'motion'

(b)   yàsaya   'you pl. swam across'

= [yà -   [s̲ -   a] -   ya
   1   8   10   stem
  adv   cnj   2pS   'motion'

(10)

(a)   ʔ ə nə ʔį̀   's/he steals Ø'
= [[ʔ ə -   nə] -   ʔį̀]
    5   7   stem
    Ø   der   'steal Ø'

(b) (i)   ʔ ə na ʔį̀   'you pl. steal Ø'
= [[ʔ ə - n -   a] -   ʔį̀]
    5   7   10   stem
    Ø   der   2pS   'steal Ø'

   (ii)   ʔ ə nu ʔį̀è   's/he wants to steal Ø'
= [[ʔ ə - n -   u] - ʔį̀è]
    5   7   9   stem
    Ø   der   m   'steal Ø'

(11)

(a)   w ə d ə ǰè   's/he talks'
= [[wə - də] - ǰè]
    5   7   stem
    Ø   der   'talk'

(b)(i)   w ə daǰè   'you pl. talk'
= [[wə - d   -a] - ǰè]
    5   7   10   stem
    Ø   der   2pS   'talk'

(b) (ii)   w ə duǰèè   's/he talks'
= [[wə - d -   u] - ǰèè]
    5   7   9   stem
    Ø   der   m   'talk'

The rule in (4) assumes that there are three conjugation or mode prefixes, sə, nə and ghə (where gh = [ɣ]). The schwa of any of these prefixes is deleted if a conjunct vowel precedes the prefix and the prefix is immediately before the stem boundary, that is, the prefix is the rightmost prefix in the conjunct domain. Although the formulation of the rule does not show it, the deletion is also conditioned by which classifier is present to the right of the stem boundary. (5a) thus shows sə conjugation in its assumed underlying form, while (5b) shows the s-coda alternant

THE SYLLABIFICATION OF VERB PREFIXES   145

produced by the application of rule (4). In the (5a) examples, the sə
prefix is not preceded by another conjunct vowel, so the rule does not
apply; in the (5b) examples the sə prefix is in the environment for
ə-deletion. Parallel examples of the alternants of the other two prefixes
mentioned in the rule are given in (6) and (7).

The rule in (8) is more straightforward, and simply deletes the schwa
of any conjunct prefix when it is followed by a vocalic conjunct prefix. In
the (a) forms of (9), (10) and (11) the assumed underlying CV forms of
prefixes are given. The (b) examples show the same prefixes as C onsets
preceding a vocalic prefix such as position 10 *a* marking 'you plural'
subject.

While these particular linear rules do provide an analysis of the facts,
they are arbitrary. Because linear rules are unrelated to syllable structure,
they must attribute at least part of the alternant conditioning to factors
such as the morphological identity of the target prefixes and the
segmental content of the conjunct domain, as rule (4) does. Using these
conditioning environments in the absence of general principles which can
explain their relevance, we can imagine a language with the same syllable
patterns as HRB but having rules such as (12).

(12)

(a) ə → $\emptyset$ / $\begin{Bmatrix} gh \\ ts' \end{Bmatrix}$ _____ C[$_1$]   Output: /da -ghə - s - [$_1$la/

$\quad\quad\quad$ [+dc S]   → *[da<u>ghsl</u>a]

(b) ə → $\emptyset$ / Vn _____   Output: /ts'e -wù - nə - s - ʔàʔ/

$\quad\quad\quad\quad\quad\quad\quad\quad\quad\quad\quad\quad$ → *[ts'ewù<u>ns</u>ʔàʔ]

(12a) deletes schwa of deictic subject prefixes provided there is a
following consonant before the stem boundary. (12b) is an overgenerating
version of nə-Absorption. These rules, I would claim, would never be
posited in a language with the syllable patterns of HRB, because they can
create triconsonantal clusters such as those underlined in the asterisked
outputs which do not adhere to the syllable structure conditions of the
language. This gap in rule possibilities, however, is unexplained in linear
theory.

The alternation facts are summarised in (13):

(13)

(a)	C (onset)	/ _____ vocalic prefix
(b)	C (coda)	/ conjunct prefix _____]
(c)	CV / {	_____ conjunct prefix ...] } [_____]

The onset consonant alternant, (13a), occurs when the following morpheme consists of, or at least begins with, a vowel; the coda C alternant, (13b), occurs when the prefix is final in the conjunct domain and preceded by another conjunct prefix; the CV alternant, (13c), occurs when the prefix is non-final in the conjunct domain *or* is the only prefix in the conjunct domain, as indicated by the use of boldface square brackets to enclose the conjunct domain.

HRB SYLLABIFICATION: A PROSODIC PHONOLOGY ANALYSIS

The prosodic theory of syllabification given in Itô (1986, 1989) assumes that syllabification is continuous, maximal and exhaustive, so that every segment must be prosodically licensed in some way, most commonly by belonging to a syllable. Syllabification consists of continuously mapping the phonological string to the syllable template of the language. A syllable template is a kind of well-formedness condition defining the possible sequences of units within the syllables of a language. These units may be variously defined. In this paper, a CV-skeletal type of template is used for HRB, but other template units are possible, e.g., onset-nucleus-coda, X-bar constituents, or moraic weight units. Beyond the simple sequencing given by the template, other parameters of prosodic and syllable theory guide syllabification, such as Extaprosodicity. All the generalisations in (13) can be accounted for in a straightforward manner using these conditions and parameters within a version of the Lexical Phonology framework (cf. Kiparsky (1982) among others).

To begin with, the pre-word-level syllable template of HRB forms core syllables, i.e. syllables of the form [CV], as shown in (14):

(14)

[CV]

This template is continuously matched to the phonological string to form syllables and thus license elements in the string.

Itô (1986) observes that there may be failure to achieve a one-to-one match between each syllable template constituent and segments in the string. Specifically, segmental material (usually a consonant) may be left over after the template is mapped across the string; this unmatched, unsyllabified material is considered to be "stray" and is unlicensed. In Itô's theory, there are two ways of dealing with stray elements: they are deleted by "Stray Erasure," a universal option, or a vowel is inserted into the string to allow a further mapping of the syllable template, thus saving the initially unsyllabifiable material. This is known as "Stray Epenthesis," a parameterised option.

Before we apply this model to HRB, a comment must be made about underlying representations. In the linear analysis, the alternating prefixes are assumed to be underlyingly CV, where the deleted V is always schwa. The general predictability of the prefix vowel in similar alternations in Navajo leads Wright (1983) to assume that alternating conjunct prefixes consist only of C on the skeletal tier. I follow this assumption. Thus, a CV template is mapped to the assumed underlying representations in (15), which repeats (5a*i*).

(15) = (5a*i*)

<pre>
                          sə dà   's/he sits'
         Input to σ mapping: [[s]   dà]
                                C   CV

σ mapping,
Stray Epenthesis: [[s]   d à]
                       C V̲   C V
                        \/   \/
                        σ   σ
</pre>

Eventually: sə dà

The input to syllable mapping includes a single C in the conjunct domain. The input is mapped to the template, and *s* is stray. V is epenthesised to save *s*, and this V eventually surfaces as ə.

Syllable template mapping, in conjunction with Stray Epenthesis, similarly accounts for all the CV alternants of conjunct prefixes, i.e., those in the (a) forms of the data in (5) - (11). In other words, whenever an alternating conjunct prefix is initial in its domain, V is epenthesised to its right to prevent the C from being stray and to allow it to be mapped to the onset of the template.

The next task is to account for the (b) examples of the data, where the alternating prefix is a coda; what *prevents* Stray Epenthesis in these forms? Since we are concerned here with the existence of codas, let us examine more generally the distribution of codas in HRB. Only two HRB syllables may have codas: the *final* syllable in the *conjunct domain* and the *final* syllable in the *word*. These two positions have something in common: both constitute edges of a domain. It has been noted with respect to all types of prosodic phenomena, including syllabification, that if edge units of a domain are allowed to be extraprosodic, then the exceptional constituencies found in, for example, word-final syllables, do not force the abandonment of otherwise regular well-formedness conditions. This same observation applies to the facts here. I therefore assume that segments at the right edge of both the conjunct domain and the word domain are extraprosodic. Extraprosodicity is a type of licensing which allows segments to remain unsyllabified and yet not be considered stray elements. In the partial derivation in (16), a representative (b) form (i.e., a form with a C coda alternant) is given which illustrates the use of extraprosodicity. *n* is final and thus extraprosodic in the conjunct domain; *l* is final and extraprosodic in the word domain. The template is mapped; *z* is unsyllabifiable, V is epenthesised to save it, and everything is thus licensed:

(16) = (2b*i*)

---

zĭxił   'you sg. kill sg. Ø'

Input to σ mapping: [[z - n̲] - x i ł]

σ mapping,
Stray Epenthesis: [[z ə -   n̲] -   x i   ł]
                       C V̲   C   C V C
                        \/ | \/ |
                         σ   Ex   σ   Ex

Extraprosodicity is not assigned when the domain-final consonant is the only segment in the domain. This constraint originates from Hayes' (1981) discussion of extrametricality in stress domains, where he states that

> extrametricality rules are blocked if their application would mark the entire stress domain as [+ex].

Hayes adds that "this condition is apparently universal, and thus should not add any cost to the grammars of particular languages" (Hayes 1981:74). I have recast this condition as the Empty Domain Condition (E.D.C.) in (17), which simply states that [x] cannot be extraprosodic if there is nothing else in its domain:

(17)

$*_a[$ $[x]]_a$ where [x] is extraprosodic
and $_a[$ $]_a$ = domain which is visible to syllable mapping
and $_a[$ $]_a$ is empty (except for [x])

This constraint comes into effect in the (a) forms of the data whenever the CV alternant is the only prefix in the conjunct domain.

How do the consonants which are extraprosodic at pre-word levels get syllabified? There are various possibilities, depending on the status of extraprosodicity and stray epenthesis at the word level, as shown in (18):

(18)

	Extraprosodicity	Stray epenthesis
Word-level	*off*/on	*off*/on
Postlexical phonology	off	off

Each of these parameters may be on or off at the word level; post-lexically, these parameters as well as all well-formedness conditions, which fall under structure preservation, are universally off. My analysis is that both extraprosodicity and stray epenthesis are off at the word-level, and that the word-level syllable template is [CVC] as shown in (19).

(19)

[CVC]

This means that, at the word level, the domain-final consonants lose their extraprosodicity, must get relicensed, and do so by being incorporated as codas into the preceding syllable as a result of mapping the word-level syllable template, which is [CVC].

An alternative analysis is to maintain extraprosodicity at the word level and not posit a separate [CVC] template; then, in the postlexical phonology, where structure preservation no longer holds and extra-prosodicity is universally off, unsyllabified consonants are syllabified regardless of templates or other syllable conditions. This is a simpler account at first glance in that it does not require a distinct word-level syllable template. However, the template in (19), as shown below, makes it possible to explain the deletion of certain conjunct-domain-final Cs in the presence of the *h* classifier in position 11, which intervenes between the final C in the conjunct domain and the stem-initial C.

The /ˋs/ conjugation prefix, which has a sə alternant, as in (5a), an s-coda alternant, as in (5b), and an s-onset alternant, as in (9b), has a fourth alternant, /Ø/, as shown in (20):

(20)

zèxį			's/he killed sg. Ø'
[[z(V) - ˋs] - h -			ghį]
7	8	11	stem
der	cnj	cl	'kill sg. Ø'

The low tone on the vowel preceding s is an indication of the underlying presence of s conjugation; notice however that s itself does not surface. In the following discussion, I summarise the analysis so far by showing how it yields the first three alternants, and then I account for this fourth null alternant by invoking the word-level template [CVC].

(21)   Summary of analysis

I: Cə alternant, e.g. sə in (5ai)
    [sə da]
    = [[ˋs   ] d a]
       C V C V
       \/   \/
       σ   σ

II: C (coda) alternant, e.g. s in (5bi)
    [tadèsła]
    = [t   a [d   ˋs] l   a]
       C V C V C   C V
       \/   \/ | \/
       σ   σ   Ex   σ

III: C (onset) alternant, e.g. s in (9b)
    [yàsaya]
    = [y à   [ˋs a] y a]
       C V   C V   C V
       \/   \/   \/
       σ   σ   σ

IV. Ø alternant, e.g. Ø in (19)
     [zèxi̧]

Pre word-level: [[z   `s] h gh i n]
                   C V   C C C V C
                   \/ | / \/ |
                   σ   Ex σ   σ   Ex

Word level: [z `   h gh i n]
              C V C C V C
              \ | / \ | /
              σ   σ

In (I), s is the only consonant in the conjunct domain, so it is not extraprosodic by the E.D.C. The CV template is mapped and Stray Epenthesis applies, adding a V which surfaces as the default vowel [ə].

In (II), s is the final consonant in the conjunct domain, so it is extraprosodic. The CV template is mapped and Stray Epenthesis applies in the conjunct domain, adding a V which surfaces as è. This vowel is assigned a low tone from s conjugation which includes a left-spreading low tone in its representation. Low-toned vowels are tensed, resulting in e as opposed to schwa as the epenthetic vowel. At the word level, the CVC template is mapped and `s becomes the coda of the penultimate syllable.

The derivation in (III) is similar to the derivation in (I) except that there is no need for Stray Epenthesis; the CV template is mapped to the string, and since s is followed by a vowel (the 2sS a of position 10), it can be unproblematically mapped to the onset C of the template.

(IV) shows one of the environments where a Ø alternant occurs: preceding the h classifier in position 11. Space does not permit a detailed discussion of the properties of h classifier. In Randoja (1990b) I discuss these properties and posit that h classifier is a consonantal timing unit prelinked to the coda syllable position. At the pre-word level the template is mapped and s conjugation is extraprosodic. At the word level, I assume that it is prelinked h classifier which gets mapped to the coda of the [CVC] template. s conjugation, now stranded between the nucleus and coda of the syllable, cannot be syllabified; Stray Epenthesis is off at the word level, so s is deleted. If there were no [CVC] template and extraprosodicity were maintained at the word level, there would be no difference between the pre-word-level and word-level representations; then, postlexically, where structure preservation no longer holds, nothing would disallow both s conjugation and h classifier from being syllabified, and therefore *s* should surface. Thus, a word-level [CVC] template is posited as part of the account of *s* deletion in this environment.

It has been shown that domain-final conjunct consonants are marked as extraprosodic by virtue of being at the right edge of the conjunct domain, and this accounts for the coda alternant of conjunct prefixes without the need for a separate vowel deletion rule. However, extraprosodicity is typically restricted to *word*-final segments and is usually not applied to edge segments in a word-internal domain as I have done. This is because in most types of word-formation, morphemes are attached con-catenatively to the edges of a word such that a former edge position becomes internal or central at the addition of morphological material. There is no phonological evidence in the typical case for the extra-prosodic status of these once-edge, now-central units, since they do not exhibit the unusual properties which the assignment of extraprosodicity is meant to capture. Thus, when no longer at the edge, they lose their extraprosodic marking. This is expressed with respect to stress in (22), known as the Peripherality Condition (Hayes 1981:195):

(22)

$$X \;\rightarrow\; [\text{-ex}] \;/\; \underline{\quad} \; Y \,]_D \qquad \text{where } Y = \emptyset$$
$$[\text{+ex}] \qquad\qquad\qquad\qquad \text{and D is the domain of the stress rules}$$

My motivation for conjunct domain extraprosodicity hinges on the following observation: the HRB morphological system is noncon-catenative, where non-thematic conjunct morphemes are the last to be added to the verb. In this final section I present arguments that conjunct domain extraprosodicity does not violate Peripherality.

Athapaskanists such as Sapir & Hoijer (1967), Kari (1979) and Rice (1989) have made an insightful distinction between three types of affixes in Athapaskan languages: thematic, derivational and inflectional. Defining characteristics of these affix types are given in (23) - (25):

(23) Thematic affixes:
  - have no isolable meaning
  - combine with the stem to give a verb's idiosyncratic meaning
  - must be listed as part of the verb's lexical entry

(24) Derivational affixes:
  - have predictable meanings
  - contribute componentially to the meaning of a verb

- are added to the verb by derivational processes
- include affixes which "choose" (determine the co-occurrence of) other derivational affixes

(25) Inflectional affixes:
- are relevant to the syntax
- consist definitely of person affixes (positions 5, 6, 10)
- may(?) consist of conjugation and mode affixes; I assume they do not, but this does not affect the analysis

Thematic affixes have no meaning in isolation from the stem, and are listed as part of the verb's lexical entry. Derivational affixes, on the other hand, have predictable meanings and are added to the verb derivationally, in a sequence which is governed almost exclusively by verb-internal dependencies. Inflectional affixes are those relevant to the syntax, specifically the person affixes. The question of whether or not conjugation and mode are inflectional is open, but the answer either way does not affect the analysis.

The question we will deal with here is how these affixes are combined in word formation. We begin with the traditional assumption that the basic lexical entry is what is called the verb theme, consisting of thematic affixes and the classifier plus verb root; this is a reasonable assumption, since neither thematic affixes nor the verb root can exist on their own and do not have independent meaning. This assumption is not new in the Athapaskan literature; cf. Sapir & Hoijer (1967), Kari (1979, 1989), Rice (1989). If a theme has no thematic affixes, the lexical entry will consist only of the classifier and root; maximally, a theme may include any combination of thematic prefixes (which in HRB are located in positions 1, 2, 5, and 7) plus the classifier and root. In the latter set of cases, the theme will be discontinuous. The theme or lexical entry is formulated as a template in (26). The order of affixation to the theme is governed by two factors. The first is verb-internal dependencies; that is, affixes which determine the co-occurrence of other affixes are added prior to the chosen affixes. The second factor is the assumption that lexical relatedness as defined in Williams (1981) holds for Athapaskan such that inflectional affixes are attached after derivational affixes. This and similar approaches to affixation sequencing are pursued in more detail in Randoja (1990a), Kari (1979, 1989) and Speas (1986) among others. (27) gives a schema of affixation sequencing where choosing and chosen relationships are indicated by arrows among the derivational positions, and then inflectional positions are added last.

(26)

Thematic template = (potentially discontinuous) lexical entry template

| 1,2 | 5 | 7 | cl + root |

(27)

Order of affixation

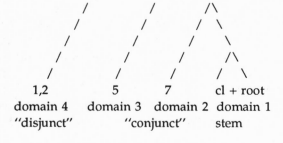

Position	Conjunct(C)/Disjunct (D)	
2	D	
3	D	
11		DERIVATION
4	D	
7	C	
1	D	
8	C	
9	C	
5	C	INFLECTION
6	C	
10	C	

A fact which is significant for phonological derivation and our present discussion is that the thematic positions indicated in the template in (26) correspond to the boundaries of four phonological rule domains. This is indicated in (28):

(28)

1,2	5	7	cl + root
domain 4	domain 3	domain 2	domain 1
"disjunct"		"conjunct"	stem

We should note also that domain 4 phonology, that of the disjunct domain, has the same general properties as domain 1 phonology, that of the stem domain; thus, the conjunct domain, subdivided into domains 2 and 3, has unique phonological characteristics. Now let us combine the information in (27) and (28). The point to notice is that, given (27) (the order in which affixes are added into the template/phonological word), domain 4 (the disjunct domain) will be the first domain to be fully mapped into the phonology. This is seen in the second column in (27), where the mapping of the Ds is completed before the mapping of the Cs is completed. After all domain 4 affixes are inserted according to their insertion frames, disjunct-domain phonology, i.e., domain 4, is entered, beginning with the mapping of the CV syllable template. Following disjunct-domain phonology, the remaining derivational and inflectional affixes are mapped into the word. At this point, the levels of conjunct-domain phonology are reached, beginning again with [CV] syllable mapping. What is relevant to our discussion is that the affixes of the conjunct domain, although internal on the surface, are added to the verb at the latest stages of word formation and therefore constitute the last part of the string to get syllabified. Thus, there is no sense in which the right edge of the conjunct domain is obliged to lose its extraprosodic status by the Peripherality Condition, because no further word formation takes place to extend the domain or create a new domain and, with that new domain, a new edge.

In summary, the goal of this analysis has been to demonstrate that universal and language-specific syllable structure conditions, as articulated in Prosodic Theory, account for HRB conjunct prefix alternations with less arbitrariness than a linear approach. Alternating prefixes consist underlyingly of a single consonant, and the application of syllable templates, extraprosodicity and stray epenthesis automatically dictates the necessary epenthesis sites without the need for epenthesis or deletion rules.

REFERENCES

Cook, Eung-Do. 1984. *A Sarcee Grammar*. Vancouver: University of British Columbia Press.

Hargus, Sharon. 1988. *The Lexical Phonology of Sekani*. New York: Garland.

Hayes, Bruce. 1981. A Metrical Theory of Stress Rules. Indiana University Linguistics Club. Bloomington.

Itô, Junko. 1986. *Syllable Theory in Prosodic Phonology*. Ph.D. Dissertation, University of Massachusetts, Amherst.

—. 1989. A Prosodic Theory of Epenthesis. *Natural Language and Linguistic Theory* 7:217-259.

Kari, James. 1975. The Disjunct Boundary in the Navajo and Tanaina Verb Prefix Complexes. *International Journal of American Linguistics* 41:330-345.

—. 1979. *Athabaskan Verb Theme Categories: Ahtna.* Alaska Native Language Center Research Paper 2. Fairbanks.

—. 1990. Some Concepts in Ahtna Athabaskan Word Formation. Unpublished manuscript, Alaska Native Language Center, Fairbanks.

Kiparsky, Paul. 1982. Lexical Morphology and Phonology. I.-S. Yange, ed., *Linguistics in the Morning Calm*, 3-91. Seoul: Hanshin Publishing.

Li, Fang-Kuei. 1933. Chipewyan Consonants. *Bulletin of the Institute of History and Philology of the Academia Sinica, Supplementary Volume I: Ts'ai Yuan Pe'i Anniversary Volume*, 429-467. Peiping.

Randoja, Tiina. 1990a. *The Phonology and Morphology of Halfway River Beaver*. Ph.D. Dissertation, University of Ottawa.

—. 1990b. The *h* classifier in Halfway River Beaver (Athapaskan). Unpublished manuscript, University of Manitoba.

Rice, Keren. 1989. *A Grammar of Slave (Dene)*. Berlin: Mouton de Gruyter.

Sapir, Edward, & Harry Hoijer. 1967. *The Phonology and Morphology of the Navaho Language*. University of California Publications in Linguistics, 50. Berkeley/Los Angeles.

Speas, Margaret. 1986. *Adjunctions and Projections in Syntax*. Ph.D. Dissertation, Massachusetts Institute of Technology.

Williams, Edwin. 1981. On the Notions 'Lexically Related' and 'Head of a Word'. *Linguistic Inquiry* 11:203-238.

Wright, Martha. 1983. The CV Skeleton and Navajo Verb Prefix Phonology. Unpublished manuscript, Tilburg University.

The Evolutionary Interaction
of Sex and Language
William D. Wade

The goal of this paper is to attempt a *plausible* explanation of a causal link in the evolution of what are usually regarded as two discrete areas of behaviour, language and sex. What follows is not, and cannot be, a compelling argument in the manner of physics or mathematics, but is rather more akin to the endeavours of weather forecasters. In projecting estimates of the weather for more than a few days into the future, or conjectures concerning the evolutionary history of a particular taxon, reliability declines sharply as a function of time.

One of the truly perplexing, and often daunting, problems of studying human behaviour, even without further complicating the issue by attempting to add to it a historical dimension, is that we are one of the most (arguably *the* most) behaviourally complex species in existence. Whenever we attempt to focus upon a single, more or less manageable manifestation of human behaviour, we quickly become aware of the influence of other variables which, if we attempt to take them all into account, inevitably produce a "hall of mirrors" effect.

Of necessity, then, we must choose between two alternatives. We can restrict ourselves to those variables we want to consider and set aside the others, simply refusing to look at them. Or, we may decide to look at behaviour in a "controlled" environment, in which we can dampen, or perhaps cancel altogether, the unwanted influences. I am biassed to believe that attempts to restrict the influence of some variables by laboratory manipulation are doomed to a significant degree of failure at the outset. Without going into the reasons, I have opted here for the first of these alternatives. In more specific terms, the goal of this paper is to argue for a relationship of mutual causality between narrowly defined aspects of language and sex.

WHY SEX?

In any species, the explanation of adaptive behaviours, no matter how complex they may be on the surface, always addresses one or both of the two most basic (i.e., not purely internal, such as temperature regulation, etc.) requirements, feeding and reproduction. In order to perpetuate itself, a species must be capable of reliably reproducing itself. Members of a species can only reliably reproduce by consistently obtaining sufficient energy to sustain a life cycle.

In Darwinian theory, species survival rests on the principle of competition, in which natural selection implacably favours species that reproduce themselves at the expense of competitors.

Psychologists differentiate feeding and reproductive behaviour with a designation such as "drive" to indicate that these are deeply embedded behaviours and, as such, not subject to the same degree of surface variability as are other categories of behaviour. Other important fundamental categories of behaviour include fear and anger, which can be related to the most basic survival functions, usually summarised as "fight or flight" behaviour. Although important to the maintenance of the life cycle, these are subservient to feeding and reproductive requirements. Fear and anger are not as universal as feeding and reproduction, which is to say that they are phylogenetically somewhat more recently established attributes of terrestrial life.

For the immediate purposes of this paper, feeding and reproduction are regarded as the most basic, pervasive, and influential categories of behaviour.

Explanations for the possible evolutionary relationship between language and feeding are commonplace. In fact, the origin of language is most often attributed to one or another aspect of feeding, whether as an adjunct to cooperative hunting or, more indirectly, as a concomitant of technology in the form of tools and weapons used to obtain and process food.

As far as I know, the possible connection between sex and the origin of language has not yet been explored, and that establishes the purpose of this paper.

THE EVOLUTIONARY SIGNIFICANCE OF SEX

Reproduction is a universal feature of living things, while sex is not. Among the older orders, various forms of asexual reproduction are common. Among mammals and birds, on the other hand, sex is universal. John Maynard Smith (1987:8-9), having cited examples of parthenogenesis among fish, amphibians and even reptiles, is unequivocal on this point:

> No wild birds or mammals are parthenogenetic... This has been
> something of a puzzle, but a possible reason has recently emerged.
> It seems that, at some gene loci, the genes derived from the father

and mother are differentially active in particular tissues. Since both activities are needed, every mammal must have a father and a mother.

Furthermore, among mammals and particularly among the platyrrhine and catarrhine primates, sexual behaviour (as opposed to reproductive behaviour) clearly serves varied, often apparently complex, social functions the implications of which for natural selection are quite apart from reproductive considerations. That does not mean that it is possible to distinguish between the two in any particular instance.

In attempting to establish a mechanism to account for differences between human and non-human sexual behaviour, the distinction between reproductive behaviour and sexual behaviour becomes, at least potentially, important. The separation between sex and reproduction is arguably more exaggerated in humans and not, perhaps, without consequences, principally in the form of neuroses that result from conflicts between deeply-rooted influences on reproductive behaviour and socially-acquired values surrounding sexual behaviour.

For these reasons, I would like to be able to distinguish between sexual behaviour and reproductive behaviour. In reality, I do not believe it possible to confront behaviour that is clearly a mixture of sexual and reproductive components and confidently isolate any aspect of behaviour as being entirely unrelated to reproduction.

Further complicating this problem is the fact that the platyrrhine and catarrhine primates are, physiologically and behaviourally, extremely variable in sexual behaviour. It is not a goal of this paper to attempt any systematic review of primate reproductive physiology and wild behaviour. Although such a review is clearly needed, about the best available treatment of this issue is that of Fedigan (1982). Generalisation in this area is very risky, and Fedigan challenges many of the common generalisations offered by primatologists attempting to account for sexuality among primates and even among quite low-level subordinate taxa (e.g., Old World monkeys or apes). Despite the attractions, consequently, we will try to avoid the minefield of accounting for hominine sexual behaviour as anything but a set of derived traits, which is more or less unique, *as a set*, to humans.

One other aspect of sex in the context of evolution needs to be briefly explored: the alternative models of selection as they affect the sexes differentially. In this domain, we get some reasonably clear guidance. Of the treatises on the evolution of sex, I have found Ghiselin's (1974) to be as comprehensive as many and more lucid than most. This work provides an excellent review of various behavioural models of sex documented by naturalistic observation, including many of the original and highly insightful contributions of Darwin and Wallace.

Ghiselin summarily represents the models of sexual selection according to the following scheme (pp. 135-136):

> *Male-male competition* would include both of the classical Darwinian forms of sexual selection. *Male combat* involves actual fighting between the males. Being the reason for the evolution of horns and tusks in males, it has on the whole been too evident to have been denied outright. *Female choice* is a competition between males by manoeuvres that "attract" the females. It has led to the evolution of sexual ornaments, but exactly which ones remains a controversial topic. Less obvious means of competition between males have largely been ignored, and new terms will now be proposed. *Male sequestering*, so called because the male sequesters the female, will here refer to instances in which the male takes possession of the female, often by brute force, and thereby prevents other males from mating with her. It is a sort of Rape of the Sabines ploy, one common among crustaceans. A less violent sort of competition than actual fighting, it nonetheless requires physical strength, and is easily combined with male combat – and just as easily confused with it. Or the male may use a version of female choice, in which he attracts the female and keeps doing so because it keeps her out of the control of other males. Some birds do this. The boundaries between seduction and rape are often far from clear. By *male dispersal* we shall mean that the males compete with one another as if in a race to be first in finding and impregnating the females. First come, first service. A scramble for genital union, putting a premium on speed and early maturation rather than on size and strength, is an alternative to male combat and to male sequestering which leads to quite different consequences. In many cases the necessary adaptations are hard to combine, so that the males must do one or the other. On the other hand male dispersal often is combined with a form of sequestering in which males act upon females so as to prevent subsequent matings, as when they use "chastity belts."

Ghiselin in his classification takes into account the possibility of female counterparts of the above classes. In my opinion, they are less generally applicable to hominines because, as Ghiselin and others mention, females generally all become impregnated whereas males have quite different degrees of success in participating. Consequently, even if, for example, *male choice* does occur, it has little evolutionary significance.

Ghiselin also points out that there is not much evidence for *female sequestering* or *female dispersal*.

Other categories of sexual selection mentioned by Ghiselin include *cooperation* and *parental exploitation*. These have relatively little to do with sexual behaviour as such and are not relevant to the central concern of this paper.

THE EVOLUTIONARY SIGNIFICANCE OF LANGUAGE

The competitive advantages of language are beyond question. A species with language enjoys an enormous advantage in competition with a species lacking language.

Selective disadvantageous aspects of language are simply not in evidence. In terms of measurable biological success, there are, at most, portents for the future, ominous only in consideration of some of the resultants, largely in the domain of technology, of language. These remain, to date, largely hypothetical.

Chomsky, who has been the most effective critic of "ape language" experimentation and steadfastly denies that non-human communication has any connection whatever with human language, nevertheless accepts the biological inevitability that human language must be the consequence of intense natural selection (1980:433):

> It seems reasonable to assume that evolution of the language faculty was a development specific to the human species long after it separated from other primates. It also seems reasonable to suppose that possession of the language faculty conferred extraordinary selectional advantages, and must be a primary factor in the remarkable biological success of the human species, that is, its proliferation.

It is virtually self-evident that a behaviour as complex, and requiring such extensive neurological investment, as language could only be the result of quite intense natural selection. Unfortunately, apart from passages carved into clay and stone within the last several millennia, there is no fossil record of language, nor does anything comparable to language appear naturally in any other species. Consequently, when we entertain arguments concerning the *evolution* of language, we have little to guide us and are necessarily in the domain of conjecture. In the absence of an alternative, there is nothing wrong with conjecture as long as it is constrained to be consistent with, or at least not at odds with, relevant theory.

Among vertebrates generally, all or nearly all communications are indicative of the immediate state of the organism and are related to very fundamental requirements that are largely mediated by the limbic and/or endocrine systems. Among primates, the most fundamental and pervasive communications take the following general form:

I am here (attractive identification, intragroup object)
I am here (repulsive identification, extragroup object)
I am threatening (anger)
I am alarmed (fear, extraspecific source)
I am being subservient (fear, intraspecific source)
I am sexually receptive (reproduction)

Setting aside the quibbles over whether human language is qualitatively or merely quantitatively distinct from other, non-human forms of communication, it is clear that contemporary human use of, and reliance on, language extends well beyond communicating about the immediate state of the communicator.

From a comparative evolutionist perspective, it is unfortunate that *Homo sapiens* has no closer relatives than the members of the genus *Pan*. Many problems concerning evolutionary changes in hominine ancestry over the last 20 million years would be rendered less enigmatic if we had cousins with whom we shared a common ancestor within, say, the last three or four million years. However, gleaning what we can from knowledge of the nearest relatives we have, we can at least establish certain commonalities with regard to the most important of adaptive behaviours.

THE INITIAL INSTRUMENTALITY OF LANGUAGE

In disparaging his own research project, Terrace (1979:219) describes one of the limitations of his subject, a young chimpanzee, thus:

Our analysis showed that Nim interrupted his teachers much more frequently than a child interrupts its parents. After seeing the extent to which Nim interrupted his teachers, it appeared that he was more concerned about telling his teachers what he wanted of them than he was about what his teachers were saying to him or about exchanging information with them.

Terrace goes on to describe how Nim restricted many of his expressions to the syntactically enigmatic form "Give + X"; his disappointment seems surprising in light of his explanation (p. 221):

Questions such as *Nim want X?*, *Nim eat X?*, and so on appeared frequently in transcripts of videotapes of Nim's teachers signing with him.

Terrace contrasts the verbal behaviour of Nim Chimsky with that of human children, perhaps unaware of the prominence that the verb "give" has in the two-word stage of language development in most human children. The difference recognised by Terrace is that of human children who have progressed beyond the two-word stage, which frequently consists of terse demands of which adults quickly tire. The progression to more lengthy utterances coincides with the child's increasing skill in manipulating ends, usually a more effective tactic than demanding.

The most powerful motivator for young children to begin to use language is their awareness of its power to achieve ends. They begin by using mere noises, to which adults respond with variable perception. They learn quickly that words achieve more precise results. Eventually, they learn to refine their verbal skills into more or less carefully articulated verbal strategies requiring complex grammatical structures. Human children are consistently able to move through this whole process quite quickly. Apart from the obvious phylogenetic distance, a possible explanation of Nim's disappointing lack of comparable progress is that he was over-indulged. If he could gain any end of which he was aware by using two-word constructions, there appears to have been no particular motive to develop his skills further.

Elsewhere in this volume, Haiman argues persuasively that human language parallels communication in other, even phylogenetically disparate species in representing ritualisation of previously instrumental acts. I find this argument so compelling that I would suggest that most (arguably all) language that is not clearly *simply* instrumental is ritualisation of *former* instrumentality.

This point is further supported by a couple of popular examples. In the film, *The Lonely Guy*, the lead character approaches an attractive woman in a singles bar and, in the style of a "companions wanted" ad, informs her of his interest in lofty literary conversation, companionable walks, mutual enjoyment of classical concerts, etc. The woman responds, "That's nice." Preparing to leave, she adds, "I just came here to get laid." The humour of the scene derives from her unexpected and unexpectedly candid rejoinder. This merely emphasises the point that instrumental communications are indeed unexpected in a context that has become saturated with ritualised social behaviour.

In another film, *Dead Poets Society*, the English teacher asks his class, rhetorically, why men write poetry. After allowing them a short interval to offer suitably erudite answers, he finally lets them off the hook with his answer: "to woo women." What is funny about this punch line is its earthy appeal to the minds of young, sexually mature but inexperienced males in place of the intellectually inflated responses they had thought would be required of them. Again, the instrumentality is clearly unexpected (who ever had an English teacher who wasn't deeply in love with ritualised language?). The relatively blunt response of the film's teacher would not be funny if it were not also fundamentally true, as memory quickly assures us in regard to a great deal of poetry. (As a separate but related issue, it is worth noting that the all-male "dead poets society" leaves unanswered the question, "Why do women write poetry?" From an evolutionary perspective, it seems unlikely that the composition of poetry was, until very recently, a form of male courtship display. If it had been, we should expect to see some evidence in sexual selection for the enhancement of male verbal behaviour. In short, we might expect human males to have evolved into glib flatterers.)

If these examples serve to underscore the differences between humans and our closest relatives in the relationship between language and its goals, we might expect a comparable lack of guile in the sexual behaviour of chimpanzees. Unfortunately (or not), chimpanzees also differ markedly from humans in the extent to which their sexual behaviour is governed by cyclical endocrine changes in females that initiate a series of effects culminating in male arousal and, ultimately, coitus. To the extent that chimpanzee sexual behaviour is both periodic and beyond volition, there is no more need for artifice in their natural sexual behaviour than in their instrumental use of borrowed human language.

If we enumerate the important ways in which we humans differ, as a species, from our anthropoid relatives, there are not many: habitually upright posture, technology and language. We share all our other attributes with one or another primate relative. The attempts to explain these characteristics are consistently directed to the feeding requirement. There is a fourth, unique biological characteristic that is descriptive only of the human female. The sexual behaviour of humans is largely volitional. That this is so is in large measure the consequence of the independence of sexual arousal in females from periodic endocrine changes. There is the further fact that, although coitus may be pleasurable to females of other species, it is evidently not a necessary feature of sexual behaviour. (In some cats, for example, the intromission of the penis into the vagina produces only intense pain in the female; this does not prevent their repeated sexual response.) Human females are not only free to engage in coitus whenever they like, they are also motivated to do so by another apparently unique human characteristic: female orgasm.

In sum, there are these two important and unique human behaviours: (1) the acquisition of volitional control over sexual arousal in females and, by extension, males; and (2) the prominence of language as a pivotal component of adaptation.

These two phenomena may have no causal relationship whatever. On the other hand, although they are both difficult to explain, they both appear to be the consequence, and perhaps the cause, of extensive neural reorganisation.

As a more or less clear example of male "attractive" behaviour, the most complex songs of humpback whales are produced by solitary males and have been attributed to sexual selection just as in songbirds.

According to Nottebohm (1984), among at least some species of songbirds, the songs that are so prominent a feature of courtship are a specialisation of the left hemisphere, as language is in most humans. Thorpe (1974:107) indicates a clear functional distinction between songs and calls in songbirds:

> Call notes are usually simple in structure, consisting of one or a few bursts of sound, in contrast to the longer and more complicated sequences of song. Call notes in the main convey information which may warn of danger, help to control the movement of a flock, indicate the whereabouts of food, and so forth. Song, on the other hand, is a type of vocalisation appropriate to, and often confined to, the breeding season; it is given primarily by the male under the general physiological control of the sex hormones and ... is often capable of a high degree of modification by imitative learning.

Marler & Hamilton (1966:87), citing Lehrman (1961), describe the requisite influence that male courtship in the ring dove has on ovulation. Although in this example the courtship display is visual rather than vocal, it is nonetheless impressive that ovulation does not seem to occur in the absence of courtship.

However tenuous, there is a demonstrable relationship, at least among songbirds, between sexual behaviour (courtship), reproductive behaviour (ovulation) and song, which is organised neurologically in ways that parallel the organisation of language in humans.

HYPOTHETICAL STEPS IN THE EVOLUTION OF HUMAN LANGUAGE

Bronowski & Bellugi (1980) proposed a series of plausible steps by which language could be treated as a phenomenon with evolutionary continuity:

(1) a delay between the arrival of the stimulus and the utterance of the message that it has provoked, or between the receipt of the incoming signal and the sending out of a signal;

(2) the separation of affect or emotional charge from the content of instruction which a message carries;

(3) the prolongation of reference, namely, the ability to refer backward and forward in time and to exchange messages which propose action in the future;

(4) the internalisation of language, so that it ceases to be only a means of social communication and becomes also an instrument of reflection and exploration with which the speaker constructs hypothetical messages before choosing one to utter; and,

(5) the structural activity of reconstitution, which consists of two linked procedures – namely, a procedure of analysis by which messages are not treated as inviolate wholes but are broken down into smaller parts, and a procedure of synthesis by which the parts are rearranged to form other messages.

The steps (1) to (4) express the behavioural ability of humans to disengage from the immediate context; without this, it would not be possible to make predicative statements – to give information about the environment in a form which does not imply an instruction to act. Step (5) expresses the logical ability of humans to influence their environment by understanding it; that is, by analysing it into parts and then making new combinations from the parts.

If these steps describe the ways in which human language has come to differ from a prior communication system characteristic of other, non-human primates, they might equally well account for the major differences between human sexual behaviour and that of other primates. As in Bronowski & Bellugi's steps (1) to (4), humans can and frequently do use language in reference to things and events of the past, or to imagine them in the future. Humans are also capable of sexual arousal based upon nothing more than the recollection of past experience, or of imagined future experience. Language is often a purely internal phenomenon in that we use language, often internally, not only to structure our thoughts about displaced things or events, but also to plan behaviour which is relevantly consequent. The fifth step of Bronowski &

Bellugi, characterised by a loss of passivity in relation to the environment, is similarly prominent in regard to the consequences of temporally displaced events and behaviours. In this regard, sexual behaviour is no different than any other human behaviour – there is the implicit ability to act upon internally generated stimuli *that is volitional*.

This may also plausibly account for why humans have evolved sexually along a course that, by and large, conforms to a model of female choice rather than of male sequestering, that is, by "attractive" male displays and behaviours rather than by force, as in other species (including primates). Many human behaviours make a good deal more sense within the framework of this model than they might otherwise. These displays are particularly in evidence during the interval of male pubescence but are certainly not absent in adults. Moreover, they are called forth at any time in the presence of a female, and are largely independent of cyclical or seasonal physiological influences. This model would, of course, be greatly facilitated by the existence of comparably evolved behaviours among human females. If we look for ways in which the sexual behaviour of human females differs from that of non-humans, the most salient feature is undoubtedly the phenomenon of female orgasm. If female responsiveness to sexual overtures that can occur at any time is based upon physiological reward rather than being the automatic result of endocrine changes, then it becomes possible to see how such a system could have evolved simultaneously with the neurological changes leading to language. One or the other may be either cause or consequence, or both, by means of mutual reenforcement.

In non-humans, sexual arousal in females depends largely on cyclical endocrine changes. There are no evident volitional influences and no effective external stimuli. In non-human males, sexual arousal is triggered by visual and olfactory cues emanating from individual females. There is no generalised arousal, nor is there any significant degree of sexual arousal in the absence of these stimuli.

Initially in human males, even a very limited possibility of sexual arousal independent of external stimuli might well have been the result of, and later on greatly enhanced by, the ability to recall stimuli, associate them with a female (or possibly females generally), and ultimately by attempts to initiate sexual contact with a female who may only be approaching her oestrous climb. In females with even a minimal capacity for favourable physiological response to such contacts, the basis could certainly exist for ultimate elaboration into extremely influential orgasmic response.

According to Masters & Johnson (1966), orgasm in human females is a learned response. It is doubtful that this kind of physiological response could develop in the context of the sexual behaviour of most non-human primates, in which coitus is often a brief, virtually perfunctory event, isolated from even immediate positive affect of any significance and without much evident potential for displacement.

CONCLUSION

Setting aside the complexities inherent in a broader perspective on human physiology and behaviour in an evolutionary framework, I have tried to argue in support of a particular interpretation, as follows:

(1) Sex and language are persistent, pervasive and complex elements of human behaviour. Both are prominent components of the human eco-niche, and unquestionably the result of intense selection.

(2) The persistence of both is a function of displacement. Without displacement, language cannot exist. Without displacement, sex is no more persistent than it is in non-human species, in which arousal is a periodic physiological function in females, resulting in external physical stimuli without which arousal does not occur in males.

(3) Early in human evolution, enhanced sex may have been an immediate reward for the investment of energy in behaviours leading toward language. The ultimate rewards are, of course, obvious but perhaps only in retrospect.

(4) An increased capacity for language could, in turn, further enhance the sexually gratifying pay-off.

(5) Once such a mutually reenforcing system is established, the process often becomes intensified, and the rate of evolutionary change accelerated.

What does such a hypothetical scheme have to recommend it? Is it simpler than other explanations? In the absence of any substantive support from the fossil record, and in the absence of comparative evidence from species closely related to us, it is impossible to say with certainty as all such explanation remains conjectural under the circumstances.

Does this explanation overturn or exclude other explanations? That is very doubtful. In fact, the causality of both human sex and human language, and other behaviours as well, is undoubtedly a good deal more complex than this brief account admits. In ignoring influences external to this argument, I have undoubtedly missed many ideas that others will consider important. The central idea of this paper is, I believe, a valuable one, and will remain regardless of whether I have argued it badly or convincingly.

REFERENCES

Bell, Graham. 1982. *The Masterpiece of Nature.* Berkeley: University of California Press.

Bellig, Robert, & George Stevens, eds. 1988. *The Evolution of Sex.* San Francisco: Harper & Row.

Berrill, N.J. 1953. *Sex and the Nature of Things.* New York: Dodd, Mead.

Bronowski, Jacob, & Ursula Bellugi. 1980. Language, Name, and Concept. T.A. Sebeok & J. Umiker-Sebeok, eds., *Speaking of Apes,* 103-113. New York: Plenum Press.

Chomsky, Noam. 1980. Human Language and other Semiotic Systems. T.A. Sebeok & J. Umiker-Sebeok, eds., *Speaking of Apes,* 429-440. New York: Plenum Press.

Fedigan, Linda Marie. 1982. *Primate Paradigms: Sex Roles and Social Bonds.* Montreal: Eden Press.

Forsyth, Adrian. 1986. *A Natural History of Sex.* New York: Charles Scribner's Sons.

Ghiselin, Michael T. 1974. *The Economy of Nature and the Evolution of Sex.* Berkeley: University of California Press.

Haiman, John. 1991. Motivation, Repetition, and Emancipation: The Bureaucratisation of Language. H.C. Wolfart, ed., *Linguistic Studies Presented to John L. Finlay,* 45-69. Algonquian and Iroquoian Linguistics, Memoir 8.

Jensen, D.J. 1978. Sequential Information Transfer: An Hypothesis about Sexual Arousal in Chimpanzees. D.J. Chivers & J. Herbert, eds., *Recent Advances in Primatology, 1: Behaviour,* 617-618. New York: Academic Press.

Lehrman, D.S. 1961. Hormonal Regulation of Parental Behavior in Birds and Infrahuman Mammals. W.C. Young, ed., *Sex and Internal Secretions,* 2:1268-1382. Baltimore: Williams & Wilkins.

Marler, Peter, & William J. Hamilton III. 1966. *Mechanisms of Animal Behavior.* New York: John Wiley.

Masters, W.H., & Virginia E. Johnson. 1966. *Human Sexual Response.* Boston: Little, Brown.

Nottebohm, Fernando. 1984. Birdsong as a Model in which to Study Brain Processes Related to Learning. *The Condor* 86:227-236.

Rancour-Laferriere, Daniel. 1985. *Signs of the Flesh*. Berlin: Mouton.

Sebeok, Thomas A., & Jean Umiker-Sebeok, eds. 1980. *Speaking of Apes*. New York: Plenum Press.

Smith, John Maynard. 1988. The Evolution of Sex. R. Bellig & G. Stevens, eds., *The Evolution of Sex*, 3-17. San Francisco: Harper & Row.

Stearns, S.C., ed. 1987. *The Evolution of Sex and its Consequences*. Basel: Birkhäuser Verlag.

Terrace, Herbert S. 1979. *Nim*. New York: Alfred A. Knopf.

Thorpe, W.H. 1970. Ontogeny of Bird Song. *Science* 167:950-956.

—. 1974. *Animal Nature and Human Nature*. Garden City, N.Y.: Doubleday.

Passives with and without Agents

H.C. Wolfart

As every schoolchild once knew, the subject of a passive sentence is referentially identical with the object of the corresponding active one. In various terminological guises, this has been the accepted truth at least since Apollonios Dyskolos.

With a slight shift in emphasis, more recent attempts at a universal definition of the passive have concentrated on agentless sentences (cf., for example, Haiman 1976) but this is hardly a new insight either. Meillet's classical formulation,

> Le vrai rôle du passif est d'exprimer le procès là où l'agent n'est pas considéré.

reflects the common attitude of most 19th-century linguists, be they Indo-Europeanists like Brugmann, typologists like Hans Conon von der Gabelentz or students of a particular language. In fact, Meillet's dictum of 1920 almost literally echoes that of Silvestre de Sacy – Iranian scholar and Arabist, teacher of Franz Bopp and general linguist – more than a century earlier (1799):

> Le premier et le principal emploi de la Voix passive, est d'exprimer une action sans exprimer le Sujet qui agit,...

Since von der Gabelentz (1861) at the latest, there has been general agreement among typologists that the languages of the Algonquian family present special problems in the recognition and interpretation of passive constructions. The many different analyses which have been proposed for individual Algonquian languages since the 17th century also indicate a great deal of uncertainty, and a number of Algonquianists have either severely restricted the domain of the term *passive* (as Bloomfield did, unlike Sapir, in his grammars of Fox, Ojibwa and Menomini) or avoided it altogether (e.g., Adam 1875 or, more recently, Hockett 1962).

Prominence for the patient, obscurity for the agent and marked verb forms are the signs of classical passive constructions. In examining the Cree verb forms which might be taken to manifest the grammatical category of VOICE, we will focus on the rôle of the agent and on the morphological and semantic structure of the transitive animate paradigm.[1]

OBLIGATORY AGENTS

The transitive verb paradigms of Plains Cree include a subset of forms which relate third and non-third persons, and this sub-paradigm falls into two halves depending on which is agent and which is patient:

(1)   *ni-* -*ânân*   'we(excl) - him'   *ni-* -ikonân   'he - us(excl)'
       ki- -*ânaw*   'we(incl) - him'   *ki-* -ikonaw   'he - us(incl)'
       ki- -*âwâw*   'you(pl) - him'   *ki-* -ikowâw   'he - you(pl)'

Paradigm fragments as in (1) are typical of the Algonquian languages, and the 17th-century missionaries (for example, Louis Nicolas [1672:24-26] in his "Grammaire Algonquine") did not hesitate to analyse as active and passive a paradigm which was, if anything, even more perspicuously symmetrical than that of Latin. In Plains Cree, the inflexion for the two presumed voices differs only in one point: where the "active" has -*â*-, the "passive" shows -*iko*-.

There are at least two arguments which speak against a voice analysis of these forms. First, their morphological symmetry obscures the fact that the members of each pair are not referentially identical: 'we see him' and 'he sees us' denote opposite events. Now, the Latin paradigms of the school grammarians (e.g., Allen & Greenough 1931:90) also present, as symmetrical, forms like *legô* 'I read' and *legor* 'I am read' which are not identical in reference. But these intransitive (or at least potentially intransitive) examples are misleading from the perspective of the agentive passive with its identity of active object and passive subject – as exemplified by Apollonios Dyskolos (*de constructione* ii, 141) with the immortal pair, ἐγώ σε ἔδειρα 'I skinned you' and σὺ ἐδάρης ὑπ' ἐμοῦ 'you were skinned by me.'

The text frequency of passives, and of agentive passives in particular, is notoriously low; in French, Dutch and Lithuanian prose, for example, passives rarely account for more than 2% of verbal predicates (with the notable exception of linguistic texts in Lithuanian where the percentage rises to 32%; cf. Gonda 1951:5, Geniušienė 1976:139). The Cree forms in question, by contrast, are of balanced frequency.

The statistical relationship between the two sets of Cree forms reflects the fact that any choice between them depends not on emphasis or style but on who does what to whom. Lexical options apart, the voice interpretation of these forms would mean that 'I hit him' could only be expressed actively, and 'he hit me' only passively. Voice as a function of pragmatic determination would be the very opposite of the traditional view of the category in which the "tripartite passive construction is only a *stylistic variant* of the corresponding active one" (Kuryłowicz 1964:73; emphasis supplied).

An even more serious problem is presented by the fact that these forms include morphemes for both patient and agent. In the presumedly active half of (2a), for instance, the first or second person is represented by *ni-* or *ki-* and the third person by the suffix *-w-*:

(2a)   *ni- -âw*   'I - him'   *ni- -ik*   'he - me'
       ki- -âw   'you(sg) - him'   *ki- -ik*   'he - you(sg)'

(2b)   *ni- -âwak*   'I - them'   *ni- -ikwak*   'they - me'
       ki- -âwak   'you(sg) - them'   *ki- -ikwak*   'they - you(sg)'

(2b) shows that the third person is also morphologically expressed in the passive; in either half of the paradigm, the third person is pluralised by *-ak*. If we accept then that a form like

(3)   *niwâpamikwak*   'they see me'

expresses both patient and agent, this would contradict the prevailing concept[2] of the passive as a construction where the agent may be suppressed or omitted.

The arguments against a voice interpretation seem about equally matched by those in favour. First, the presumed passive forms are highly marked by an inflexional morpheme /ekw/[3] whose many derivational extensions (cf. Wolfart 1973, 1979, 1980) are, moreover, clearly passive. Rather than present a lengthy argument to show that *-iko- ~ -ikw- ~ -ik-*, in examples (1) and (2), is marked as opposed to *-â-*, let us simply look at another dialect. Outside the Plains dialect (from which all examples are drawn unless otherwise identified), the conjunct endings for the inclusive first person plural and the second person plural follow the pattern of example (4), with the *-it-* forms evidently being the marked members of the opposition:

(4) Plains Cree:

       -âyahk   'that we(incl) - him'   *-ikoyahk*   'that he - us(incl)'
       -âyêk   'that you(pl) - him'   *-ikoyêk*   'that he - you(pl)'

   Woods Cree (Howse):

       -ahk   'that we(incl) - him'   *-itahk*   'that he - us(incl)'
       -êk   'that you(pl) - him'   *-itêk*   'that he - you(pl)'

The suffix *-iko-* which in Plains Cree appears in the marked member of the opposition occurs in a variety of other contexts as well; its passive meaning is particularly obvious in the derivation of intransitive stems such as,

(5a)   *ohcinâkosi-*   'be (animate) seen from there',

(5b)   *itihtâkwan-*   'be (inanimate) heard thus'.

An extended suffix *-ikowisi-*, to cite another example, derives a class of intransitives from transitive stems, e.g.,

(5c)   *itêyim-*   'think so of someone',

(5d)   *itêyimikowisi-*   'be so thought of by the supernatural powers';

more than merely passive in meaning, these verbs express a state of impotence or submission (perhaps even grace).

The most important argument for a passive interpretation of the forms in question is the relative prominence of agent and patient. Like the other Algonquian languages, Cree has a person (or animacy) hierarchy such that the second person ranks higher than the first, and the first higher than the third: 2 > 1 > 3. This hierarchy is reflected in the fixed order of the affixes in nouns and verbs. Thus, in example (2), the first-person prefix *ni-* precedes the third-person suffix *-w-* irrespective of which is agent and which is patient.

In the iconic order of the spoken chain, the prominence of being marked by the earlier affix consequently belongs to the agent in 'I hit them'; in 'they hit me', on the other hand, the most prominent person is the patient.

In addition to paradigmatic symmetry and the marked status of the presumed passive subset, then, the latter forms exhibit another fundamental characteristic of passive constructions: they place the patient in focus.

The case for voice, however, faces not only the two obstacles which have already been discussed: the obligatory presence of agents and the lack of referential identity. It is further weakened if the manifestations of the agent-patient hierarchy can be distinguished from those of the person hierarchy (cf. the discussion of "markedness assimilation" in Haiman 1985:147-151). In that case the marked forms need not be interpreted as expressing the primacy of the patient as much as the appearance in the rôle of the patient of the higher-ranking person.

The diagrammatic iconicity of the sequentially fixed person morphemes is a crucial element of this competing analysis (cf. Wolfart 1973:24). At least since Howse's Cree grammar of 1844, the agent-first forms (with the higher-ranking person as agent) are called DIRECT; forms are INVERSE if the patient takes precedence (and the higher-ranking person appears in the marked context of being the patient). Having become the accepted interpretation of Algonquianists (notably Bloomfield's), the direct-inverse analysis has also been applied (cf. Hale 1973, Comrie 1980, Heath 1976) to other languages of North America, Siberia and Australia.

AGENTLESS SENTENCES

The most effective way of focussing attention on the patient is to ignore the agent altogether, and agentlessness is the dominant characteristic of passive constructions in many languages.

Where agentive[4] complements occur, their text-frequency tends to be low: Schwyzer found none in Hesiod and only five instances in the first six books (amounting to approximately 5,000 lines) of the Iliad (1943:52, 56); they are no more common in the comedies of Plautus[5] which, after all, use a rather more colloquial style. The 4,000 verses of the Chanson de Roland contain only three clear-cut cases (Kallin 1923:167) and even for modern prose texts in English, Dutch and French (cf. Gonda 1951:4-5) the percentage of constructions with agentive complements never exceeds 30% of all passive constructions. Kuryłowicz (1964:73) attributes the low incidence of such constructions to their optional nature which stands in sharp contrast to the pragmatic necessity of using an agentless form if the agent is either not known or not to be mentioned.

In a number of languages, the agent must not appear at all in a passive construction. To the commonly cited examples of Classical Arabic, Latvian and Pashto (cf. Socin 1904:95, Endzelin 1923:766ff. and Penzl 1955:127-128 [but note, per contra, Shafeev 1964:49]), we can add one of the passive constructions of Plains Cree.

Inflexional forms without agents are restricted to third-person patients, as in example (6):

(6)   *wâpamâw atim* 'the dog is seen'/'there is seeing (of) the dog'

An agentive complement cannot occur.[6]

Although the morphological analysis of *wâpamâw* and such associated forms as *wâpamâwak* and *wâpamimâwa* presents no problem,

(7)   *wâpamâw*   'he(proximate) is seen'
       wâpamâwak   'they(proximate) are seen'
       wâpamimâwa   'he/they(obviative) is/are seen',

their paradigmatic position is, at the very least, problematic. The absence of an overtly recognisable passive morpheme such as /ekw/ and the lack of paradigmatic symmetry would be remarkable in themselves. But, as if that were not enough, these forms are completely parallel, down to the "voice" morpheme *-â-*, to the presumed active forms such as

(8)   *niwâpamâw*   'I see him(prox)'
       niwâpamâwak   'I see them(prox)'
       niwâpamimâwa   'I see him/them(obv)'.

The only difference is the absence of the personal prefix.

In fact, the forms in (7) are not only syntactically agentless but morphologically as well: the only participant to be expressed is the third person, by the suffix -w-.

So we have the paradox of a construction which (a) clearly focusses on the patient and (b) is syntactically and morphologically inagentive (and thus seems to meet the most stringent definition of passive) – yet, in its morphological structure, is clearly parallel to active forms.

While the paradox cannot be resolved by recourse to translational paraphrase, we should not overlook the fact that sentences like (6) can be interpreted either personally or impersonally; from a Cree point of view, there seems little to choose between 'the dog is seen' and 'there is seeing (of) the dog.' (Dealing with parallel forms in Algonquin, Nicolas [1672:17] relies on the [French] equivalent of 'one sees the dog' and the term, «verbe medium».)

The impersonal reading is particularly appropriate for compound stems which include preverbs like *wî* 'intention' or *kakwê* 'effort,'[7] e.g.,

(9)   *kâ-kiskêyihtahk ê-wî-kakwê-nipah*iht (P6-16)
      'he knew that there would be an attempt to kill him'.

(The basic verb stem is *nipah-* 'kill someone'; the suffix -*iht* is the conjunct order equivalent of -*âw*.)

Examples such as (9) throw into relief another paradox (which is easily translated because of the meaning of 'kill'): although forms like *wâpamâw* or *ê-nipahiht* are agentless, they are formed from stems which are explicitly transitive. This is the main reason why a number of Algonquianists (e.g., Hockett 1962, Wolfart 1973) have preferred to interpret these forms as inflected for an "indefinite subject." In contrast to possessive noun themes, however, which include a special indefinite possessor prefix *mi-*, these forms show neither a prefix nor any other evidence of a personal agent.

There can be no doubt that impersonal constructions are closely related to agentless passive constructions. In Latin, as Ernout puts it (1908:290; emphasis supplied),

A tous les temps et à tous les modes du passif infectum et perfectum, la troisième personne peut être employée d'une façon absolue, pour exprimer l'action verbale purement et simplement, sans indication du sujet agissant. *Les verbes intransitifs et les verbes transitifs participent indistinctement à cet emploi.*

For Indo-European, this relationship has given rise to a developmental hypothesis, with the majority (e.g., Brugmann, Meillet, Wackernagel and many others) claiming priority for the impersonal and with only a small minority (primarily Wistrand 1942 but also Schwyzer 1943 and Gonda 1951) supporting the claim of a personal – and, perhaps, even agentive – passive.

In the Indo-European languages, the fundamental difficulty lies in the absence, for the most part, of a morphological distinction between transitive and intransitive verbs. In Latin, for example, all four possible constructions are well attested, with even the impersonal passive taking an agentive complement:

personal without agent:
    Tullia amâtur.   'Tullia is loved.'

personal with agent:
    Tullia â Marcô amâtur.   'Tullia is loved by Marcus.'

impersonal without agent:
    amâtur et egêtur âcriter   'there was loving and desiring,
        (Plautus)   heatedly'

impersonal with agent:
    adcurritur ab ûniversîs   'there was running towards
        (Tacitus)   by everybody'

While *amâre* is clearly ambivalent, it is hardly accidental that examples for personal and impersonal constructions usually rely on active and stative verbs. For Classical Arabic (Socin 1904:95, Harder-Paret 1962:66) we find the following illustrations:

    qutila zaidun   'Zaid was killed'
    ġuḍiba 'alaihim   'there was anger towards them'

In Cree the distinction of transitive and intransitive verbs is expressed both derivationally and inflexionally. Intransitive verbs have impersonal forms which cannot be interpreted in any other way; whether

(10)   *ê-mêtawêhk*

is translated as 'there is playing', 'they play', 'one plays' or even (as the traditional label of these forms might suggest) as 'someone plays' is a matter of English style rather than of Cree grammar: Cree makes a clear distinction between forms like (10) and constructions with *awiyak* 'someone' or *pêyak* 'a certain' which are used with third-person verb forms.

The inagentive passive form of the transitive animate paradigm may also be translated or "understood" as impersonal, as in example (9). But it is fundamentally distinct from a fully impersonal construction since it expresses a patient which is always personal.

OPTIONAL AGENTS

The two candidates for passive status which we have considered are found in much the same form throughout the Algonquian languages. In the one, the agent is both permitted syntactically and morphologically expressed, in the other it is neither. Of the intersections of these two criteria, we can exclude (on a priori grounds) the morphologically expressed-- agent for which a nominal complement would not be permitted. The fourth type, however, actually occurs in Cree:[8] the agent may be specified by a nominal complement but it is not expressed morphologically in the verb.

In the third-person sub-paradigm only one referent is morphologically expressed.[9] In (11a) it is the agent, in (11b) the patient which is marked by the third-person suffix -w- (cf. fn. 3):

(11a) *wâpamêw*   'he(prox) sees him/them'
     wâpamêwak   'they(prox) see him/them'
     wâpamêyiwa   'he/they(obv) sees/see him/them'

(11b) *wâpamik*   'he(prox) is seen by him/them/it'
     wâpamikwak   'they(prox) are seen by him/them/it'
     wâpamikoyiwa   'he/they(obv) is/are seen by him/them/it'

Third-person passive forms like *wâpamik* or *nipahik* 'he is killed by him/them/it' do not specify the agent beyond the fact that it has to be a third person; as examples (12a) and (12b) show, it need not even be animate:

(12a) *nama wîhkâc nipahik nêhiyaw piyêsiwa.* (P4-15)
     'Never is a Cree killed by the Thunderers.'

(12b) *nama wîhkâc nêhiyaw nipahik iskotêw.* (P4-15)
     'Never is a Cree killed by fire.'

(Note the obviative ending -a in the animate noun *piyêsiwa* 'Thunderer' and its absence in the inanimate *iskotêw* 'fire'.)

In these examples, the verb form *nipahik* is accompanied by two nominal complements: the patient *nêhiyaw* 'Cree' and the agent *piyêsiwa* or *iskotêw*. While the agent is less prominent than the patient, then, it does not recede into the background quite as much as the agent of an Indo-European passive.

The prepositional phrases of Indo-European relegate the agent to an explicitly distant rôle; in impersonal passive constructions the reference of the prepositional phrase is so remote that Ernout (1908:329; emphasis supplied) denies it the status of agent:

L'ablatif de noms de personnes, accompagné de *à* ou *ab*, indique non pas par qui se fait l'action, ce qui se rend par l'instrumental ou par la préposition *per...*, *mais de qui elle provient.*

Analysing a sentence from Caesar,

> *cum item ab hostibus constanter ac non timide pugnaretur,*

in some detail, he claims (1908:292):

> Ce serait un non-sens de considérer, quoiqu'on le fasse généralement, *ab hostibus* comme le "sujet logique" de *pugnaretur*; si César avait voulu exprimer un sujet, il aurait écrit simplement "cum item hostes... pugnarent". L'idée mise en relief ici n'est pas que *les ennemis* combattent, mais que l'on combat avec constance et courage.

Without pursuing this argument further, we recognise that at least two types of agentive complements must be distinguished in typological studies: DISTANT agents, expressed for example in oblique cases or in prepositional phrases, and CLOSE agents of the Algonquian kind.

Whether or not an agent is implied, the most important aspect of the *-ik* passive is that it may but need not take an agentive complement, as illustrated in examples (13a) and (13b):

(13a) *namôya wâpam*ik. (P80-9)
       '[The other] did not see him.'

(13b) *namôya wâpam*ik *wîtimwa.* (P252-15)
       'His sister-in-law did not see him.'

The third-person *-ik* forms thus satisfy all the traditional criteria for being considered passive: the patient is in focus, the agent need not be expressed and the predicate may be interpreted as intransitive (since only one participant is morphologically expressed). In addition, they are also marked morphologically: even though they express only one person, the third, they use the suffix /ekw/ to indicate that the first-mentioned – and therefore highest-ranking – person is the patient.

The special status of the *-ik* forms is clearly recognised in the Cree grammar of Joseph Howse. While the forms which relate third and non-third persons are analysed as *direct* and *inverse*, the third-person forms are distinguished (1844:57, 255) explicitly as *active* and *passive*.

Even though the "stylistic" choice (Kuryłowicz) between *wâpamik* and its counterpart *wâpamêw* is not entirely unrestricted,[10] these third-person forms occupy a pivotal rôle in the system and might well be seen to manifest an opposition of voice.

AN EMBARRASSMENT OF PASSIVES

Within a single inflexional paradigm, then, we find three sets of forms
which have at one time or another been analysed as passive. (In dealing
with the "grammatical passive" [Paul 1920:280] only, we exclude a
number of derivational formations with a variety of passive and middle
meanings; we also restrict our attention to the structure of the inflexional
paradigm, leaving aside the syntactic arguments of Jolley 1982 and
Dahlstrom 1986.) Without a doubt it is the prominence of the patient,
shared by all three sets, which has let them be analysed as passives.

Figure 1. Cree "Passives"

	I AGENTIVE	II INAGENTIVE	III OPTIONALLY AGENTIVE
patient prominence	+	+	+
marked morphology	+	−	+
agentlessness	−	+	±

At the extremes there is a syntactic opposition between an AGENTIVE
"passive" (I) which requires the agent to be expressed inflexionally and
an INAGENTIVE passive (II) which does not permit any mention or
specification of the agent, either morphologically or syntactically. Their
opposition is neutralised in the OPTIONALLY AGENTIVE passive (III) which
does not express the agent inflexionally but freely permits an agentive
noun phrase.

In paradigmatic terms, the three presumed passives function at
different levels of contrast. The inagentive (II) and the optionally agentive
(III) are opposed to one another within the sub-paradigm of forms
involving third persons exclusively. The agentive forms (I) stand apart
since they relate third and non-third persons. Being least passive-like,
these forms are also most readily interpreted in terms of the person
hierarchy (i.e., as direct and inverse) rather than as instances of voice.

The inflexional paradigm does not exhaust the syntactic-semantic
contrasts which may be expressed by distinct but similar forms. The
inagentive passive (II), for example, being restricted to third-person

patients, is supplemented by forms for first- and second-person patients drawn from another paradigm (cf. Wolfart 1973:59-62):[11]

Figure 2. Sub-paradigms

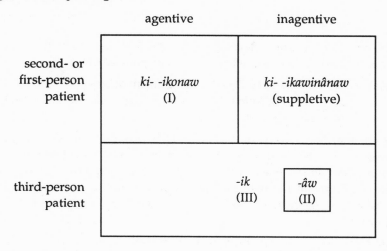

	agentive	inagentive
second- or first-person patient	ki- -ikonaw (I)	ki- -ikawinânaw (suppletive)
third-person patient	-ik (III)	-âw (II)

These suppletive forms are highly marked as secondarily derived; in example (14), the derivational suffix -ikawi- is followed by a form of the inclusive plural suffix (-nânaw instead of -naw) which does not otherwise appear in the mixed (third-and-non-third) sub-paradigm:

(14)   kiwâpamikawinânaw   'we(incl) are seen'

For the two third-person passives, by contrast, the conflict lies squarely within the transitive animate paradigm.

In the third-person sub-paradigm, then, the one active form -êw is opposed to two passives: the inagentive (II) in -âw and the optionally agentive (III) in -ik.

(15a)   wâpamâw   'he is seen'
                                                           (II)
          wâpamêw 'he sees him/them'
                                                   wâpamik   'he is seen by
                                                           (III)   him/them/it'

The same pattern recurs in the conjunct order, as in example (15b), where the suffix -ât is opposed to both -iht and -ikot:

(15b)   *ê-wâpam*iht 'that he be seen'
                                           (II)

ê-wâpamât 'that he see him/them'

                                           *ê-wâpam*ikot 'that he be seen
                                           (III)   by him/them/it'

The two third-person passives evidently differ in their syntactic range, as
is most clearly illustrated when they occur paratactically:

(16a) *namôya nipah*âw; *kîwêhtah*âw, *ê-kîwêhtah*ikot *ayahciyiniwa*. (P60-34)
       'But he was not killed; he was taken back; the Blackfoot took
       him home with them.'

While the first two verb forms in (16a) do not permit a nominal
complement, the third stands in construction with the obviative agent
noun *ayahciyiniwa* 'Blackfoot'; in preserving the repetition of the verb
stem *kîwêhtah-*, an alternative translation might emphasise the resumptive
function of the final clause: 'he was taken back, taken back by the
Blackfoot'.

(16b) *tâpwê âta ê-pê-nitom*iht, *opawâkaniyiwa ê-nitom*ikot, *namôya tâpwêhtam*.
       'True, though he was summoned [there], though their dream-spirit
       summoned him, he gave no heed.' (P262-16)

Following the inagentive verb in (16b), the "afterthought" clause, with its
agent noun *opawâkaniyiwa* 'their(obv) dream-spirit (obv)', echoes the same
basic stem. In the concluding clause, the patient of the two concessive
clauses functions, pivotally, as the agent.

    There are many contexts, on the other hand, where both third-person
passives are found. Examples (17) and (18) are also taken from running
text:

(17a) *âsay mîna asam*âw. (P106-16)
       'Again he was given food.'

(17b) *êkwa asam*ik; (P300-23)
       'Then they gave him food;'

Note that even Bloomfield, whose translations are usually quite literal,
gives the same translation for (18a) and (18b):

(18a) *asam*âw *okiniya, pimîhkân*. (P280-4)
       'He was given wild quinces to eat, [in the form of] pemmican.'

(18b) *â, sêmâk asam*ik *pimiy*. (P236-1)
       'Oh, at once he was given fat to eat.'

Since the sentences in (17) and (18) seem themselves indistinguishable, one might expect to find differences in the preceding context. But as examples (19a) and (19b) suggest, which are part of a much longer scene, any differences would have to be sought in the discourse structure and not in the syntax:

(19a) *nôtinitowak. namôya kinwês nôtinitowak. nipah*âw *awa takwâhnaw.*
       (P150-4)
       'They fought. Not long did they fight. The bull was killed.'

(19b) *nôtinitowak; mîna êwako nipah*ik. (P150-8)
       'They fought; this one, too, [the bear] killed.

There are at least some contexts, then, in which the two passives – inagentive and optionally agentive – seem to stand in direct opposition.

VARIABILITY AND PARADIGMATIC CHANGE

The overlap in the range of the two passives and their existence within the same verbal paradigm appear to undermine the stability of that paradigm. In the Cree dialects of western James Bay, the forms of the inagentive passive have disappeared entirely from the independent paradigm. When prompted, speakers at Albany and Moose Factory reject these forms "as being 'incomplete' " (Ellis 1971:85) since they do not have a personal prefix. (Note, however, that all third-person forms lack prefixes in Cree.[12]) The function of the inagentive passive forms is taken over by intransitive stems which are highly marked as derivational.

The fact that two derived stems, *-âkaniwi-* and *-âkaniwan-*, are used in free variation suggests that the inflexional form has been replaced only recently. This inference is confirmed by the coexistence, in the paradigm of the conjunct order, of the derivational form based on an intransitive stem in *-âkaniwi-* and the inflexional (and opaque) suffix *-iht*. Ellis specifically reports (1971:85) that the new forms are "common, especially in conversational style."

In Plains Cree, there is no sign of the displacement of the inagentive passive from its inflexional paradigm:

(20) VTA paradigm Plains Cree   James Bay Cree

      independent   -âw   *-âkaniwi- ~ -âkaniwan-*
      conjunct   -iht   *-âkaniwi- ~ -iht*

Outside the transitive animate (VTA) paradigm, however, suppletive (and transparent) forms are common enough.

In the intransitive paradigm (VAI), James Bay Cree shows a single, invariant derived stem based on the suffix *-(nâ)niwan-*; (in Plains Cree, the derivational suffixes are preceded by -nâ- except after â- and ê-stems):

(21)   VAI paradigm   Plains Cree   James Bay Cree

    independent   -ni- ~ -niwi- ~ -niwan- ~ -niwin- -niwan-
    conjunct   -hk   -niwan-

For Plains Cree, the range of variants used in the independent order, as
shown in (21), suggests recency. The conjunct order still uses an
inflexional form exclusively.[13]

Transitive verbs with inanimate objects (VTI) present a similar picture.
(Since the inagentive forms of these paradigms raise some special
syntactic-semantic problems, we restrict our attention to their
morphology.) James Bay Cree uses derived stems based on -kâtê-
throughout, and the same formation appears in the independent order of
Plains Cree. This is the paradigm where the inroads of the suppletive
pattern are deepest; the inflexional form in -amihk is in competition with
a derivational form based on -kâtê-:

(22)   VTI paradigm   Plains Cree   James Bay Cree

    independent   -kâtê-   -kâtê-
    conjunct   -amihk ~ -kâtê-   -kâtê-

In at least one dialect, then, in James Bay Cree, the replacement of all
"indefinite agent" forms, including the inagentive passive forms, by
overtly intransitive stems, highly marked as derived, is almost complete;
and the grammatical field is being left to the optionally agentive
passive.[14]

A similar process has already begun, it would appear, in Plains Cree.
Transitive verbs with inanimate objects occupy the most ambiguous
position among the verbal paradigms of Cree because of a pervasive
conflict between syntactic transitivity and a morphological structure
which expresses only a single participant. It is precisely at this weakest
point of the paradigmatic system that we find the first incursion of a
lexical passive.

Whether such a shift (from grammar to lexicon) will spread to the
transitive animate paradigm, which is quite distinct from all the others,
remains a matter for speculation. The mechanism, however, seems clear
enough: the suppletive forms based on -ikawi- will either support the
maintenance of -âw within the paradigm, or the joint pull of -ikawi- and
the push of paradigmatic instability will combine to remove -âw from the
paradigm and, with it, the inagentive passive.

COMPETING THIRD-PERSON PASSIVES

For the time being, Plains Cree has two agentless constructions, both flourishing, for a third-person patient.

Their relative status within the paradigm can be distinguished without any reference to typological considerations (or the unjustly notorious "straitjacket" of traditional Latin grammar).

The inagentive (II) is paradigmatically anomalous in at least two ways. First, while all other members of the paradigm come in symmetrical pairs, it stands alone. Second, among the forms with the theme marker -â- and a third-person patient, this is the only one (as noted expressis verbis by Ellis's James Bay informants) not to have a prefix.

The optionally agentive passive (III), by contrast, occupies a stable paradigmatic position, with the /ekw/-forms balanced by those in -ê-, as half of the symmetrical third-person sub-paradigm.

The language-specific and strictly synchronic approach adopted in this essay should not blind us to the wider implications, above all the general drift towards explicitly passive forms. Within the transitive animate (VTA) paradigm and across the dialects, the inagentive forms (II) are first supplemented and then supplanted by forms of derived intransitive stems which are overtly passive in their morphological make-up. This development might be viewed as an argument for the salience of the patient and thus, perhaps, against the Indo-European hypothesis (cf. Leumann-Hofmann-Szantyr 1965:418) of an originally impersonal passive.

The third-person passive (III) of Cree occupies a pivotal position at the intersection of agentive and inagentive forms. If it could be shown that this passive, rather than constituting a fundamental part of the verbal system, results from a re-interpretation of existing material, this might support the claim of Indo-Europeanists like Wackernagel and typologists like von der Gabelentz that (in Wackernagel's [1926:121] words) "die passivische Diathese nur so etwas nachträglich Hinzugewachsenes und Herausgebildetes ist."

Typological questions aside, paradigmatic imbalance and variability within Cree suggest that we are witnessing at close range the disappearance from the verbal paradigm of quasi-passive inagentive forms and their replacement, partial and tentative though it may still be, by a morphologically marked, inflexionally symmetrical and optionally agentive passive.

NOTES

[1] Thus, the Cree evidence will be introduced from the traditional perspective of the Word-and-Paradigm model rather than in terms of the passive as a universal syntactic category.

This essay is a renewed attempt to outline in fairly general terms a case which I first argued, along with several related claims, in a series of papers and lectures given during 1979 and 1980.

I wish to express my thanks, long overdue, to R. Harris and B. Schlerath, my hosts at Oxford and Berlin; among those who have offered critical comments, I am especially grateful to A.F.L. Beeston, R.T. Carter, I. Goddard and J. Haiman (who must not, of course, be blamed for my failure to accept all their strictures). The research on which this study is based has variously been supported by the Research Board and the Northern Studies Committee, University of Manitoba, and the Social Sciences and Humanities Research Council of Canada.

[2] This view is stated in its most extreme form by Silverstein (1976:140) who claims that "there are no languages where there is *obligatory* expression of the agent."

[3] The virgules indicate morphophonological representation; as a result of various sandhi rules, /ekw/ may surface as -iko-, -ikw- or -ik- and, after stems ending in -aw-, also as -âko-, -âkw- or -âk-. (In word-final position, neither the /-w-/ of /ekw/ nor the third-person suffix -w- which may follow it appear in the surface form.)

[4] In all typological contexts the term *agentive* is to be understood in its traditionally wide sense of 'including mention of an agent.' The distinction between agentive phrases with and without prepositions, and the like, will be taken up below.

[5] Rich documentation for early Latin is offered by Ernout; for example (1908:329):

Cet emploi [l'ablatif de noms de personnes, accompagné de
â ou ab] est d'ailleurs très rare chez les écrivains archaïques:
dans les cinq comédies de Plaute étudiées, il n'y en a que
deux exemples après un temps de l'infectum.

[6] If the context demands amplification, another clause is added paratactically, e.g.,

wâpamâw atim, niwâpamâw.   'The dog was seen, I saw it.'
For textual examples see (16).

[7] For Delaware and Blackfoot it has been claimed (Goddard 1969:120, Frantz 1976:211) that the preverb may "characterise" either the "indefinite subject" or the patient.

For examples where Bloomfield uses an impersonal translation cf. P228-31 or S63-17.

P stands for Bloomfield 1934, *S* for Bloomfield 1930; the orthography has been normalised but all sentences except (9) are given in Bloomfield's translation.

8   It may, of course, also be found elsewhere; but the morphological information summarised in Goddard 1967 would need to be supplemented with syntactic evidence from the individual languages.

9   Cf. Wolfart 1978:266 and ibid., fn. 10. In that paper, strictly synchronic arguments are marshalled to show that *wâpamêw* and *wâpamik* are single-place forms. Historically, they reflect an ABSOLUTE paradigm while the double-participant forms represent a distinct OBJECTIVE paradigm (cf. Goddard 1967:94).

10 Only the -*ik* form is possible when the agent noun is possessed by one of two third-person referents within a clause, e.g.,

    kîhkâmik otânisa. (S11-31)
    'His(prox) daughter(obv) upbraided(inv) him(prox).'

11 There are some indications that the optionally agentive passive is similarly supplemented by the "inanimate actor" forms (cf. Wolfart 1973:61), notably the syncretism of -*ik* and -*ikow*.

12 While this observation is directly relevant to *wâpamêw* in all dialects, a number of dialects have *wâpamikow* where the lack of a prefix is, apparently, balanced by the intransitive-like suffix.

    Uhlenbeck (1917:189) went so far as to derive the entire paradigm from the prefixless form:

    Zoo berust het geheele paradigma van Ojibway *ninwâbama* 'ik zie hem', *kiwâbama* 'jij ziet hem', enz., op den éénen passieven vorm *wâbama* 'hij wordt gezien',...

13 If -*hk* were derivational as well, as Frantz (1976:201) has proposed, one would expect parallelism between the two modal orders: in fact, we find neither conjunct -*niwahk* nor independent -*n*.

    Even in Menomini, where the independent form is much more like the VII stem, the similarity is superficial. Contrast the negative forms *kan pôsenan* 'there is no embarking' (VAI "passive") and *kan kemêwanon* 'it is not raining' (VII) which indicate -*n*- vs. -*nw*-; cf. Bloomfield 1962:8.3, 9.2, 9.3.

14 Although this topic would take us beyond the scope of the present essay, there are some signs which suggest that the optionally agentive passive has already begun to undergo a parallel development in the direction of a derived intransitive stem.

REFERENCES

Adam, Lucien. 1875. Esquisse d'une grammaire comparée des dialectes cree et chippeway. *Congrès International des Américanistes, Compte Rendu* 2:88-148. Nancy & Paris.

188   WOLFART

Allen, J.H., & J.B. Greenough. 1931. *New Latin Grammar for Schools and Colleges*. Revised edition. Boston: Ginn & Co.

Apollonios Dyskolos. 1910. *de constructione libri IV*, ed. G. Uhlig. R. Schneider & G. Uhlig, eds., *Apollonii Dyscoli quae supersunt*, vol. 2. Leipzig: Teubner.

Bloomfield, Leonard. 1925. Notes on the Fox Language. *International Journal of American Linguistics* 3:219-232, 4:181-219 (1925, 1927).

—. 1930. *Sacred Stories of the Sweet Grass Cree*. National Museum of Canada Bulletin 60. Ottawa: King's Printer.

—. 1934. *Plains Cree Texts*. American Ethnological Society Publications 16. New York: Stechert.

—. 1958. *Eastern Ojibwa: Grammatical Sketch, Texts and Word List*. C.F. Hockett, ed. Ann Arbor: University of Michigan Press.

—. 1962. *The Menomini Language*. New Haven: Yale University Press.

Comrie, Bernard. 1980. Inverse Verb Forms in Siberia: Evidence from Chukchee, Koryak and Kamchadal. *Folia Linguistica Historica* 1:61-74.

Dahlstrom, Amy Louise. 1986. *Plains Cree Morphosyntax*. Ph.D. Dissertation, University of California, Berkeley.

Ellis, C. Douglas. 1971. Cree Verb Paradigms. *International Journal of American Linguistics* 37:76-95.

Endzelin, J. 1923. *Lettische Grammatik*. Heidelberg: Carl Winter.

Ernout, A. 1908. Recherches sur l'emploi du passif latin à l'époque républicaine. *Société de linguistique de Paris, Mémoires* 15:273-333 (1908-09).

Frantz, Donald G. 1976. Unspecified-Subject Phenomena in Algonquian. W. Cowan, ed., *Papers of the Seventh Algonquian Conference, 1975*, 197-216. Ottawa: Carleton University.

von der Gabelentz, Hans Conon. 1861. Über das Passivum: Eine sprach-vergleichende Abhandlung. *Abhandlungen der Königlich Sächsischen Gesellschaft der Wissenschaften* 8, Phil.-Hist. Klasse 3.

Geniušienė, Emma Š. 1976. Das Passiv des Litauischen und seine Verwendung. R. Lötzsch & R. Růžička, eds., *Satzstruktur und Genus verbi*, 139-152. Studia Grammatica 13. Berlin: Akademie-Verlag.

Goddard, Ives. 1967. The Algonquian Independent Indicative. A.D. DeBlois et al., *Contributions to Anthropology: Linguistics I (Algonquian)*, 66-106. National Museum of Canada Bulletin 214. Ottawa: Queen's Printer.

—. 1969. *Delaware Verbal Morphology: A Descriptive and Comparative Study*. Ph.D. Dissertation, Harvard University.

Gonda, Jan. 1951. *Remarks on the Sanskrit Passive*. Orientalia Rheno-Traiectina 4. Leiden: E.J. Brill.

Haiman, John. 1976. Agentless Sentences. *Foundations of Language* 14:19-53.

—. 1985. *Natural Syntax: Iconicity and Erosion*. Cambridge: Cambridge University Press.

Hale, Kenneth. 1973. A Note on Subject-Object Inversion in Navajo. B.B. Kachru et al., eds., *Issues in Linguistics: Papers in Honor of Henry and Renée Kahane*, 300-309. Urbana: University of Illinois Press.

Harder, Ernst, & Rudi Paret. 1962. *Kleine Arabische Sprachlehre*. 9th ed. Heidelberg: Julius Groos.

Heath, Jeffrey. 1976. Substantival Hierarchies: Addendum to Silverstein. R.M.W. Dixon, ed., *Grammatical Categories in Australian Languages*, 172-190. Linguistic Studies 22. Canberra: Australian Institute of Aboriginal Studies.

Hockett, Charles F. 1962. Preface. L. Bloomfield, *The Menomini Language*, v-x. New Haven: Yale University Press.

Howse, Joseph. 1944. *A Grammar of the Cree Language*. London: J.G.F. & J. Rivington.

Jolley, Catherine A. 1982. On the Plains Cree Passive: An Analysis of Syntactic and Lexical Rules. B.D. Joseph, ed., *Grammatical Relations and Relational Grammar*, 1-33. Working Papers in Linguistics 26, Ohio State University. Columbus.

Kallin, H. 1923. *Etude Syntactique sur l'expression du rapport de l'agent dans les languages romanes*. Uppsala Dissertation. Paris.

Kuryłowicz, Jerzy. 1964. *The Inflectional Categories of Indo-European*. Heidelberg: Carl Winter.

Leumann, Manu, Johann Baptist Hofmann & Anton Szantyr. 1965. *Lateinische Grammatik 2: Lateinische Syntax und Stilistik*. München: C.H. Beck.

Meillet, Antoine. 1920. Sur les caractères du verbe. *Revue philosophique* 89:1- (cited after *Linguistique historique et linguistique générale I*, Paris, Honoré Champion, 1921).

Nausester, W. 1907. Beiträge zur Lehre vom Deponens und Passivum des Lateinischen. *Novae Symbolae Joachimicae: Festschrift des Königlich Joachimsthalschen Gymnasiums* [Berlin], 135-168. Halle.

Nicolas, Louis. 1672. Grammaire Algonquine ou des Sauvages de l'Amerique septentrionalle [sic]... Manuscrits Americains 1. Bibliothèque Nationale, Paris (1672-74).

Paul, Hermann. 1920. *Prinzipien der Sprachgeschichte*. 5th ed. Halle: Max Niemeyer.

Penzl, Herbert. 1955. *A Grammar of Pashto: A Descriptive Study of the Dialect of Kandahar*. Washington: American Council of Learned Societies.

Sapir, Edward. 1917. Review of Het passieve karakter van het verbum transitivum..., by C.C. Uhlenbeck 1917. *International Journal of American Linguistics* 1:82-86.

Schwyzer, Eduard. 1943. Zum persönlichen Agens beim Passiv, besonders im Griechischen. *Abhandlungen der Preussischen Akademie der Wissenschaften*, Jahrgang 1942, Phil.-Hist. Klasse 10.

Shafeev, D.A. 1964. A Short Grammatical Outline of Pashto. Indiana University Research Center in Anthropology, Folklore and Linguistics, Publications, 33 (also *International Journal of American Linguistics*, vol. 30, no. 3, pt. 3). Bloomington: Indiana University.

Silverstein, Michael. 1976. Hierarchy of Features and Ergativity. R.M.W. Dixon, ed., *Grammatical Categories in Australian Languages*, 112-171. Linguistic Series 22. Canberra: Australian Institute of Aboriginal Studies.

Silvestre de Sacy, Antoine Isaac. 1799. *Principes de grammaire générale, mis à la portée des enfans* [sic] *et propres à servir d'introduction à l'étude de toutes le langues*. Paris.

Socin, A. 1904. *Arabische Grammatik*, 5th ed. by K. Brockelmann. Berlin: Reuther & Reichard.

Uhlenbeck, C.C. 1917. Het passieve karakter van het verbum transitivum of van het verbum actionis in talen van Noord-Amerika. *Koninklijke Akademie van Wetenschappen, Verslagen en Mededeelingen*, Afdeeling Letterkunde, Vijfde Reeks, Tweede Deel, 187-216. Amsterdam.

Wackernagel, Jacob. 1926. *Vorlesungen über Syntax, Erste Reihe*. Basel: Birkhäuser Verlag.

Wistrand, Erik. 1942. Über das Passivum. *Göteborgs Kungl. Vetenskaps- och Vitterhets-Samhälles Handlingar*, följd 6, ser. A, bd. 1, pt. 1.

Wolfart, H.C. 1973. *Plains Cree: A Grammatical Study*. American Philosophical Society, Transations, n.s., vol. 63, pt. 5. Philadelphia.

—. 1978. How Many Obviatives: Sense and Reference in a Cree Verb Paradigm. E.-D. Cook & J. Kaye, eds., *Linguistic Studies of Native Canada*, 255-272. Lisse: Peter de Ridder Press / Vancouver: University of British Columbia Press.

—. 1979. Passive Nouns. Sub-Faculty of Linguistics, University of Oxford.

—. 1980. Marked Terms for Marginal Kin. W. Cowan, ed., *Papers of the Eleventh Algonquian Conference*, 283-293. Ottawa: Carleton University.